"*Taboo* brilliantly treads on the sacred cows we've been conditioned to accept as established truths. Systemic racism, racist police, white privilege—Wilfred Reilly dismantles these claims by analyzing the data. But he doesn't stop there. The same dispassionate and careful analysis is applied to the narratives of the white identitarian alt-right. *Taboo* is the much-needed book for an America intoxicated with victimhood."

—**ANDY NGO**, journalist at The Post Millennial

"Dr. Wilfred Reilly's book on social taboos is compulsory for anyone seeking to better understand the most off-limits political, social, and cultural realities."

—**PETE TURNER**, former U.S. Army spy and host of *The Break It Down Show*

"I'm sure [Reilly's] compelling and honest approach to the subject of race relations in our country [...] will further the needed discussion in a constructive and healing manner."

—**BILL MARTINEZ**, host of nationally syndicated talk radio show *Bill Martinez Live*

"The conventional wisdom is that people on the right are more likely to deny scientific facts than people on the left. That may have been true once, but not any more, as Wilfred Reilly demonstrates in this book. One of the paradoxes of the age we're living in is that scientific denialism is now more prevalent among educated liberals than among uneducated conservatives. If you ask what the difference is between a man and a woman, the ordinary, unlettered person, unencumbered by fashionable dogma, will be able to tell you. An educated person will embark on a long, rambling speech and then, midway through, think better of it for fear of being cancelled by their colleagues."

—**TOBY YOUNG**, associate editor of Quillette

"As he did in *Hate Crime Hoax*, Will Reilly has again proven himself to be a master truth-teller and myth-buster. With clear thinking; straightforward writing; and a style that is witty, funny, and a pleasure to read, Reilly boldly confronts the social, cultural, and political barriers that have prevented an honest discussion of race and class in America. We are living in a time of a dangerously increasing mass belief in corrosive myths of 'systemic racism,' 'white privilege,' 'racist police shootings,' and others. Perpetuated by media and the elites, the result has been a growing self-hatred of the United States, disdain for its values, and disbelief in its foundation. *Taboo* challenges these false assumptions, replacing them with truth—the first step in winning back the hearts and minds of the American people. Will Reilly is an important thinker, a powerful writer, and a patriot."

—**MAURY RICHARDS**, police chief of Martinsburg, West Virginia, and author at The Daily Caller

"Professor Reilly's book *Hate Crime Hoax* blew my mind. Too often we avoid the difficult, but in Will Reilly's new book, *Taboo: 10 Facts You Can't Talk About*, he takes us step by step into the vitally important discussions … the important facts that others avoid. The media aren't doing it, but fortunately Professor Reilly is in a way that we can all understand."

—**LOUIE B. FREE**, host of *BrainFood from the Heartland*

Taboo

T A B O O

10 FACTS
[You Can't Talk About]

WILFRED REILLY

REGNERY
PUBLISHING
A Division of Salem Media Group

Regnery® is a registered trademark of Salem Communications Holding Corporation

ISBN 978-1-62157-928-1
ebook ISBN 978-1-62157-991-5
LCCN: 2019955192

Published in the United States by
Regnery Publishing
A Division of Salem Media Group
300 New Jersey Ave NW
Washington, DC 20001
www.Regnery.com

Manufactured in the United States of America

10 9 8 7 6 5 4 3 2

Books are available in quantity for promotional or premium use. For information on discounts and terms, please visit our website: www.Regnery.com.

To the concept of Logos—the idea that all that matters in an argument or discussion is the provable truth, and that no areas of inquiry are "off limits"

Contents

Introduction

Real oppression has almost vanished from the United States, but its ghost remains troublesome. My last book, *Hate Crime Hoax*, dealt with a very specific issue: the prevalence of hoax hate crime accusations in the U.S.A. However, as I put the book together, I became more aware of a broader narrative about America lurking behind the eagerness of the mainstream media to report on almost literally every incident of alleged brutal racism, of mighty activist groups like the Southern Poverty Law Center (SPLC) using the incidents as fundraising tools, and of many ordinary liberal citizens immediately accepting them as true. I call this background zeitgeist the Continuing Oppression Narrative, or C.O.N.

The core idea of the Continuing Oppression Narrative is that not much has changed in America: racism may have become socially taboo following the civil rights movement of the 1960s, but it has "gone underground" rather than vanishing, and in fact hardly declined at all. This one central thesis underlies all of the lesser ideas that, together, make up the C.O.N. Some of *those* might be: American police are waging a "war on Black people," killing probably thousands of us annually; ethnic violence remains common in America, with interracial crime making up a substantial percentage of all crime with whites initiating most of it; the continued prevalence of bigotry is indicated by small but real gaps between the races (and sexes) in terms of variables like income; and subtle new forms of racism like "white privilege" and "cultural appropriation" oppress minorities as much as old-school prejudice ever did. At least partly in response to these claims, recent years have witnessed a surge in the size and noisiness of the "alt-right," a rival identitarian movement which claims that Caucasians are genetically superior to people of color and that successfully integrated societies are almost impossible.

Each one of the claims just mentioned is wrong, and many are nonsensical. In any coherent sense of these terms, actual day-to-day race relations in the United States are fairly good at this point in history. The country has been legally desegregated since the *Brown v. Board of Education* Supreme Court decision in 1954, the Civil Rights Act made racism literally illegal back in 1964, and pro-minority affirmative action became the law of the land after the Philadelphia Plan in 1967. The specific arguments made above also all fail. According to the *Washington Post*, less than 1,000 people of all races are killed by police in a typical year, perhaps 250 of them will be Black, and 100 or fewer will be "unarmed."[1]

More broadly, serious interracial crimes of any kind are fairly rare—85 percent of white murder victims and 93 percent of Black ones are killed by someone of the same race—and the interracial crimes that do occur in the U.S.A. are more than 70 percent minority-on-white. White privilege and "cultural appropriation" turn out hardly to exist at all when examined using modern empirical methods, and the gaps between races which are used to argue that modern bigotry is prevalent often completely vanish when nonracial variables like crime rate and average age are adjusted for. The alt-right's claims are at least as weak as the social justice left's: Caucasian societies globally (Albania? Iraq?) often perform no better on metrics of IQ or crime rate than Asian or West African ones, and racial integration has been the norm in large civilized countries at least since the Roman Empire.

Given the impact of the ideas just discussed, however, it is worth unpacking each one in a bit more detail. Probably the primary *cause célèbre* of the modern activist left is the idea that American police and other law enforcement officers (LEOs) are unfairly targeting Blacks and other minorities—and that, at the extremes, LEOs are essentially murdering African Americans at will. This claim is astonishingly prevalent in mainstream contemporary discourse. The platform of the Movement for Black Lives, one of the founding documents of the Black Lives Matter (BLM) movement, states bluntly that "police killing of our people"[2] is an existential threat to the Black community, and BLM activist Cherno Biko has told Fox News that a Black American is baselessly "murdered" by police "every 28 hours."[3]

The mainstream media often pass on such claims essentially verbatim, with the BBC, the *Washington Post*, *Vanity Fair*, and HuffPost, among many others, all running recent major stories about alleged police inhumanity toward African Americans. HuffPost's piece was titled "Here's How Many Black People Have Been Killed by Police Since Colin Kaepernick Began Protesting" and sub-headed "It's Been Just One Month." The slant—or bias, if you will—of the coverage is clear.

However, Black Lives Matter's claims about the frequency of unprovoked police violence specifically targeting African Americans are almost all demonstrably false. A glance through real data on police violence—easily available via sources such as *The Guardian*'s "The Counted" project and www.killedbypolice.net—indicates first that LEOs kill very few people in a typical year. In 2015, when the BLM movement took off nationally, only about 1,200 people of all races died during encounters with police. Only 258 of these people were Black, and, according to my calculations, exactly 17 *unarmed* Black folks were killed by *white* officers during the year.

It is true that the percentage of people killed by police who were Black (21.5 percent) is higher than the percentage of Blacks in the general population (13–14 percent), and this minor discrepancy has remained true in the years since 2015. However, it also has to be pointed out that rates of overall crime, violent crime, and arrest vary between races. The Black violent crime rate is at least twice the white violent crime rate. Adjusting for any of these differences—a very simple thing to do using modern "regression" analysis—completely eliminates disparities in Black-white rates of police shooting victimization. Even before this is done, it is just undisputed that 70 percent or more of cop shooting victims are not Black. The left-leaning mass media often seem to deal with this fact by actively concealing it. An in-depth look at Google and Bing search results indicates that the large non-Black majority of police shooting incidents receive less than 10 percent of all media coverage of police violence.

The broader argument that interracial crime and ethnic conflict—mostly targeting minorities—are frequent also fails. Like BLM's allegations about police violence, this argument is made constantly in modern middle-class discourse. In recent years, dozens of basically regular-ass citizens have gained international notoriety for allegedly abusing Blacks or other people of color (POC). "BBQ Becky" called the police on Black folks for just grilling in an Oakland public park after a shouted tirade; "Pool Patrol Paula" physically attacked a Black kid for swimming with the white folk; "Permit Patty" abusively drove a young Black girl selling water away from her business, shouting questions about the legality of street vending; "Coupon Carl" shamed a Black businesswoman by rudely questioning the legitimacy of the coupons she was trying to use at the CVS store he managed … and so on.

These stories are almost invariably presented as part of a disturbing, larger trend of racial harassment. Literally anyone who has used Twitter or Facebook has seen hashtags like #ShoppingWhileBlack, #GrillingWhileBlack, and—perhaps most poignantly—#LivingWhileBlack. Is it, we are asked to wonder, almost impossible simply to be a well-off Black person in the U.S.A. of 2019?

As I can personally attest: nah. Again, the narrative collapses totally when examined for more than a second. First, many of the accused "white racists" in the viral cases beloved by the media seem to have actually done nothing offensive at all. For example, "BBQ Becky" was angry only because a large group was hosting a full-on cookout in a dog run area of the park where charcoal grilling was prohibited. Furthermore, easily available data on interracial crime completely debunk the idea that rampant white-on-Black violence and abuse, in general, are major problems in America.

First, serious interracial crime, like fatal police violence, is quite rare. Crime tends to be stupid and mundane: more than 84 percent of white murder victims and 93 percent of Black murder victims are killed by persons of their own race, most of whom they knew. The same pattern holds true for most truly serious crimes: out of the roughly 12,000,000 crimes reported to U.S. police in a typical year, only about 600,000 will be (1) interracial (2) violent crimes. Furthermore, and this truly Must Never Be Said, the huge majority of interracial crimes are POC-on-white, and especially Black-on-white. In 2013, for example, whites and Blacks experienced similar rates of interracial crime, with 13.7 percent of crimes against whites being committed by Blacks and 10.4 percent of crimes against Blacks being committed by whites. However, the larger size of the white population means that more than 560,000 anti-white interracial crimes—versus 103,563 anti-Black interracial crimes—took place. Again, the mainstream media seem to almost intentionally ignore this pattern, with coverage of interracial crime being massively focused on outlier "white"-on-Black cases like the Trayvon Martin shooting.

The next, and probably broadest, component of the Continuing Oppression Narrative is the contention that gaps in performance between groups almost invariably reflect racism or other prejudices. This idea, while less influential on a day-to-day basis than BLM's claims about the violent nature of American society, may be the true cornerstone thesis of cultural Marxism. Even in the absence of any visible racism whatsoever—even in a country where real racism is against the law—the fact that Black men (for example) earn less money than white guys do can be taken as evidence of a subtle, pervasive bigotry. The same argument is made in the context of one hundred other dependent variables—from SAT scores to rates of incarceration to levels of familial wealth—and activists extend it beyond race. In the context of male/female relations, for example, the lingering disparity of 20 percent or so between the earnings of men and women is attributed to sexism by many feminists and labeled the gender pay gap.

Here, again, empirical analysis shows that many things "everybody knows" about racism and sexism are simply wrong. In almost every case, mathematically adjusting for cultural variables which we almost never discuss in modern PC America eliminates the gaps that are generally attributed to discrimination. It is in fact true that Black men make less than 85 percent of the white male wage. However, as government economist June O'Neill and conservative researcher Dinesh D'Souza pointed out back in 1995, adjusting for Black-white differences in age, region,[4] and education closed the earnings gap to a ratio of almost 90 to 100. Adding in standardized aptitude test scores and simple work experience closed it to 99 to 100. Similarly, adjusting for factors like (1) *whether women are working at all*, (2) what sort of career people choose, and (3) the number of hours spent in the office weekly totally eliminates the gender pay gap.

To a certain extent, this almost seems obvious, once said. If employers could hire an *identically qualified* Black guy or businesswoman for 80 percent the cost of a white guy, why wouldn't every single edgy firm in the country do exclusively that—and gain a massive market-share lead on the competition by immediately shaving 20 percent off labor costs? Why have we never heard of even one single tech bro doing it? The answer is simple: the basic premise of the left-wing argument about what performance gaps mean is wrong.

The final major claim of C.O.N. advocates is that racism never truly ended or declined in the modern U.S.A. but simply changed form. Activists speak constantly about new forms of "subtle racism," such as "white privilege" and "cultural appropriation." Essentially, white privilege is the idea that all whites enjoy a significant advantage over equally situated people of color—if not all people of color—because of their white skin, which confers an "invisible knapsack" full of benefits on members of the national majority group. These benefits allegedly range from the minor, such as the ability to more easily find Band-Aids matching one's skin tone, to very major advantages, such as rarely having race work against you during a job or university admissions interview. A sort of sidekick to white privilege, cultural appropriation is the idea that whites hurt POC by borrowing things from their cultures without permission and "appropriating" them into mainstream American life.

These concepts also fail as logical constructs. The great flaw of the idea of white privilege is its crude and univariate nature. Obviously, it surely is true that being a Caucasian blonde might sometimes be an advantage during a job interview. However, as writers ranging from myself to conservative thinker Dennis Prager to the staff of *The Atlantic* have pointed out, a whole range of other factors predict success in life as much as or more than race does. A short list of these might include sexual orientation, sex, attractiveness, height, weight, IQ, aggression, birth order, urban (as opposed to rural) status, Northern (as opposed to Southern) status, Christianity (as opposed to "oppressed" minority religions), "cisgender" status, and social class.

Prager convincingly points out that perhaps the most important privilege in modern society is simply being raised by a stable two-parent family. The poverty rate is 7 percent for the Black children of married couples and almost 25 percent for the white children of single moms. My own calculations indicate that, with non-racial factors fully controlled for, the effect of simply not being white on the life outcomes of minority Americans is on the order of 2–3 percent. In fact, in the affirmative action era, Black and Hispanic Americans not infrequently seem to have the advantage when competing for a particular collegiate spot or Fortune 1000 job.

The idea of universal white privilege is plausible, but wrong. In contrast, the idea of cultural appropriation—that it is racist for white people to borrow things from "minority" cultures—sounds and is insane. The great flaw of *this* idea is its absurdity. Simply put, almost everything that any given human being uses was originally invented by the citizens of a nation other than his or her own. In the U.S.A., as anti-racists themselves used to proudly point out, our beer is German, our favorite take-out food is Chinese, half of our cars are Japanese, and our very numbers are of Arabic origin. Logically, if borrowing from other cultures was truly morally wrong, we Black Americans would have to toss away our pants and shoes—most civilized African peoples preferred robes and sandals—and every Japanese businessman would have to immediately trade in his beloved Brooks Brothers suit for a kimono and sword.

Even a narrower definition of cultural appropriation limiting it (as some activists try to do) only to borrowing from groups which one's own society has oppressed or warred with would still block half of human exchange, if no longer all of it. Under that standard, no Turk could eat Greek gyros, no American could buy rugs from the Middle East, and no resident of Mongolia or Western China could drink vodka, which is made in the Russia their ancestors once conquered. Cultural appropriation—in essence an attempt to define human trade itself as somehow racist—fails utterly as a logical construct.

Partly in response to the absurdities of the contemporary activist left, a rival identitarian movement, the alt-right, has recently arisen among working-class and middle-class whites. Many more white Americans have begun to perceive discrimination against their in-group in recent years, with Harvard University and the Robert Wood Johnson Foundation concluding in 2017 that 55 percent of Caucasians believe there exists "substantial discrimination against white people in America today."[5] This belief has had political and social consequences, with traffic up exponentially at alt-right websites like American Renaissance and VDARE.

On those platforms, "white advocates" expound their own Bizarro World version of the C.O.N., contending that there is currently an epidemic of racist Black violence targeting whites, claiming that many American and global elites secretly desire the "genocide" of whites, and presenting their voices as a "red-pilled" alternative to the dishonest mainstream news media. Alt-righters generally argue that genetic inadequacy—not white racism—is responsible for the problems in minority communities and posit that racial and religious diversity is a bad thing which leads only to conflict. Some advocate for the creation of separate, all-white ethno-states within or outside the contemporary boundaries of the U.S.A.

Like those of the hard left, most of the identitarian claims of the alt-right (except, perhaps, those concerning media bias) are provably false. As we have already seen, there is no epidemic of interracial crime of any kind in the U.S.A. There were indeed about five times as many Black-on-white crimes as white-on-Black crimes—560,600 to 103,563—during the representative year that I use for data analysis purposes. However, there were also roughly 12 million *total* crimes, and it is worth noting that there are almost exactly 5 times as many whites as African Americans in the United States.

If this even needs to be said, the genetic explanation for the success of American Caucasians also fails totally and begins to collapse as soon as we look beyond the boundaries of this country. Regions of the world populated almost totally by members of the Caucasian racial group include *Eastern* Europe (Albania, Moldova, the former Yugoslavia), the Middle East (Iran, Iraq, Afghanistan, Palestine), and the "Stans" in Central Asia (Uzbekistan, Kyrgyzstan, Borat's country). These countries may all have rich and wonderful histories, but they are hardly the safest, richest, or most stable countries on earth. The Protestant ethic and the free public schools have a great deal more to do with the high average performance of white, Asian, and West Indian Americans than does their genetic heritage alone.

The rightist argument against at least "managed" diversity is nearly as weak. Frankly, diversity within societies does correlate with slightly increased conflict, but it also correlates with improved cultural and artistic climate, cuisine, athletic competition, dating options, and even patent rate. And, for good or ill, "cosmopolitanism" has been a characteristic of large civilized societies at least since ancient Rome. Finally, the alt-right's argument for ethno-states may be the craziest of the crazy positions taken by its members. Actually establishing these, with (say) whites getting Washington and Oregon but Blacks getting Alabama, would require breaking the greatest nation in world history up into a series of tiny countries with names like the Republic of You and Me, and I'm Not Sure about Me. No thanks! Simply put, white right-wing identitarianism is not a viable alternative to multi-culti left-wing identitarianism.

Equally simply put, the Continuing Oppression Narrative fails totally. Any coherent review of real, non-fringe data reveals that only

1,000–1,200 people of all races are killed by LEOs in a typical year, with fewer than 300 of these being Black and fewer than 100 being "unarmed." Interracial crime of all varieties is not exponentially more common, with more than 80 percent of the victims of serious crimes such as murder, across all races, being targeted by someone of the same race. Performance gaps between groups sometimes still do exist but seem almost never to be due primarily to old-school racism. For example, the earnings gap between Black and white males closes almost totally if we compare equivalent men and adjust only for the variables of age, region, education, and aptitude test scores. Finally, "new-school" conceptualizations of racism (such as cultural appropriation and white privilege) turn out to be almost totally meaningless when analyzed using modern empirical methods. For good measure, the identitarian visions that *rival* the C.O.N. logically fail as well.

All of this matters. Americans in the "conversing classes" are in an interesting, if not historically unique, position. We do not in fact have an ongoing race (or class, or gender) war in modern America … but we hear unceasingly that we do. It is no exaggeration to say that the existence of entire sizable sectors of society—continuing affirmative action, minority set-asides, the budgets of powerful activist NGOs like the SPLC—is justified largely by the claims that the Old Wars never ended and that bigotry remains epidemic in modern America. The leftist-dominated organs of national discourse often seem to intentionally promote this belief by, for example, devoting less than 10 percent of all coverage of police violence to the 70 percent or more of cases involving a non-Black victim. This leads to an odd situation where things in reality are going extraordinarily well—minority unemployment recently hit an all-time low—but many Americans believe themselves to be surrounded by escalating tension and strife.

This book aims to break that cycle. In the introduction to last year's *Hate Crime Hoax*, I said that I wanted to take "the first step back to a saner national conversation" about hate crimes. I then pointed out that, for all of the media frenzy about these incidents, there are fewer than seven thousand actual felony or misdemeanor hate crimes reported in a typical year, and many of these turn out to be fakes. This book has the same goal of clarification, but on a larger scale. In it, I make all of the points briefly summarized above, as well as others dealing with sane immigration policy and the nature of racism, in order to dismantle the C.O.N. and strike a blow against the identitarian left (and right). Doing so requires discussing things that are taboo in our culture today, such as race and crime, the reality and measurement of IQ, racism among minorities, what the practical versus moral goals of society must be, and even the differences between men and women. Thus the title of this book.

Tackling taboos is difficult, but necessary. Very often—MOST often—they are used not to shield strong and valid ideas from pointless attacks, but rather to protect weak ones from worthwhile criticism. The censor tends not to be an individual fully confident he is right, but rather one who is terrified to the core that he is wrong. Only by ignoring the censor's taboos and beginning to speak can we challenge bad ideas, overcome them, and replace them with better ones.

Let's start talking.

CHAPTER 1

Taboo Obvious Fact #1:
The Police Aren't Murdering
Black People

Probably the archetypal taboo-but-obvious fact of the American race debate is this: there is no "epidemic" of African Americans being murdered by police in the U.S.A. The claim that there is such an epidemic is made constantly by members of movements like Black Lives Matter (BLM), the New Black Panthers (NBP), and Antifa. But it is flatly false. Serious empirical analyses done by everyone from myself[1] to the Manhattan Institute's Heather Mac Donald to www.killedbypolice.net—an entire web resource set up to study this topic—invariably conclude that fewer than 1,200 people of all races and sexes are killed annually by American police officers. In a typical year, such as the representative year of 2015, roughly 250 (258) of these people will be Black. It is true that the Black percentage of the individuals killed by police, 22–24 percent, is slightly higher than the 13–14 percent representation of Blacks in the overall U.S. population. However, this roughly 10 percent gap is wholly explained by the fact that the Black crime rate, violent crime rate, arrest rate, and police encounter rate are all significantly higher than the equivalent rates for whites. There is no evidence for any of Black Lives Matter's major claims.

The argument that Blacks are being murdered essentially at will by rogue cops—and white vigilantes, but more about that later—is made astonishingly often by serious people. The website of the Movement for Black Lives argues that "the police killing of our people"[2] is an existential threat to the Black community, and that law enforcement officers kill hundreds or thousands of innocent Black people every year as part of a wave of "sustained and increasing … violence against Black communities."[3] More broadly, the platform of the Movement for Black Lives, one of the foundational documents of Black Lives Matter, argues that Black people are criminalized and "dehumanized" across every arena of society, including "justice and education systems," social service and welfare agencies, and even pop culture.[4] All of this is done intentionally; the conscious goal is preventing "the growth of another nationwide (civil rights) movement." The only possible solution to such abuse is the complete remaking of American society: lifetime free access for all Black people to every level of education, including "open admissions to public colleges" for Blacks, combined with "re-payment to Blacks of all wealth ever extracted from a majority-Black community" via "racism, slavery, food apartheid, housing discrimination … and capitalism."[5] And so on.

The largest outlets in the mainstream Western media (MSM) often pass on claims like these essentially verbatim. The official website for Britain's BBC, for example, recently ran what prints out as a single-spaced, nine-page story under the headline "Why Do US Police Keep Killing Unarmed Black Men?" Inside the piece, activist Samuel Sinyangwe is quoted as saying that the plague of cop murders is a real one. Quoth he: "What my data show is that Ferguson is everywhere."[6] In a majority of cities in the U.S.A., "you're seeing Black people being killed by police." Sinyangwe goes on to provide some specific descriptive statistics, noting that "Black people are (proportionately) three times more likely to be killed by police in the United States than white people," and claiming that far more unarmed Black people are killed by police than unarmed white people.

Another writer, Lorie Fridell, offers one possible explanation for this, arguing that police officers as a group are guilty of an implicit bias linking Blacks—totally undeservedly, of course—to crime. Discussing her work studying police bias, she says that her two strongest conclusions are (1) that most LEOs are well-intentioned, but (2) that bias among police officers is pervasive—not a matter of "a few officers in a few departments." According to Fridell, officers and many other Americans possess a strong, unconscious bias linking Blacks to urban crime, and this prejudice is probably implicated in many instances where police use deadly force against African Americans. In a remarkable side note, Fridell, almost in passing, concludes that this "bias" seems to be at least as strong among minority officers as white ones. Falsely believing that a suspect was armed in a series of threat perception modules was slightly but significantly more common when the "suspect" was Black, even if all of the tested officers were themselves Black or Hispanic. Fridell does not stand alone in this secondary finding: multiple serious scholars have found that Black and Latino officers are in fact *more* likely to discharge their weapons at criminal suspects of all races than white officers are.

Interesting stuff. In the same BBC article, law professor and former cop Seth Stoughton offers another possible explanation for the alleged epidemic of itchy police trigger fingers: a "warrior" cop culture that endangers Blacks and other civilians. He argues that a culture of perceived urban warfare among officers—the belief that LEOs are "soldiers engaged in battle with the criminal element"—has contributed to a large number of potentially avoidable shootings. To Stoughton, this component of police culture begins before officers are actually on the job. It starts with "police recruitment videos that show officers shooting rifles, strapping on hard body armor, using force. That attracts a particular type of candidate." Police academies then further entrench an attitude of readiness for combat, telling recruits that policing is a dangerous profession and that almost the first rule of law enforcement is to go home at the end of every shift. As a result, allegedly, Blacks and others die.

Roughly a year after Fridell and Stoughton were quoted in the BBC piece, *Vanity Fair* ran a fifteen-page article headlined "What the Data Really Says about Police and Racial Bias." On occasion, the piece actually discussed ... well ... what the data really say about the police and racial bias. For example, *Vanity Fair* author Kia Makarechi mentioned a well-known and impeccably researched study conducted by Washington State University faculty, which demonstrated that police officers were *less* likely during hyperrealistic video simulations to shoot unarmed Black suspects than unarmed white suspects.

However, the main thrust of the article was exactly what you might expect: that racism springs eternal. The key focus of at least eight of the eighteen points discussed by Makarechi is that disparities exist in the rates at which American Blacks and whites are stopped, searched, and arrested, and that this indicates racial bias. In San Francisco, for example, Black people account for less than 15 percent of the city's population but made up 42 percent of those searched by police in 2015. In New York City, 88 percent of the 4.4 million persons stopped by the police between 2004 and 2012 were Black or Latino, despite the fact that those groups together made up less than 60 percent of the city population. In poor, charred Ferguson, Missouri, police bias is argued to be especially egregious: African Americans make up perhaps 60 percent of the little city— an exact count is for some reason apparently difficult—but represented nearly 90 percent of documented use-of-force cases involving the Ferguson Police Department during a lengthy study period. And so on.

The *Vanity Fair* and BBC pieces were epic in scale and have been widely discussed, but smaller-scale articles accusing the police of abusing Blacks are also printed with some frequency. Radicals and mainstream media journalists (assuming that there is generally a difference between them) almost universally argue that a pervasive culture of prejudice and bias underlies the reality of occasional police shootings. A 2016 HuffPost piece provides a classic example of the genre. The title of the story, which ran a week or two after the start of that year's National Football League season, was "Here's How Many Black People Have Been Killed by Police since Colin Kaepernick Began Protesting." Its subhead was "It's Been Just One Month." Inside the article, distraught authors Travis Waldron and Julia Craven noted that "at least 15" Black people died during confrontations with American police during the period between when third-string former San Francisco 49ers quarterback Colin Kaepernick first began to protest police brutality by kneeling and the publication date for their piece.[7]

Waldron and Craven paid special attention to forty-year-old Terence Crutcher of Tulsa, Oklahoma, saying that "like so many other Black men," he was "unarmed with his hands in the air" when police shot and killed him. On the other hand, and typically, the HuffPost article completely ignored the literally dozens of white and Hispanic men killed by police during the same window of more than thirty days during which Crutcher was shot.

Activists and reporters claiming that Black men are being murdered in job lots by American LEOs can cite some empirical quantitative research which purports to validate this claim. The best known of the scholarly pieces on point is probably the impressively titled "A Multi-Level Bayesian Analysis of Racial Bias in Police Shootings at the County-Level in the United States, 2011–2014," published by Cody T. Ross in 2015. Inside the article, Ross used a series of impressive methodological techniques (and plain long division) to conclude that Blacks are roughly three times as likely to be shot by cops as whites are. Citing his paper directly: "The median probability across counties of being Black, armed, and shot by police is 2.94 times the probability of being white, armed, and shot by the police." Unarmed brothers had it even worse: "The probability of being Black, unarmed, and shot by police" was roughly 3.49 times the probability of being white, unarmed, and shot by police.[8]

These gaps between the rates at which Blacks and whites were shot by police officers appear to be unlinked to the overall crime rate in a particular county, although they were strongly influenced by the population size of a particular county-wide or city-wide area of analysis and by income inequality between Blacks and whites in a county, among other variables. Dr. Ross rather explicitly linked his findings to "racial bias."

Ross's work is solid, but he made one major omission, which provides as good a jumping-off point as any for a logical rebuttal of BLM's argument. At no point did he examine the relationship between (1) *the gap between* white and Black crime rates in each county and (2) *the gap between* white and Black rates of being shot by police. Ross argued, probably correctly, that there is no relationship between rising crime rates themselves and the ratio of police shootings of Blacks versus whites. But there is no particular reason that there would be. In a typical high-crime but diverse city where folks of all races commit crimes frequently, LEOs would be expected to shoot criminal suspects at a higher rate than in a low-crime city and shoot suspects of all races at a similar rate. What would be expected to almost exactly predict the Black-to-white ratio of police killings is the ratio of the Black serious crime rate to the white serious crime rate. Since he never tested this relationship, Ross could not actually conclude that gaps between Black and white rates of violent encounters with police are due primarily to racism.

Now to the facts. In reality, very few people are shot by American LEOs, and rates of police shootings by race seem to have almost nothing to do with racism once crime rates are adjusted for. The first point here is itself notable, in light of the absolute frenzy around police violence in the U.S.A. While doing research for my previous book, *Hate Crime Hoax*, I was stunned to discover that only about 1,200 people of all races were killed by LEOs during a very representative year (2015), around the time the BLM movement took off nationally. Only 258 of these people were Black. According to my calculations, exactly SEVENTEEN *unarmed* Black people were killed by *white* cops in 2015.

While I stand by my data, most research teams who tackled the same question have—astonishingly—found even lower annual rates of both overall and Black-victim shootings by police officers. The *Washington Post* lists 997 people shot and killed by police in 2015—of whom 259 were Black—along with 963 in 2016 and 987 in 2017. All major sources appear to agree that well under 10 percent of all American homicides—and only a minuscule 4 percent of Black homicides—involve a police officer or other law enforcement officer acting in any official capacity.

It is true that the percentage of people killed by police in a typical year who happen to be Black, usually 22–25 percent, is about 10 percent higher than the percentage of Blacks in American society (roughly 13 percent). Another technically accurate—if wholly dishonest—way to say what I just said is to claim that Blacks are "overrepresented by 78 percent" among police shooting victims because 25 percent is 178 percent of 14 percent. Media outlets are fond of doing exactly this. Even those rare articles that admit the huge majority of individuals shot by LEOs are Caucasian whites and Hispanics tend to seize on statistics which indicate Black overrepresentation among police shooting casualties and discuss them at length. What could this overrepresentation mean but RACISM? But, in fact, the answer to that question is incredibly simple. Rates of crime, violent crime, hostile police encounters, and arrests vary dramatically between Blacks and whites, and adjusting for any of those rates eliminates the apparent disparity in police shootings.

Although it is—again—somewhat taboo to discuss this, the fact that Black Americans currently have a higher crime rate than white Americans is not in serious dispute. According to the widely cited 2012–2013 Department of Justice figures dealing with violent crime (the first set of such figures to treat Hispanics as victims and offenders in categories separate from whites), Blacks committed 13.7 percent (560,477) of the 4,091,071 total violent attacks directed at whites during the research year, 62.2 percent (594,508) of the 955,800 violent attacks directed at Blacks, 21.2 percent of the 995,996 violent attacks directed at Hispanics/Latinos (211,151), and 19.3 percent (85,063) of the 440,741 violent attacks directed at Asians or Native Americans—for a total of 1,451,199 violent criminal attacks.

In contrast, whites committed 56 percent of the attacks directed against whites (2,291,504), 10.4 percent of the attacks directed against Blacks (99,403), 21.7 percent of the attacks targeting Latinos (216,131), and a surprising 40.3 percent of all attacks with an Asian or Native

American victim (177,619). The white total of violent criminal assaults in this typical year was 2,784,657, or roughly twice the Black total. However, since there are roughly five times as many whites in America as Blacks, the DOJ and a range of political commentators—ranging from Tim Wise on the left to Jared Taylor on the very extreme right—have concluded that the Black rate of serious/violent crime is roughly 2.5 times the white rate.

This discrepancy between Black and white rates of crime is especially pronounced in large urban areas, where whites tend to be richer than the national average and minorities tend to be poorer—and where most police shootings occur at the hands of tough big-city forces who obviously must be armed and ready to protect themselves. Far-right-leaning but methodologically skilled social scientist Edwin Rubenstein has pointed out that, during the full year of 2014, a Black New York City resident was 31 times more likely than a white resident to be arrested for murder (a Hispanic resident was 2.4 times as likely). For the crime of "shooting"—simply firing a bullet, often randomly, within city limits—the Black-to-white ratio was an astonishing 98.4-to-1, and the Hispanic-to-white ratio was 23.6-to-1. Extrapolating from the data just cited, Rubenstein claims that a (mythical) all-white New York City would see a 90 percent drop in the murder rate, 81 percent drop in the rate of robbery, and a 97 percent decline in plain, random shootings of guns. In an all-white Chicago, murder would drop by 90 percent, robbery by at least that much, and rape by 81 percent.[9]

It is important not to take these numbers too seriously or draw "alt-right" conclusions from them. When Chicago *was* an almost all-white town with income demographics fairly similar to today's, the city was hardly a global bastion of peace. In fact, the whole place was run by the Mafia. Al Capone's boys carried out the St. Valentine's Day Massacre in 1929, and the city overall—much smaller than today—saw a total of 498 murders that year, in addition to hundreds of unresolved disappearances. Today, high-crime white areas such as the Appalachian regions of West Virginia and Kentucky need no help from those of us with a nice natural tan to post staggering crime totals. In 2016, the U.S. city with the highest per capita rate of serious violent crime was actually midsized Oceana, West Virginia, where an astonishing 4,176 major crimes—many linked to the ongoing opiate epidemic—occurred for every 100,000 residents. However, with all of that said, the plain fact is that a Black crime rate which is 2.5 times the white crime rate and rises to 10 times the white crime rate in many major cities obviously explains most or all Black-white disparities in terms of unpleasant encounters with police. Police tend to patrol hardest where there is a lot of crime; this is not rocket surgery.

Although the point just made is rarely heard in the mainstream media, a good number of serious statistical analyses have arrived at it. Perhaps most notably, Roland G. Fryer, the youngest African American ever to receive tenure at Harvard, found—using cutting-edge modern regression methods and actually *controlling* for variables such as suspect and officer demographics, the characteristics of each police encounter, and the presence or absence of a weapon—that "there are no racial differences in [rate of] officer-involved shootings." Remarkably, with all relevant variables actually controlled for, "Blacks were 27.4 percent less likely to be shot at by police relative to non-Black, non-Hispanics"[10]—or American whites, as we used to call 'em.

After reaching this conclusion, Fryer went out of his way to make a wonky but critical point. Quoth he: "Evidence for bias [in past studies] is mainly a result of misspecified regression equations."[11] In layman's terms, Fryer's point means that an apparent disparity between two groups—Black people actually *are* about twice as likely as whites to get shot by cops—can be due either to (1) prejudice or (2) some *other* variable that also happens to differ between the two groups. Simplistic mainstream media analyses of Black-to-white shooting disparities almost invariably conclude that these are the result of racism. However, sophisticated analyses, such as Fryer's well-done piece or even my quick quantitative adjustment for crime rates, come to the conclusion that no significant bias exists. Black and white guys with the *same* characteristics are treated essentially the same during encounters with LEOs. As Thomas

Sowell has pointed out for decades, the simple existence of disparities in group performance is not evidence of discrimination.

To its credit and my surprise, the *New York Times* has reported extensively on Fryer's work. In a lengthy feature story titled "Surprising New Evidence Shows Bias in Police Use of Force but Not in Shootings," Quoctrung Bui and Amanda Cox devote a fair amount of ink to claiming that some of Fryer's secondary findings do indicate bias on the part of police. Their opening sentence is: "A new study confirms that Black men and women are treated differently in the hands of law enforcement." Relative to whites, African Americans are slightly more likely to be "touched, handcuffed, pushed to the ground, or pepper-sprayed by a police officer."

But these claims seem to be a rather desultory attempt to "spin" Fryer's conclusions. Subsequent analysis of the Fryer data by Bui and Cox reveals that differences in police behavior across all of the variables just mentioned were tiny. *Before* adjusting for any of the factors analyzed by Fryer, Blacks were only 18 percent more likely to be pushed or shoved and a mere "16 percent more likely to be handcuffed without being arrested" than whites or persons of all other races. More importantly, the *Times* journalists—reporting from a perhaps left-leaning, but honest, perspective—did not even attempt to challenge Fryer's primary conclusion. "When it comes to the most lethal form of force, police shootings," the authors note, "the study finds no racial bias." Even Fryer's finding that Blacks are often less likely to be shot than equivalent whites is succinctly and accurately cited: "In various models controlling for different factors and using [exact] definitions of tense situations, Mr. Fryer found that Blacks were … less likely to be shot or there was no difference."

Over at *National Review*, veteran writer Nick Selby made a different, interesting, and relevant point (which future chapters will return to): there is no logical reason to expect that all large groups will *generally* have the same crime rates, leaving racism as the most logical explanation for group disparities in arrests or fatal encounters with police. Again, we encounter the Taboo Obvious: although one is not supposed to say this in mixed company, different racial, regional, and gender groups are obviously good at different things and perform differently across a whole range of metrics for cultural, economic, societal, historical, and perhaps even (*clutches pearls*) genetic reasons.

Take my group. In the U.S.A. as a whole, Blacks make up 13–14 percent of the population, but more than 65 percent of NBA basketball players, only 1.4 percent of doctors, 38 percent of barbers, and 16 percent of professional restaurant cooks and chefs. And, as a young and disproportionately urban population with a slightly below-average level of income and a history of racial oppression and violent ethnic conflict, it is indisputable that we make up more than 13 percent of violent criminals. As Shelby pointed out, the "unspoken assumption" of liberal academics is that rates of police shootings should exactly match America's overall racial demographics, but this is a foolish and dangerous assumption. He noted what I did myself a few pages ago: that adjusting for variables like median age and crime rate essentially closes the Black-white police shooting gap.

In the context of these real-world facts, many of the police shooting cases made globally famous by BLM take on new meaning. Instead of being archetypal examples of a disturbing national trend, almost all of them are revealed to be rare and aberrational situations, often involving very unsympathetic behavior on the part of very unsympathetic people. The shooting of Alton Sterling provides an excellent example of this dichotomy. Sterling, a thirty-seven-year-old Baton Rouge man, was shot dead by two white police officers during a scuffle on July 5, 2016. Police had responded to a report that a large Black man in a red shirt—Sterling—was selling bootleg CDs and DVDs on a busy block in Baton Rouge, and that he might have a gun. When the two officers, Howie Lake II and Blane Salamoni, arrived on the scene, they became involved in a verbal confrontation and then a physical fight with Sterling. When the two men attempted to restrain Sterling's arms, Sterling reached for something—presumably his gun—in his pocket. Both officers discharged several shots, which killed Sterling.

The Alton Sterling case received global coverage, and the almost universal MSM take was that the harmless and popular local CD bootlegger, a "gentle giant" à la Michael Brown, had been murdered or the next thing to it. On July 5, the day after Sterling's death, several hundred demonstrators marched through the streets of Baton Rouge, shouting, "No Justice—No Peace," setting off fireworks, and blocking major intersections. The next day, Black Lives Matter Louisiana held a candlelight vigil downtown, with attendance by some estimates reaching into the thousands. Local and national media, prominently including CNN and MSNBC, covered both events sympathetically. Even the president, then Barack Obama, got involved. Mr. Obama exhorted "all Americans to do better" just days after the shooting of Sterling and declared that "Americans should feel outraged at episodes of police brutality." A less measured fan of Sterling's was BLM activist Micah Xavier Johnson, who opened fire on police on July 7, 2016, at a Dallas protest specifically linked to the Baton Rouge shooting. Johnson, a trained sniper-style marksman, killed five sworn officers ("the Dallas Five") and wounded eleven others before being terminated with a robot-delivered explosive device.

The passion generated by the death of Sterling was real and should not be mocked. However, a quick look at the real facts shows that it was largely unmerited. Sterling seems to have been a career criminal whose death by violence was tragic, but hardly surprising. First, any close reading of Baton Rouge police records reveals that the initial man-with-a-gun call about Sterling was not a simple claim of public carry or illegal possession. Instead, Sterling was accused of *brandishing his weapon and using it to threaten a man* in a dispute over illegal CD sales. When police arrived, they quickly discovered that Sterling was still armed. The sequence which ended with Sterling being shot began, according to witnesses, when one of the two officers involved noticed his weapon and screamed, "GUN! Gun! He's got a gun!" Shortly after the final, fatal shots were fired, this street report was confirmed: a loaded (illegal) .38 revolver was retrieved from the front pants pocket of the fallen Sterling.

The fact that Sterling had a gun during his fatal confrontation with police was hardly unusual. Multiple witnesses and other neighborhood residents who participated in the interviews and legal procedures which followed the shooting testified that Sterling often went about armed. The owner of the store closest to where the shooting occurred stated on the record that Sterling had begun carrying a pistol "at least days" before the scuffle, because "he been robbed." In all probability, he had been packing far longer than that. Almost unbelievably, Sterling had been involved in at least one *previous armed fight with police.* A 2009 Baton Rouge Police Department affidavit of probable cause states that, on one previous occasion, he resisted arrest to the point of having to be "wrestled to the ground," and that a loaded semi-automatic pistol actually fell out of his waistband in the middle of that physical fight.

Although previous offenses are not necessarily relevant to the facts of Sterling's death, and accounts differ as to whether BRPD officers were aware of them at the time of their 2016 fight with Sterling, it is hard not to notice that the gentle giant's 2009 gun charge was not a one-off mistake. Alton Sterling had a rather remarkable criminal record. Among other things, he was—in the technical, legal sense of this term—a child molester. According to a Louisiana records search, Sterling was convicted on September 20, 2000, for "carnal knowledge of a juvenile," an in-state female in her early teens.

He was subsequently charged on August 12, 2015, and April 8, 2016, for failure to ever register as a sex offender. In addition to that minor peccadillo, Sterling was criminally charged over the years with battery (January 6, 1998), public intimidation (May 4, 2000), domestic violence/woman beating (September 4, 2001), burglary (May 24, 2005), receiving stolen property (July 11, 2005), enhanced burglary/burglary of an inhabited dwelling place (September 12, 2005), criminal damage to property (March 17, 2006), domestic abuse yet again (April 4, 2008), and illegal possession of a weapon (October 12, 2009).

On just one occasion in the summer of 2009, a raid on Mr. Sterling's street-corner music business resulted in charges for (1) resisting an officer,

(2) drug possession, (3) receiving stolen goods, (4) sound reproduction without consent (in other words, piracy), and (5) the esoteric Louisiana charge of "carrying a weapon with CDs." Even Sterling's gun turned out to have been stolen, resulting in an additional separate charge for (6) illegal possession of a firearm.

Without claiming that the BRPD was aware of all these past indiscretions—although I found them easily, and a quick search on a police car's dashboard computer would have pulled the same list up—situational awareness of even two or three of them would have caused officers to quite properly regard any struggle with Sterling as a clash with a dangerous felon rather than a normal, peaceable citizen. Under these circumstances, violently resisting police while again illegally armed was a foolish mistake by Sterling, which had awful but predictable consequences.

Looked at through a skeptical and pro-American eye, many or most other BLM claims of murder and martyrdom collapse similarly. The death of Freddie Gray provides a good second example of this trend. One of the most iconic BLM victims, Mr. Gray was a twenty-five-year-old African American man arrested by the Baltimore Police Department on April 12, 2015, for a minor offense listed in most records as "possession of an illegal knife." While being transported to the city's Western District station in a police van, Gray was not secured with a locking seat belt and somehow sustained serious spinal injuries. At least some media members have suggested that Gray's injuries were the result of a "rough ride"—an unsanctioned practice where a hand-cuffed prisoner is placed into a police vehicle without a seatbelt and driven around erratically.

Whether or not exactly this occurred in his case, Gray lapsed into a coma during the ride and was taken to the University of Maryland's R Adams Cowley Shock Trauma Center. There he was diagnosed with several back injuries, including three fractured vertebrae and a spinal cord partially severed at the neck. Despite intensive and caring treatment, including several surgeries, Gray died on April 19, 2015—exactly a week after his arrest.

Even in comparison to Sterling's death, Gray's death caused a frenzy of protest and unrest, leading directly to the Baltimore riots of 2015. On April 25, 2015, a major protest against Gray's death in downtown Baltimore turned violent, with large-scale brawling between activists and LEOs resulting in at least thirty-four arrests and the hospitalization of fifteen officers with fairly serious injuries. Two days later, after a packed funeral for Gray, civil disorder intensified into out-and-out rioting, with a large and unruly crowd burning multiple Black-owned businesses as well as a flagship CVS pharmacy. Images of rioters dancing atop burning police cars went viral globally, and Maryland governor Larry Hogan deployed the National Guard to Baltimore, announcing an all-night curfew that lasted until May 3. The general, center-left public attitude toward the Freddie Gray matter was probably summed up by a student of mine, who said, "That brother was a total innocent. They murdered him because he had a damn pocketknife."

Not quite. Reality turns out to be considerably more complex. First, and contrary to many BLM claims, police did not encounter Gray because "they was out patrolling for any Black man." According to the *Baltimore Sun*'s Kevin Rector, officers ran into Gray near Baltimore's notorious Gilmor Homes projects, an area known for through-the-roof levels of "home foreclosures, poverty, drug deals, and violent crime." Police were at Gilmor Homes in force in the first place because Black activist and Baltimore state attorney Marilyn Mosby had recently pleaded with them to target the area, specifically requesting "enhanced" patrolling of the 3–4 block zone where LEOs encountered Gray.

As a direct result, BPD lieutenant Brian W. Rice and several officers under his command were conducting a bicycle patrol of the projects on April 15, 2015. At 8:39 a.m., these policemen rode by Gray and he made eye contact with them. Gray immediately proceeded to run away as fast as he could, "fleeing on foot unprovoked after noticing the police presence," according to the police report in the case. After a lengthy chase, he was taken into custody without any use of force.

Gray probably had good reason to run. A quick glance at his criminal record indicates that, in the seven years since turning eighteen and becoming a legal adult, he had been arrested and charged with felonies or serious misdemeanors eighteen times. Eight of these arrests were for possession of either narcotics or "a controlled dangerous substance" with the intent to distribute, while another seven were for simple possession of a controlled dangerous substance (this usually means cocaine, PCP, or heroin) or marijuana.

To spice things up a bit, Gray had also been arrested for assault, destruction of property, felony burglary, trespassing, illegal gambling, fleeing from and escaping the police, and (unsurprisingly) violation of probation terms during the period under review. But the main thrust of his body of work was obvious: Gray was an active drug dealer, targeting an almost exclusively African American clientele. As BPD deputy commissioner Jerry Rodriguez said, stating the Taboo Obvious, Gray was someone with a lengthy drug record who was apprehended "in a high crime area known to have high narcotic incidents." Whether or not he had drugs on him the day of his final arrest, he probably did not run from the police because of their "cisgendered patriarchal whiteness," or some such.

Of course, none of this would justify BPD officers intentionally restraining a helpless Gray and driving him around bumpy back roads until his neck broke. City cops sometimes do things like that, and that fact is deplorable. However, a rather exhaustive search of the record fails to confirm that any such thing happened. Gray's arrest was not a violent one, and he was placed in a transport van, as per policy, within eleven minutes of being detained. Once in the van, he certainly was not driven to a remote area and beaten bloody. The *Baltimore Sun*, Wikipedia, and BPD accounts of the Gray situation all note that the van made at least four confirmed public stops with Gray inside.

On one occasion, it stopped at a public outdoor market. During another, at 8:46 a.m., Gray was unloaded and placed in leg irons because he was behaving angrily and erratically. During a third, at 8:56 a.m., *another prisoner was placed in the van.* No sources indicate that this man observed anything unusual about Gray's condition, and he has in fact stated that he noticed nothing untoward about BPD treatment of Gray. When Gray arrived at the Western District police station at 9:21 a.m., his injuries were apparent—but he was then immediately treated by paramedics, rather than (say) being hustled off to an isolated cell to die.

It is true that police in the Freddie Gray case were in technical violation of a 2015 Baltimore ordinance requiring that criminal suspects be "safely seat-belted in" while in custody during transport. This has been widely noted by the MSM, was a mistake, and must be acknowledged. However, this rule, often presented as though it were the hoariest of BPD policies, had been enacted *six days* prior to Gray's arrest. Many cops, frankly, were probably unaware of it, while others openly argued that it endangered them. Police lawyer Michael Davey noted at one point that, in situations involving a combative or recalcitrant prisoner, "It is not always possible or safe for officers to enter the rear of those transport vans that are very small." This was very specifically an issue in the Gray case: "This one was very small."

Not being properly restrained may have contributed—and probably did contribute—to Gray's injuries. But whether or not the BPD officers driving that van and processing its occupant bear some moral responsibility for harms sustained by an "irate" prisoner who had to be restrained on at least one occasion, police officers lurching while driving and injuring a drug dealer's neck does not a lynching make. Baltimore juries essentially agreed with this claim. Of the officers involved in the Freddie Gray matter, Lieutenant Rice and Officers Edward Nero and Caesar Goodson went to trial and were fully acquitted, while Officer William Porter survived a mistrial. All remaining charges against an original group of six officers, including Garrett Miller and Sergeant Alicia White, were dropped by July 27, 2016. In January 2017, a federal judge allowed a lawsuit by five of these six officers to proceed against the Baltimore state's attorney, seeking damages for malicious prosecution, defamation, and invasion of privacy.

A key factor in the Gray case—and a reason why regional support for the six accused officers remained high despite what sometimes seemed like the best efforts of the media—was the fact that the police involved were clearly not racist murderers. Perhaps most notably, three of the six individuals charged in connection with Gray's death *were themselves Black*. Specifically, Lieutenant Rice and Officers Nero and Miller are Caucasian, while Sergeant White and Officers Goodson and Porter are African American.

Sergeant White, a Baltimore resident and BPD veteran since 2010, was the second-highest ranking officer involved with the arrest of Gray, and also the individual who would have been directly responsible for "calling for medical assistance" in his case if she thought it necessary. As a source related to one of the African American officers told Britain's *Daily Mail* about the diverse backgrounds of the police team: "That totally undermines the idea that this was about race. The only people who are saying that this is about race are the outside media. This is not another George Zimmerman, it's not another Ferguson. This is completely different."

The Sterling and Gray cases are hardly unique. Even those BLM shootings which do turn out to have been absolute tragedies—and there certainly are some—rarely or never seem to have actually been motivated by old-school racial hatred. The case of Philando Castile provides an excellent example of this phenomenon. Castile, a popular and professional school district employee who worked as a nutrition services supervisor at the J. J. Hill Montessori Magnet School, was shot five times by a St. Paul, Minnesota, area police officer while out for an evening drive on July 6, 2016. Castile's shooting, horrifically, was witnessed not only by his long-term girlfriend, Diamond Reynolds, but also by his four-year-old daughter. That Castile's shooting was a tragic mistake has never been seriously contested by anyone. His family settled a wrongful death lawsuit with the city for $2,995,000 not long after the incident, and Reynolds received an additional $800,000 and an official apology.

Nevertheless, as always, the cry on the breeze was intentional racism. By 12:30 a.m. on July 7, "less than three hours after the shooting," according to Wikipedia and the *Star Tribune* in Minneapolis, dozens of protesters had gathered near the scene of Castile's shooting. They were initially peaceful, but visibly angry. Within days, the peaceful veneer was gone. On July 8, an estimated 2,000 demonstrators completely shut down Interstate 880 in California. By July 9, outright physical fighting had broken out between police officers and contingents of St. Paul demonstrators.

One hundred and two people were arrested and charged with crimes on that date, and twenty-one officers—fifteen city cops and six Minnesota state troopers—were injured or hospitalized. Molotov cocktails were reportedly thrown at law enforcement officers, who used CS gas to disperse the crowd. Around the same time, another contingent of demonstrators literally set up camp outside the Minnesota Governor's Residence to protest "racism." Perhaps in response, the governor issued a remarkable statement in which he asked, "Would this have happened if these passengers had been white?" He answered his own question: "No, I don't think so."

In this case again, however, passionate claims of racism did not align with what turned out to be reality. As in the Freddie Gray case, most of the prominent figures involved with the death of Castile were people of color. The officer directly responsible for firing the fatal shots was a Hispanic man named after an American Indian chief, Jeronimo Yanez. His partner, Joseph Kauser, was white, but also an anti-racist city kid who had been personal friends with Yanez since the 2012 graduation of both men from the police academy at Minnesota State University, Mankato. Even the Ramsey County district attorney who made the tough decision to charge Yanez with several felonies (the lawman was acquitted on all counts in June 2017) was a non-Caucasian, popular Asian American prosecutor, John Choi. Possibly as a result of the diversity of its prosecutorial and policing population, the specific department responsible for Castile's shooting, Minnesota-St. Anthony's, had not experienced an officer-involved shooting in the *thirty years* before the death of Castile. Literally nothing indicates that any of the men involved were racist bigots.

It also emerged that Yanez, a respected four-year veteran of an urban police force, did not simply panic and shoot a Black man because of (say) vague perceptions of Black crime. As it happens, a violent handgun robbery of a Super USA convenience store had taken place less than four blocks from where Castile was pulled over, roughly an hour before the stop occurred. The primary suspect in the robbery, according to the website Conservative Treehouse, was described as a "Black guy" with "shoulder-length dreadlocks," "glasses," "a small mustache," and some but not much facial hair on his chin. This is virtually an exact description of Castile.[12]

According to police audio which emerged in 2016 and has been reported on by the *Star Tribune*, Yanez very specifically pulled over Castile because he thought that Castile was this armed robber. "A veteran St. Anthony's police officer patrolling Larpenteur Avenue"—that's Yanez—is on record radioing the occupants of a nearby squad car and explaining that he and his partner planned to pull over Castile's car and check the identities of both driver and passenger. To quote him directly: "The two occupants just look like people that were involved in a robbery. The driver looks ... like one of our suspects, because of [his] wide-set nose." The other officer concurred, and the stop was made.

After Yanez pulled him over, things were complicated further by the fact that Castile was a legal gun owner, who generally had his pistol with him and did on July 6. After being asked for his license and registration, Castile's first response was to tell Yanez that he was carrying a loaded firearm. Yanez's response was, "DON'T reach for it, then"—to which, tragically, Castile replied, "I ... I was reaching for it." The exchange became confusing, with Reynolds saying, "He's not...." and Castile adding, "Now, I'm not pulling it out." At or near the end of this exchange, Castile reached into his pants for his license, and Yanez—who thought he was the armed robber—fatally shot him. The death of Mr. Castile was indisputably a terrible tragedy. However, literally nothing links it to bigotry or malice, or very arguably even to indisputable misconduct.

An honest look at the BLM cases reveals few or no racially motivated murders, a fair number of regrettable tragedies which disproportionately involve overworked minority officers detailed to high-crime hoods, and—we must speak bluntly here—a ton of bloody, physical fights that could have been easily avoided by even reasonably sane, normal behavior on the civilian's part. It is very possible, indeed likely, that stressed city cops did not perfectly conform to the perfect ideal of police procedure during the Alton Sterling and Freddie Gray situations. The thinker Simonides of Ceos once pointed out that searching for a perfect man, especially among warriors, is likely to be a long and fruitless process. But it is equally true and far more relevant that, had Alton Sterling not been an illegally armed convicted felon who engaged in a physical fight with officers after having the cops called on him for waving his gun at a *third* man, he would be alive today. Similarly, had Michael Brown not attempted to grab a uniformed officer's gun during a street fight after being stopped for walking down the middle of a busy street, just hours after committing a brutal strong-arm robbery of another minority citizen, the "gentle giant" would still be with us.

All of us should and must condemn actual police brutality, but the plain fact is that it is fairly easy not to get shot by the police. With the exception of youthful fistfight charges and the like, the probable majority of people, across all races, have never been arrested even once. While such police behavior may not always be justified in the most technical legal sense, most citizens are probably not surprised or horrified to learn that felons who attack cops run a higher-than-average risk of being shot by them. Critically, almost none of the BLM cases turn out to actually involve unarmed, non-criminal Black men who were on their way home from church or a game of hoops before being executed by white cops. Not a single one of the cases discussed in great depth so far fits that bill, and few others do.

As a thought experiment, it is worth contrasting the media feeding frenzies surrounding the imperfect-but-reasonable behavior of LEOs during the shootings of felons like Alton Sterling and Mike Brown with the almost total absence of any media coverage of police shootings of white Americans. Whether or not Blacks are shot at a slightly disproportionate rate by sworn officers, it is essentially undisputed that at least 75 percent of the males killed by police in a typical year are white or Hispanic Caucasians. However, in a truly remarkable example of media bias, these cases receive, by my best estimate, less than 10 percent of all national media coverage of police violence. This is true even where the circumstances of a particular situation would have almost certainly led to widespread protests and rioting had the victim been Black. The Dylan Noble case, unfortunately for Mr. Noble, provides an archetypal example of this.

Dylan Noble was a nineteen-year-old Fresno, California, man shot by police on June 25, 2016. According to the sole *New York Times* account of the case, Noble caught the attention of police officers for driving fast: "His tires screeched at a traffic light, throwing up smoke from burning rubber." Officers decided to detain Noble as part of a standard traffic stop and pursued his truck for two to three blocks before pulling the teen over at a Chevron gas station. The two officers involved ordered Noble to leave his truck and put his hands in the air, which he apparently did. Noble was then immediately ordered to lie down on the ground. Some sources have claimed that he was being treated as high risk because of his physical resemblance to a suspect described in an earlier "man with a rifle" call into Fresno PD.

At this point, Noble apparently began to disobey orders, standing up and "drifting away" from the truck and officers while muttering to himself. Still standing upright, he reversed course and began moving toward the LEOs, with one hand out of view behind his back. Noble was told to stop his advance five or six times, with one officer telling him he could be shot if he continued moving forward. After hearing this warning, Noble, looking confused, took a final step forward and muttered a phrase generally rendered as: "I hate my [fucking] life."

Men of their word, the Fresno officers opened fire, striking Noble with two shots and knocking him to the ground. While flat on the ground, Noble was shot twice more—once with a service pistol, and once with a backup duty shotgun carried by one of the officers. The gap in time between Noble's first being pulled over and his being shot dead was "about three minutes." The dead Noble, once flipped over and searched, was revealed to be totally unarmed: "He didn't even have a knife."

The Dylan Noble case would seem, at first glance, to be an almost ideal candidate for a storm of coverage from Black Lives Matter, Blue Lives Murder, Antifa, and the rest of the anti-police crowd. While nothing really indicates that Fresno cops acted dishonorably—they shot a fighting-age male who kept disobeying orders—the same could be said for almost all BLM matters. Questions about the use of excessive force seem unavoidable, whether or not they might also be answerable. Noble was shot twice while flat on his back, including one blast from a shotgun. While defending his officers, even Fresno police chief Jerry Dyer called a video of the Noble shooting "extremely disturbing to watch," and noted that there were "many questions ... out there" about the case.[13]

However, for whatever reason (*cough, the color of Noble's skin, cough*), no storm of outrage ever materialized. Instead, MSM coverage of the Noble case was notably and remarkably unsympathetic. The headline of the *New York Times* piece which provided most of the quotes used in the last few paragraphs was "Fresno Police Shooting Video Shows Dylan Noble Ignoring Orders to Stop," and the article devotes two of its four pages largely to Chief Dyer defending the FPD. An even harsher headline led the *Los Angeles Times* feature on the case: "Dylan Noble ... Was Drunk and Had Traces of Cocaine in His Body, Autopsy Shows." This article devoted several pages to the fact that Noble had a blood alcohol count (BAC) reading of 0.12 at the time of his death, which is equivalent to about three beers, and might have used cocaine at some point in the recent past. Neither of these headlines is, technically speaking, in error. Noble was not a hero, but rather a traffic criminal who resembled the suspect in a shooting and was killed after a tense encounter with police. However, Michael Brown was not a hero either. It is hard not to contrast the coverage of Noble with the pictures of Brown in his graduation gown or Trayvon Martin is his trademark hoodie, which have become American cultural artifacts.

A brief review of the record indicates that the Dylan Noble case is not unusual. A great many poor white men are shot by police, and MSM coverage of these affairs tends to be spotty and non-sympathetic. The Dillon Taylor case provides another tragic example. Taylor was a Caucasian male shot dead by Salt Lake City police on August 11, 2017, in large part because he was wearing headphones. The Taylor case began when officers responded to a report of a white male brandishing a gun outside a convenience store and arrived on the scene to confront Taylor, along with his brother Jerrail Taylor and cousin Adam Thayne. According to police records, the other two men were immediately cooperative, but Dillon appeared upset and did not respond to orders. Jerrail Taylor has argued, passionately and on several occasions, that this was due not to hostility or arrogance but simply to the fact that Dillon Taylor was listening to music: "He couldn't hear what the police were telling him to do, and so he just kept walking." By the time Dillon noticed the bustling scene around him and turned off his music, according to Jerrail, "I saw them point guns at my brother's face, and I knew what was going to happen."

And happen it did. Officers instructed Taylor to lie down on the ground, and he apparently attempted to comply. But, after what had now become a minutes-long standoff with someone thought to be a potential shooter, the Salt Lake City officers "fired at him from close range before he had a chance." To quote Jerrail: "There was [a short wait]. He went to pull up his pants to get on the ground, and they shot him." Taylor crumpled to the ground and was dead within minutes.

Objectively speaking, Dillon Taylor was an extraordinarily sympathetic victim of police violence. Not only was he gunned down in front of his own brother and cousin, he had also recently gotten engaged, and his pretty fiancée was three months pregnant with the couple's first child. Although no angel—he had an outstanding misdemeanor warrant for a probation violation—Taylor had apparently taken major recent steps to turn his life around. He was not in fact in possession of a gun when shot; police seemed to have mistaken his cellular phone for a firearm. He was, by all accounts, completely sober when shot.

For all of that, MSM coverage of the potentially high-profile Taylor case was amazingly scanty. While a quick Google search for "Trayvon Martin" turns up a well-maintained Wikipedia page as well as *four* feature articles from CNN and major pieces in the *New York Times* and *Washington Post*, doing the same for "Dillon Taylor" yields results like a personal Facebook page labeled "Justice for Dillon." Taylor's own archived Twitter account makes the list of the top ten results, as does the IMDb profile for a film director with the same name. One of the few relatively mainstream articles to discuss the matter, Andres Jauregui's piece over at HuffPost, bears a rather remarkable title: "Officer's Fatal Shooting of Unarmed Man Dillon Taylor Was Justified, According to Prosecutors."

The coverage of the Dillon Taylor case was so bizarrely slanted— when it was there at all—that the conservative Federalist Papers website felt compelled to discuss it in a major article called "Unarmed White Man Killed by Black Cop; Here's How the Media Reacted." Quoting another conservative source, author Steve Straub said bluntly, "While national news media continue to focus on race in Ferguson, Missouri ... they apparently don't think a similar case in Utah with the races reversed is that newsworthy." As that "similar case" teaser indicates, Straub made a point which almost no MSM discussion of the Taylor matter bothered with: the Dillon Taylor shooting was *also* an incident of interracial police violence. Officer Bron Cruz, the man most directly responsible for Taylor's death, was "a Black police officer," although most local media outlets to touch on his race preferred referring to him as "non-white." To Straub, both this fact and the case itself were ignored because "[t]here's a mindset out there [that] only people of color can be victims. A white person can never be a victim."[14]

Quite possibly, that claim is valid. Whatever the reasons for this might be, I and others have certainly concluded that "high-profile" police shootings of whites generally receive something in the order of one-tenth as much media coverage as high-profile police shootings of Blacks. Interestingly, even police shootings of Hispanics—a group logically more oppressed than native-born Blacks "IN TRUMP'S AMERICA"—receive virtually no mass media coverage. On July 11, 2016, the well-put-together niche website attn.com compiled a list of widely ignored police shootings of Hispanics, which included some truly remarkable cases. In one of them, a twenty-four-year-old mother of three, Melissa Ventura, was shot while holding a knife that she may have been using to defend herself from violence. In another, nineteen-year-old street racing star Pedro Villanueva was killed when *undercover* California Highway Patrol officers shot into his moving car. In still another case, eighteen-year-old Anthony Nunez was killed by San Jose officers who were attempting to *stop him from committing suicide*, after he had already shot himself in the head, because he was still touching his gun and seemed potentially threatening.[15]

All of these cases, and at least two other police shootings of Latinos, took place in a single week between July 3 and July 9, 2016. Again, none of the victims involved seem to have been spotless heroes. Drag racing, for example, is highly illegal. However, it seems a safe bet that some or all of them would be widely regarded as heroes today had they been left-leaning Black criminals. Danielle DeCourcey, author of the attn.com piece, specifically attributed the lack of attention paid to shootings of Latino taxpayers to the absence of BLM-style movements in working-class Latino communities. Latinos tend to have a generally positive view of the police, often mentally contrasting them with their corrupt Latin American equivalents. "Over there, the police are always asking for bribes," source Yolanda Dominguez is quoted as saying. "Here, they try to help."

Perhaps more importantly, political and religious leaders in the Latino community tend to focus more on finding constituents jobs or pathways to U.S. citizenship than on calling out "racism." Black churchmen, for example, play a large role in drumming up political conscious-ness about alleged racial issues facing the Black community, while the more traditional churches in Latino areas usually do not take on this function. Some Hispanics seem to resent this, with attorney Amin David, who was quoted at length in the attn.com piece, saying, "I really applaud the African American churches. They really know the buttons to press." However, as this book goes to press, the situation appears unlikely to change. No movement focused on making dead criminals into heroic symbols of oppression seems likely to soon achieve mainstream status in Latino or poor white communities.

By this point, we have established that roughly 80 percent of all individuals shot and killed by the police in a typical year are whites or Latinos, and that these cases generally receive substantially less media coverage than very similar cases of Blacks being shot by police. Simply put, there is no epidemic of specifically Black people being shot by police. However, as authors dating back at least to Aristotle have noted, things which do not exist—the Greek gods, for example—often have as great an impact on society as those which do. Whether or not it was ever actually true, the perception that cops have recently been murdering Blacks in job lots and must be forced or persuaded to stop has had a truly massive impact on the modern profession of policing.

The most obvious real-world effect of the fictional BLM narrative has been that cops are doing less police work and are retreating from the effective broken windows policing that so dramatically lowered crime rates in the early 1990s, due almost entirely to fears of being labeled racist. In my home city of Chicago, discretionary police stops dropped by an astonishing 90 percent between 2015 and 2016 as, to quote a widely circulated DNAinfo headline, "Gun Violence Skyrocket[ed]." According to Chicago Police Department spokesman Tony Guglielmi, there were 157,346 total recorded police stops between the start of 2015 and the end of March of that year. But during 2016, the total number of stops recorded in the first quarter of the year dropped to 20,908. Unsurprisingly, police also found fewer illegal guns in 2016—1,316 of them, down more than 100 from the previous year's total.[16]

Predictably, Chicago crime soared through the roof. According to Guglielmi's data, "Shootings across the city are up 80 percent" from 2015 to 2016. By March 31 of the latter year, 123 people had already been killed and an additional 652 were wounded in more than 600 single- or multi-victim shootings across the city. Sounding forlorn, Cook County state's attorney Anita Alvarez warned that my hometown was on pace to have 700 murders in 2016, the highest total in 20-plus years.[17] Furthermore, the crime wave was not confined to murder and a few other serious felonies, and thus could not fully be explained by a gang war or other localized phenomena. Instead, ABC7 Chicago accurately summed up the situation as: "Wall-to-Wall: FBI Stats Show All Chicago Crime Up."

According to data put together by the *federales* and confirmed by the Chicago Police Department and ABC's news team, total violent crimes in Chicago jumped a remarkable 24 percent during the year 2016 alone. Aggravated assaults increased 23 percent, while rates of robbery (including armed robbery) were 28 percent higher than they were in 2015. For good measure, property crimes jumped at least 6 percent. Overall, ABC7 reporters Chuck Goudie, Ross Weidner, and Christine Tressel thought it fair to say that sex crimes, assaults, robberies, and burglaries were "all up in the first half of last year," with no reason to believe that this would change in the second half. This trend was not confined to Chicago itself. Crime jumped by nearly a third across the entire Chi-Town metroplex, increasing by 28 percent in northwest sub-urban Elgin, Illinois, and by 31 percent more than twenty miles away in the southern suburb of Joliet.[18] In this latter case, rather remarkably, newly aggressive criminals were apparently not deterred by the fact that Joliet is home to one of the Midwest's largest state penitentiaries.

For that matter, the new normal for crime was not confined to Illinois or the Midwest. Around the same time the first DNAinfo article on rising Chicago crime rates came out, Heather Mac Donald provided a multi-page piece headlined "The New Nationwide Crime Wave" to the *Wall Street Journal.* In it, she pointed out some striking facts. Following the 2014 shooting of Michael Brown and the resulting unrest, a more than twenty-year-long decline in American crime rates essentially ended. For the first time in twenty-one years, the year 2015 witnessed a sharp and sustained increase in predatory gun violence across America. According to the Baltimore Police Department, quoted at some length by Mac Donald, gun violence within the city was up more than 60 percent over "this time last year." In Milwaukee, homicides increased an astonishing 180 percent between May 17, 2014, and May 17, 2015. In St. Louis, the increase was less than 30 percent, but robberies also jumped 43 percent and non-fatal shootings—several involving gunmen simply emptying pistols into crowds—were up 39 percent. Similar patterns prevailed in Atlanta (murders up 32 percent), Los Angeles (25 percent), and New York, New York (13 percent, plus a roughly 10 percent increase in shootings). "Crime is the worst I've ever seen it," said St. Louis alderman Joe Vaccaro.

Mac Donald's conclusions proved, unfortunately, to have staying power. In a follow-up 2017 piece headlined "All That Kneeling Ignores the Real Cause of Soaring Black Homicides," she pointed out that the murder rate continued to increase every year between 2014 and 2017. While aldermen representing white ethnic or Hispanic wards, like Mr. Vacarro and Chicago's "Proco" Joe Moreno, could hardly have been thrilled with the damage done to their neighborhoods by this trend, Black Americans were even harder hit. To use Mac Donald's data, "nearly 900 additional Blacks were killed in 2016 compared with 2015," bringing the total of Black homicide victims in the latter year to almost 8,000 (7,881). That increase came "on top of the *previous* 900-victim increase" among Blacks alone, which occurred between 2014 and 2015. Remarkably, in a reversal of a long-standing trend, the 7,900 Black Americans killed in 2016 were 1,305 more than the total number of whites and Hispanics killed in 2016, despite the white population being roughly five times as large as the Black population.[19]

Police spokespeople have been remarkably open about the strong connection between BLM-style lobbying and the increase in crime. Multiple Chicago police sources blamed "flagging officer morale" for the 2015–2016 drop in stops and the resultant rise in shootings. "I'll leave that up to the common sense of the citizens as to why things are not as productive," said Fraternal Order of Police president Dean Angelo, but "I've never seen morale this bad in my career." Another high-ranking source, who asked not to be identified, was even blunter: "Maybe [officers are] doing their job ... but it's the bare minimum. The data shows they're not engaging in proactive policing." Police sources saw this as a regrettable, but understandable, state of affairs. One asked, "In this environment, why would an officer make a stop unless they see a gun, or witness a shooting[?]" Nationwide, political figures like former FBI director James Comey essentially agreed, with Comey coining the term "Ferguson effect" to describe downturns in proactive policing following riots and other vibrant exercises in civic engagement.

Words and actions have consequences. At some level, it is hard not to be almost inspired by the BLM movement. As a teacher, I have always had a soft spot for young people making beautiful signs, marching down the public ways, and engaging their elders. When not shouting such things as "Pigs in a BLAN-KET ... Fry 'em like BA-CON!"—a popular marchers' chant calling for the death of police—BLM activists often seem to almost embody this kind of youthful idealism. But like the hippie communalism of old, the Black Lives Matter movement has a tragic flaw. The basic claims of BLM are simply not true. Fewer than 1,200 people were killed by police in the year the movement began; only 258 of them were Black, and exactly 17 were unarmed Black men shot by white officers. Because they were directed at a nonexistent problem, the sweeping solutions of these proud young activists did far more harm than good. In a typical Midwestern city, shootings increased by half while police stops dropped 80 percent. Whatever the movement's intentions, it is hard not to come to an unpleasant and unavoidable conclusion: Black Lives Matter got a ton of Black people killed.

Taboo Obvious Fact #2: There Is No "War on POC" ... and BBQ Becky Did Nothing Wrong

An important corollary to the Taboo Obvious fact that there is no epidemic of (white) police officers murdering (helpless, unarmed) Black men is the Taboo Obvious fact that there is no race war at all going on in America—and certainly not one led by whites. The center-left mainstream media are constantly chock-full of stories about Blacks and other people of color (POC) facing abuse at the hands of whites—Permit Patty, Pool Patrol Paula, BBQ Becky, and so on. However, interracial violent crimes of any kind are extremely rare. In the case of murder, an astonishing 85 percent of white victims and 93 percent of Black ones are killed by an assailant of their own race. The pattern is essentially the same for most other serious crimes, with the notable exception of robbery. Furthermore—and this is almost never said—when interracial crimes do occur, they slant at least 75–80 percent POC-on-white. Both of these largely undisputed facts have held true for the last several decades.

As I discussed during the last chapter's review of FBI data from 2012 to 2013, Blacks alone commit more than five hundred thousand crimes of violence against whites in a typical year, while whites commit about one hundred thousand violent crimes against Blacks. The MSM essentially present their own version of reality by totally ignoring this trend. Although 76 percent of the individuals killed by police are whites or Hispanics, these cases receive less than 10 percent of national media coverage. Eight out of ten cases of interracial violence are POC-on-white, and these cases also probably receive less than 10 percent of national media coverage of interracial violence.[1] This chapter unpacks the real, indisputable, and, in many cases, surprisingly positive facts surrounding interracial crime in the United States.

It is absolutely indisputable that, for the past two to three years, major media outlets such as CNN and MSNBC have run literally dozens of stories focusing on the harassment of Blacks by whites. Backed up by hashtags like #AnotherOne and #LivingWhileBlack, various chattering hairdos have claimed that it is almost impossible to simply exist in the U.S.A. as a person of color. Even the names and nicknames of white harassers involved in particular street-fighting incidents have "gone viral" and become part of the American zeitgeist. Who could forget, for example, Pool Patrol Paula?

The Pool Patrol Paula case became national news after a South Carolina woman named Stephanie Sebby-Strempel was arrested on assault charges in June 2018 for harassing a fifteen-year-old African American boy at a community pool. According to the lad, Darshaun RocQuemore Simmons, "She called me the N-word and she called me a punk." To quote a piece on the CBS News website, the woman then "verbally and physically assaulted" him, forcing the kid to leave the pool area and engage local LEOs. While he remained calm throughout what was basically a minor scuffle, responding in a contained and gentlemanly fashion, young Mr. Simmons now claims that he had to enter counseling to "try to process" the alleged assault. The city of Summerville, South Carolina, may have to do the same. After a legitimately angry complaint from Simmons's father, Bryan, that no lifeguard or other adult at the pool "stepped up and [stopped] this lady," activists have called for the town to implement citywide diversity training. At any rate, the confrontation, which Simmons recorded on his smartphone, went viral almost immediately on YouTube and Twitter, causing Sebby-Strempel to be arraigned on assault charges, locked up on a bond of sixty-five thousand dollars, and fired from her position with cosmetics retailer Rodan + Fields.

Pool Patrol Paula did not police the water alone! On July 6, 2018, MSN ran a three-page article on a white man who called the police on a Black woman who was using the private pool in his condominium complex. According to the woman, Jasmine Edwards, complex resident Adam Bloom politely asked her for "her address, and then for an ID," and called the police after this request escalated into an argument. According to Bloom and the lawyer he ended up having to retain, videos which exist of this incident don't capture the context. Bloom was the Glenridge condo community's "pool chair" and became involved after another condo board member asked Edwards for her address when he did not recognize her. Edwards responded to that question by giving an address on a street where no residences had yet been built, which struck Bloom's colleague as suspicious. When confronted by both Bloom and an officer who responded to the scene, Edwards—who apparently does live in the Glenridge community—produced a key to the gated pool area. Bloom and the officer declared themselves satisfied, and the police closed the call and left.

But the race relations crisis was only beginning! Edwards, who had videotaped the entire incident on a smartphone, posted the video clip to Facebook under a header calling it a "classic case of racial profiling." The video was shared tens of thousands of times, and Bloom was quickly fired from his executive job at Sonoco Products. As something of a stab to the back, Glenridge also let him go as pool chair. Bloom "resigned" on July 5, 2018, and the homeowners association released a page-long formal statement saying that Bloom escalated the pool situation and "does not reflect the inclusive values Glenridge seeks to uphold as a community." Even the sports website BSO reported on the case as coverage went truly national, describing the incident as part of "a growing trend of white people calling the police on Black people for the most ridiculous of reasons."[2] When this case was last covered by a major media outlet, Bloom's lawyer, John Vermitsky, stated that his client had received multiple death threats and been forced to leave his home and move his wife and children to a safe location. Bloom could not be reached for this book.

The alleged harassment of innocent minorities extends well beyond the pool. Another random white taxpayer earned the label "Permit Patty" after calling the police on an African American girl selling water on a San Francisco sidewalk. This woman, actually named Alison Ettel, told CNN that she was trying to make a business deadline on the day the incident occurred and became irritated by "constant yelling about $2 bottles of water for sale under her window." According to Ettel, as transcribed by CNN reporter Dan Simon: "I was working from home. I was on some extreme deadlines.... there was somebody shouting outside continuously.... I couldn't concentrate at all."[3] Ettel claims she called 911 only after going outside and engaging the girl and her mother, who refused to leave, and that she called primarily to ask whether street vending without a permit is illegal.[4] It seems unclear, from the record, whether any LEOs in fact showed up to confront the industrious young woman.

However, a video of Ettel's call to the cops, posted to social media by Erin Austin, the girl's mother, rapidly went viral. From this one, we got the hashtags #SellingWaterWhileBlack and #LivingWhileBlack. Austin was notably unsympathetic to the harried Ettel's attempt to explain the situation, saying, "Just the fact that she called the police on a child, that's evil." Race, allegedly, made the situation even worse: "To call on a child of color, knowing that people have been killing Black kids ... that says to me you don't care about my child's life."

Austin also denied any misbehavior on the part of her daughter, saying, "She's not a loud kid. She's not screaming!" Many people apparently agreed with Austin's assessment. As has become typical in these cases, Ettel lost her job, resigning as CEO of Treatwell Health—which, ironically, is a far-left-leaning California company that sells medicinal cannabis products. According to *TIME*'s Gina Martinez, she has also received multiple death threats. A fair number of people appear to see even this as justified. In her recording of the confrontation with Ettel, Austin can be heard saying, "You can hide all you want. The whole world's gonna see you, boo."[5] Those exact lines have apparently been repeated in some of the calls and messages to Ettel.

Alison Ettel may have gotten famous for "harassing" Black people, but no one got famous like BBQ Becky. "Becky," actually named Jennifer Schulte—"Becky" is a half-joking term used to describe unexceptional white women, with implications that the target is ignorant and privileged—achieved international notoriety after calling police on a group of African Americans barbecuing in a park. This incident occurred on April 29, 2018, when Schulte noticed the party grilling in a "dog run" area of an Oakland park where charcoal fires are not allowed. She apparently asked the group to leave the area or use alternative fuel, and this request escalated into a two-hour argument with barbecuers Kenzie Smith and Michelle Snider.[6] Near the end of the confrontation, Schulte called police, alleging that Snider had shoved her and then begun "following and harassing" her as the argument escalated. Police, apparently more than a bit bemused, arrested nobody. Schulte was evaluated for a "5150" short-term psychiatric hold but was found fully sane, and the Snider party was simply apprised of the grilling regulations and asked to leave the park for the day.

Obviously, however, things did not end there. Snider contended both throughout and after the scuffle that the incident was explicitly racist in nature and—again—that it is almost impossible for POC simply to lead normal lives in America. "This[7] is exactly what is the problem with Oakland today," she said in her social media video. "This lady wants to sit here and call the police on them for having a barbecue at the lake, as if this is not normal. [Police] have got other things to do than sit here and listen to another white lady complain about Black people in Lake Merritt Park."[8]

In solidarity with Snider, virtually the entire East Oakland Black community responded by throwing a giant barbecue "in all areas" of

Fort Merritt. According to CNN's Gianluca Mezzofiore, hundreds of people danced to West Coast hip-hop and classic soul music on May 20, 2018, while local Democratic political candidates worked the crowd making their pitches for November. One of these candidates was BBQ Becky's actual fisticuffs opponent, Kenzie Smith, who was nominated to a spot on Oakland's powerful Parks and Recreation Advisory Committee following their encounter and ran for city council in 2018 while backed by a five-figure war chest. Beyond Smith, event organizer Jhamel Robinson noted that "(Everybody) showed up. We had 30 street vendors, local businesses, six DJs playing hip hop ... there were dance contests and local council candidates."[9] Even famed 1960s activist Angela Davis put in a cameo appearance. The most commonly used name for the event? #BBQingWhileBlack.

BBQ Becky's was by far the most famous viral video depicting whites apparently harassing or attacking Blacks for "just living life," but it was by no means the last. Back in Chicago, a white CVS manager earned the nickname Coupon Carl—and nationwide opprobrium—after calling the police on a Black woman he believed was using a fraudulent coupon. According to Camilla Hudson, store manager Morry Matson refused to accept a coupon she had received in the mail to replace a defective product, saying that it looked questionable. A confrontation began and, in a video viewed more than 263,000 times on YouTube and Facebook, a shaky-handed Matson can be seen dialing local law enforcement and trying to report his irate customer. "She's ... African American," he says awkwardly, to which the angry Hudson counters, "I'm BLACK. Black isn't a bad word." Like most involved in such social media mob situations, Matson was fired, losing his salaried management job with the pharmacy just days after the call.

In an interesting twist to this particular story, Matson himself turns out to be part of an oppressed minority group. A gay man, he was in fact an Illinois chapter president for the Log Cabin group of moderate gay Republicans at the same time his argument with Hudson took place. Although no far-left liberal—Matson had done delegate work for The

Donald in the past—he was actually a popular candidate for 48th Ward alderman when the incident occurred, running on a platform of initiatives such as a jogging and cycling trail in his home district and ensuring that parents of all races can "send their children off to school without fear." None of this sufficed to save him. As noted, by July 15, CVS had opted to let Matson and another employee go and issued a lengthy statement reading in part: "We sincerely apologize to Ms. Hudson for her experience in one of our stores. Our Region Director … contacted Ms. Hudson as soon as we were made aware of this incident. CVS has begun an investigation, and we will take any corrective action that is warranted to prevent it from happening again."

Conservatives are now beginning to publicize similar incidents of public harassment and assault, and the media is nearly as prone to provide these with widespread coverage. On July 5, 2018, for example, an incident where a San Antonio teen was attacked inside a Whataburger restaurant for wearing a MAGA hat went internationally viral. According to Chris Sommerfeldt of the *New York Daily News*, sixteen-year-old Hunter Richard was "having dinner with a couple of friends" when an unidentified adult Hispanic male came up to him, tore his red Donald Trump hat off his head, and started cursing at him. The man then grabbed Richard's drink and "emptied it over him," dousing the kid with soda. The attacker's last words before walking away with the hat were, "This is going to go great in my fucking fireplace, bitch," to which Richard fired back, "Have fun with it."[10]

This situation, perhaps surprisingly, received extensive national attention, with the suspect in the hat attack eventually being identified as thirty-year-old Texas man Kino Jimenez, and San Antonio police rapidly prepping a warrant and arresting him for theft. Whataburger formally condemned the attack, saying, "We were shocked to see this video, and certainly don't condone this type of customer behavior in our restaurants." Multiple center-right media sources attempted to create the impression of a wave of anti-Trump attacks, with journalist Kate Taylor pointing out, "In May, a 22-year old said he was harassed and threatened by employees at a Cheesecake Factory in Miami, Florida, for wearing the 'MAGA' hat," and noting a few other incidents.[11]

The popular impression that interracial crime is constant, with minorities (and, for that matter, conservatives) barely able to walk down big-city streets without risking a mob attack, is rather remarkably wrong—and the idea that widespread *white-on-Black* crime, specifically, is currently at epidemic levels borders on the insane. First, serious interracial crime of any kind—whether it be Black thugs attacking tough rural whites or vice versa—is quite rare. According to Aaron Bandler of the right-leaning but statistically sound Daily Wire, 93 percent of Black homicide victims are killed by other Blacks, and roughly 85 percent of white homicide victims are killed by other whites. Bandler's simple point takes one sentence to make. The International Business Times says essentially the same thing at greater length, with Lydia O'Neal noting, "Homicides in which the offender and victim were of the same race have vastly outnumbered interracial homicides for the past ten years. FBI data show that while 500 Black-on-white killings and 229 white-on-Black killings were reported in 2015, 2,574 homicides were committed by whites against other whites, and 2,380 by Blacks against Blacks."[12]

Generally speaking, the same principle governs crimes less serious than murder, although to a lesser extent. According to previously mentioned Department of Justice numbers for 2012–2013, which have been cited by everyone from Tim Wise to Jared Taylor, there were 4,091,971 violent crimes committed against white victims. Only 560,600, or 13.7 percent, were committed by Blacks, while more than 56 percent were committed by other whites—along with 11.9 percent by (mostly Caucasian) Hispanics and 7.8 percent by unknown (and generally white) assailants. Crimes against whites were dominated by whites. Similarly, of 995,800 crimes against Blacks, only 10.4 percent—roughly 100,000—were committed by whites.

Interestingly, both Black and white scumbags were disproportionately *unlikely* to attack targets of the other major race. Whites make up 62 percent of the population but represented only 38.6 percent of those targeted by Black crooks—a 38 percent underrepresentation. White goombahs seem even more politically correct: Blacks make up fully 13 percent of the population but were only 3.6 percent of those attacked by white criminals. This figure represents a *72 percent* underrepresentation of Blacks among the targets of white criminals. All told, out of 6,484,507 reported violent crimes, only 664,163 (10.2 percent) were examples of "traditional" interracial crime involving whites and Blacks attacking one another. Again, these figures emerge from federal government data which have not been seriously contested.

So far, nothing too terribly controversial has been said. But there's more! On those rare occasions when serious interracial violence does occur, it is almost invariably POC-on-white, and especially Black-on-white. My own data indicate that in the representative year under review, there were 560,600 Black-on-white violent crimes and only 103,000 white-on-Black violent crimes. Well-known anti-racist author Tim Wise[13] comes to the same conclusion using a different data set. He pointed out that, in 2008, "there were indeed far more Black-on-white violent crimes (B-W) than white-on-Black violent crimes (W-B) … about 429,000 in the first case and only about 91,000 in the other. [This means] that out of about 520,000 single-offender interracial violent crimes that year, 82.5 percent were Black-on-white (B-W) while only 17.5 percent were white-on-Black (W-B). My goodness!"[14]

To some extent, these figures should not be especially surprising. There are *more* whites than Blacks, and they have more money. It is not especially surprising that robbers, for example, prefer to target a group that is five times larger and has twice the amount of money on average versus a slightly tougher group that is one-fifth the size and has half as much money.[15] However, my figures and Wise's at the very least put the lie to the claim that there is an epidemic of Pool Patrol Paulas. Not only is interracial crime rather rare, but Blacks and other people of color commit the large empirical majority of it.

Many conservative columnists argue openly that the center-left mass media in the U.S.A. "spin" data and story lines involving interracial crime in a partisan and biased fashion, creating the illusion of an epi-demic of anti-POC violence while, if anything, the reverse exists. In a widely quoted column, journalist Jason Lewis of the *Star Tribune* in Minneapolis listed a number of shocking Black-on-white crimes which received far less coverage than 2013's comparable Trayvon Martin epi-sode. In one case, for example, a thirteen-year-old Kansas City boy was "doused in gasoline and set on fire" by perpetrators who told him, "You'll get what you deserve, white boy."

In another matter, an eighty-eight-year-old decorated veteran of World War II was "brutally beaten to death with flashlights" outside a Spokane, Washington, bar by two Black teenagers. In a third, three would-be gang members, two of whom were Black men, gunned down popular Aussie exchange student Chris Lang essentially for the fun of it. In perhaps the most remarkable case, two women, aged twenty-four and thirty-two, were *raped for hours by a dozen "youths"* in a Delaware park "widely known for such brazen crimes." Their frantic cries for help were apparently ignored not just by multiple passersby but also by the media, which ran only a few local stories on the matter.[16]

Conservative pundit Ann Coulter contends that rape, specifically, is an arena of crime where stark cross-racial differences in commission are not merely ignored, but are actively covered up by the left-leaning media. Quoth she: "They don't report on the much more common Black-on-white crime, but the very rare man-bites-dog story of white-on-Black crime—that gets covered hysterically not because it is a man-bites-dog story, but they act as if 'No, this is all too common, it's the racism in America.'" In the context of interracial rape and sex crime cases, "The number of Black-on-white rapes ... [going back] 15 years, there are about 1,000-to-2,000 a year Black-on-white rapes. The number of white-on-Black rapes is either 0.0 or [a] sample too small for a number."[17]

Lest slander spread, it is important to point out one flaw in Coulter's data, which are widely cited by alt-right and "alt-lite" outlets. The figures Coulter cites come from the annual National Crime Victimization Survey (NCVS) put together by the Department of Justice's Bureau of Justice

Statistics (BJS). The annual BJS survey is not a census-like sampling of all Americans, but rather a skillfully done poll of 160,000-odd randomly selected individuals. In a typical year, U.S. population demographics indicate that 13 percent of these people (say 19,200) would be Black, half of those (9,600) would be women, perhaps one-tenth of the women would have been raped at some point prior to the survey (960), and—using the BJS's own figures for all violent crime—10.4 percent of the rapists of Black women would have been white men (97 cases).

It is an ethical constraint among virtually all social scientists with whom I have ever worked to report very small-N figures of less than one hundred as "stat. 0" or "too small to be accurately measured." The annual rate of white-on-Black rape is clearly not "0." In fact, the figures just cited indicate that it may be fully half the rate of Black-on-white rape. However, it is an indisputable mathematical fact that 2x is still bigger than x, and it is hard not to contrast the wall-to-wall coverage often provided to atypical incidents of white-on-Black violence with the limited or nonexistent coverage of more common cases where the races cut the other way.

Some of the incidents of interracial violence marginalized by the contemporary MSM are truly remarkable and horrifying. The purpose of this book is not sensationalism—and, again, 90-odd percent of murders and other violent major crimes are intraracial—but it is worth discussing a few such cases in detail. Almost certainly the most emotionally staggering recent case of Black-on-white racist violence was the "Knoxville Horror," the rape-murder of Tennessee college students Channon Christian and Hugh Christopher Newsom. The case began during the late evening of January 6, 2007, when Christian's vehicle was carjacked as she drove along with Newsom on the way to a date. The carjackers, George Geovonni "Detroit" Thomas, Letalvis Darnell "Rome" Cobbins, and Lemaricus Devall "Slim" Davidson, drove Newsom and Christian to a rental home occupied by one of the assailants, where both young people were raped, tortured, and murdered.

It is worth going into a bit more detail here. Of the two youngsters, Newsom was killed first, and more humanely. According to the testimony of Knox County's acting medical commissioner, he was sodomized with an object and anally raped by a person while trapped in the ramshackle rental house. He was then tied up, blindfolded, gagged, "and stripped naked from the waist down" before "being shot in the head, neck, and back" and being set on fire while he was apparently still alive. When Newsom finally expired, his body was wrapped in rags, dumped near a set of railroad tracks, and abandoned. The burnt corpse was discovered the next day.

Christian had it much worse. According to the medical examiner, she died "after hours of torture," suffering "injuries to her vagina, anus, and mouth" from repeated sexual assaults. When the kidnappers were finally done with their sport, bleach and other household cleaning chemicals were poured down Christian's throat and scrubbed into her skin "in an attempt by her attackers to remove DNA evidence." She was then tied up with strips of bedding and window curtains, her face was covered completely with a trash bag, and her body was wrapped inside five large Hefty-style garbage bags. Still alive, she was placed inside a residential unit's dumpster, where she slowly suffocated to death. A female conservative writer describes her as having been literally "thrown away like trash. White trash."

The murders of Christian and Newsom were pursued skillfully and aggressively by Knoxville police. By December 8, 2009, attackers Cobbins, Davidson, and Thomas had been convicted and sentenced either to death (Davidson) or to life in prison without the possibility of parole. Their female accessory, Vanessa Coleman, received fifty-three years in prison for helping facilitate the horrific crimes. A fifth defendant, Eric Boyd, was sentenced to eighteen years inside for aiding in a carjacking that ended up resulting in a fatality, and for failing to report the location of a known criminal fugitive.

Astonishingly, this situation—a case in which two attractive and successful individuals were kidnapped, raped, tortured, and murdered by four to five persons of a different ethnicity and social class in a racially tense Southern city—received almost literally no mainstream media coverage. Roughly ten years later, a Google search for "Knoxville Horror" (conducted on October 2, 2018) turns up the following results: a Wikipedia article, the local Knoxville News website, the alt-right site VDARE, a Snopes fact-check describing certain citizen accounts of the Knoxville Horror as factually imperfect, a very short piece from the right-wing website The Blaze, and—almost unbelievably—discussions of a popular Tennessee festival centered around actual horror films. The most in-depth national reporting on the whole gruesome affair came from another frankly alt-right site, Jared Taylor's American Renaissance, which used area blogger Nicholas Stix as its sole stringer working the case. This was not Trayvon Martin–level coverage.

In terms of both the extreme brutality of the violence involved and the almost total paucity of national news coverage, the Knoxville Horror does not stand alone. The Brittanee Drexel case provides an even more remarkable example of extreme and ignored POC-on-white violence. In this situation, an underage teen spring breaker was kidnapped by a mostly or entirely Black group of males, "made into a sex slave, raped, shot, and then eaten by alligators." A blunt summary of the end of the case on the Fox News website states: "A teenager who vanished from Myrtle Beach, S.C., in 2009 was repeatedly raped in a gang 'stash house' for several days—then she was shot dead and fed to alligators when her disappearance generated too much media attention, the FBI said."[18]

Most details of this incident, which took place in 2009, came to light following the 2016 jailhouse confession of an inmate named Taquan Brown, apparently to FBI agent Gerrick Munoz. According to Brown's on-the-record testimony to officials, he saw a line of men "sexually abusing Brittanee Drexel" when he went to a gang house in McClellanville, South Carolina, to make a drug deal. When he went into the backyard of the house to give money to one of the men there, he observed Drexel bravely try "to make a break for it." However, her desperate escape attempt failed, and one of the captors pistol-whipped Drexel and dragged her back inside the house. Brown then heard two loud shots, probably from a large-caliber pistol. The next time he saw Drexel, her dead body was being wrapped up and taken out of the house. Several witnesses, including Brown, told investigators that the corpse was dumped into a "well-known McClellanville pond teeming with hungry alligators."

So far as I have been able to tell, no one was ever directly punished in connection with the Brittanee Drexel case. A dogged 2009 search for the missing spring breaker, which included police dive teams and highly trained body-sniffing dogs, turned up essentially nothing. Even following Brown's confession years later, the man he fingered as having killed Drexel, Timothy Da'Shaun Taylor, continued to deny any responsibility for the murder. In 2017, he was sentenced to ten to twenty years in prison on an unrelated felony robbery charge, and he has remained incommunicado from prison. Drexel remains unavenged.

She also remains largely uncovered. Running a Google search for "Brittanee Drexel murder" turns up almost entirely local South Carolinian media—the *Democrat and Chronicle* newspaper, the *Post and Courier*, Fox13Now, 13wham.com, SC WMBF News, and so on—alongside the alt-lite website narrativecollapse.com. The top thirty search results for the Drexel case also include the sensationalistic website Popucrime and a friend's personal Facebook page mourning Drexel's loss. MSNBC, CNN, and for the most part even Fox News are nowhere in evidence.

Spending only one hour digging through media at the Fox13Now level reveals literally dozens more graphic stories of interracial crimes which For Some Reason never became the international scandals which they would have been were the races of the participants reversed. In April 2017, for example, the regional California press reported that a gunman motivated almost solely by racial hatred had used his .357 revolver to kill three white men during a broad-daylight shooting spree in downtown Fresno. According to reporters for the *Los Angeles Times*, shooter "Kori Ali Muhammad" (real name Kori Taylor) expressed "hatred toward white people and the government" and proselytized to his family about a potential race war in America before launching his attack. The avowed racist regularly referred to white people as "devils" on social media and had literally dropped an anti-white rap album earlier in the year. One song on the record referred to him explicitly as an armed "Black soldier."[19]

When Muhammad finally snapped, he "stalked the streets" of center-city Fresno and fatally shot three white males with his handgun. Before surrendering to the authorities—which he was allowed to do unharmed—Muhammad screamed "Allahu akbar,"[20] expressed contempt toward his white victims, and apparently threatened the governor of California, according to Fresno PD chief Jerry Dyer. There was no doubt whatsoever about the shooter's motivations, and local authorities announced that Muhammad's attack would certainly be investigated as a hate crime. Chief Dyer was quoted as saying: "If in fact he's lashing out at white people—white males in this case—that would constitute a hate crime."

In addition to the killings on April 18, 2017, the FPD also named Muhammad as the primary suspect in the shooting of *another* white male, an armed security guard, roughly a week prior. This truly remarkable string of crimes—a racially motivated murder spree that killed four people—received exclusively regional coverage. Eight of the first ten search results for the matter are Fresno, Sacramento, or suburban Los Angeles newspapers or TV stations. The first two are articles in the *Fresno Bee.*

The mass media are, to an extraordinary degree, responsible for the widespread false belief that interracial crimes are (1) at all common and (2) majority white-on-Black. Many journalists, and indeed entire publications—I see you, The Root—seem to devote themselves almost entirely to using questionable stories of racism to fan the flames of controversy in America. Perhaps most notable in this regard is Shaun King, a ... remarkably light-skinned Black man who writes for The Intercept, formerly graced the back pages of the *New York Daily News*, and talks about essentially nothing other than the "oppression" of American Blacks in 2019.

In one entirely typical column last year, King called the National Football League's decision to play for five hundred days without benchwarmer Colin Kaepernick "the biggest injustice" since Muhammad Ali was stripped of his boxing title during the civil rights era. He went on to label the reluctance of teams to sign the protest-leading quarterback the worst thing to happen to any athlete in his lifetime, referring to Kaepernick as "a legend and a cult hero" and declaring his willingness to boycott the NFL for the rest of his natural life. At no point did King mention the great man's actual record: 2–16 over the last eighteen games he started as an NFL quarterback. Even this piece might not have been peak Shaun King. On another occasion, he criticized the Georgia Department of Corrections as racist because the heavily integrated law enforcement agency shot a Christmas photo in a snowy-looking cotton field.[21] King's Facebook discussion of this atrocity ("A COTTON FIELD!") received thirteen thousand "likes" and roughly ten thousand shares.

This sort of thing can be almost funny. King is frankly a whip-song writer—is that racist?—and he has the right to publish whatever nonsense he wants to about sports and racism. The blatant bias of this man and many other popular press journalists, however, becomes ethically and legally troubling when they engage serious stories where serious consequences for individuals and even for the U.S.A. depend on what the facts of the case at hand actually are. This was recently and dramatically illustrated when King failed to thoroughly fact-check a tall tale he was told before reporting the wholly false story of a white police officer viciously raping a Black woman.

King was one of many journalists, and arguably the most prominent among them, to share the story of Sherita Dixon-Cole in the late spring of 2018. Dixon-Cole's tale was a dramatic one. After being stopped for suspicion of driving under the influence on May 20, 2018, Cole claimed that the arresting officer, whom I will not name here, "began grabbing her clothes and sexually molesting her" before dragging her behind a building and raping her. This information was fed to King by local Texas civil rights attorney Lee Merritt, and King "failed to verify Cole's claim ... and went on a Facebook rant of over 700 words," according to John Dempsey's excellent account at *Townhall*. King's Facebook post went massively viral, was shared more than 55,000 times, and helped to spread the story globally.[22] Directly following the post, both the actual arresting officer in the Dixon-Cole case and another Texas trooper with a similar name began to receive graphic threats of death, assault, and sexual violence.

But then the nearly inevitable happened. By May 25, the Texas Highway Patrol had released footage from the arresting officer's vehicle and body cameras, showing clearly that nothing untoward had happened to Dixon-Cole at all. Dempsey correctly described the tape, which is easily viewable online, as depicting "another routine traffic stop" which ended in an uneventful misdemeanor arrest. Almost surely in an attempt to avoid further charges of racism, municipal and Texas state officials declined to file any false report charges against Dixon-Cole, citing the technical fact that she apparently made her nonsensical claims to correctional officers while briefly in custody, rather than to sworn "police or peace officers." So far as I have been able to tell, Dixon-Cole has never apologized for her claims.

Nor has King offered a *mea culpa* for his—although he did pen a rambling seven-hundred-word column for Medium about the whole thing, saying in part: "Many good people fought for this person … out of the goodness of our heart. We were right to fight—this system requires us to fight for every ounce of justice we ever get—but someone truly abused us in this circumstance."[23] And so on. Dempsey, rather more succinctly, sums the whole thing up: "Shaun King doesn't care about what happened. He only cares about pushing a social justice warrior story. If King cared about the truth, he would have asked to see the video before going on an embarrassing Facebook diatribe full of lies."

On the SJW left, King does not write alone. Multiple widely respected center-left media venues do little but promote—my lawyer advised me to delete the phrase "make up"—questionable stories about racism. The Afro-centric online magazine The Root, one of the top ten thousand web sources in the world according to the Alexa ranking service, may be the most absurd offender in this regard. The publication regularly runs articles like the piece on July 17, 2018, called "So Trump Is a Traitor: What Difference Does That Make to Black Folks?" That piece opens: "Wow! Did you see the season finale of America yesterday[?]," and goes on to describe the Trump White House as a combination of a reality TV show and cesspool of nightmarish racism. To quote verbatim: "All the Black characters keep getting written off the show or are sniveling Uncle Ruckus types. The rest of the cast are a bunch of mustache-twirling racists and wife beaters—it's almost as though once HBO cast *Confederate* aside, they decided to just integrate the show into the White House and save production costs."[24]

That was only the beginning. Author Jason Johnson went on to state that, while the president of the United States is "clearly" a traitor, his (wait for it) RACISM is much more of a problem. Indeed, allegedly, the two go together. The *real* motivation behind flamboyant Trump gestures like meeting privately with strongman Russian leader Vladimir Putin is … wait for it again … his dislike of Black people. To quote Johnson: "Putin is revered by white nationalist, nativist and white supremacist movements around the world. What happened on Monday … [is] the solidification of a new, white nationalist pact that trickles down from the White House to Republicans in Congress to the National Rifle Association." The goal of this unholy alliance? Nothing less than "the elimination or the subjugation of Black people." This article received literally tens of thousands of social media likes, loves, and retweets. Hell, I just gave it some more publicity here![25]

This is abject insanity. No edgy conservative writer—from Ben Shapiro to Milo Yiannopoulos to Steven Crowder—could get away with using dozens of extreme racial slurs ("sniveling Uncle Ruckus") while *calling the sitting president a traitor* and claiming that mainstream entities like Congress and the National Rifle Association are planning to *exterminate his entire race*. H'what? But this sort of thing is remarkably common on the ctrl-left.[26] Another pro-Black online zine in the Alexa top twenty thousand, Very Smart Brothas, recently ran a major article focused on the unusual claim that "Texas Shouldn't Execute Chris Young for Murder Even Though He Is Guilty of the Crime."

Why not? RACISM, that's why! First, there is essentially no doubt that Texas criminal Chris Young committed the brutal murder of a minority businessman, convenience store owner Hasmukh Patel. Cameras in the store literally recorded Young shooting Patel and then fleeing. However, author Lawrence Ware argued that America's history of abusing Blacks would render his punishment invalid. According to Ware, the U.S. justice system has been and remains a staggeringly racist enterprise. His evidence: "Black folks make up 13 percent of the population, yet they make up 35 percent of those executed."[27] Predictably, Ware did not discuss crime rates. However, he did find time to talk reparations. This was another piece of evidence he provided that detailed the flaws of U.S. jurisprudence: "I'm still waiting for my 40 acres and a mule to atone for the violence this country has inflicted on me." In conclusion: "Chris Young ... is a human being," who should not be killed despite being a convicted murderer. His (Black) life *matters*!

Another major, absolutely mainstream popular press article, penned by Greg Howard for Deadspin, went beyond criticism of the sitting president or a specific legal case to conclude that "America Is Not for Black People." Howard opened his exegesis thus: "The United States of America is not for Black people. We know this, and then we put it out of our minds, and then something happens to remind us." On this occasion, that something was officer Darren Wilson's shooting of Michael Brown as the linebacker-sized teen[28] grabbed for his gun. Or, alternatively, as Howard described it: "An unarmed [young] man was executed by police in broad daylight."[29]

Beginning with the premise that American police are gleefully murdering Black people, Howard went on to explain *why* this is the case. To him, several primary factors were involved. First, Officer Friendly is long gone; policemen should now be thought of as "domestic soldiers" rather than peacekeeping members of the communities they patrol. Technology plays a big role here: "Officers have tanks now. They have drones. They have automatic rifles, and planes, and helicopters." Furthermore, some police academies have added military-style "boot camps" to their training. Add in an utterly unmerited dislike of Blacks, which Howard seemed to attribute to most LEOs, and the conclusion is obvious: "Police officers are capturing, imprisoning, and killing Black males at a ridiculous clip, waging a very literal war on people like Michael Brown." At no point during this explanation did Howard, who is a very technically skilled writer, mention any of the actual empirical facts relevant to a serious examination of police violence—such as the fact that 76 percent of those killed by LEOs are whites or Latinos, or the fact that only about one thousand Americans are shot by police in a typical year.

Nonsense like this has consequences. The feverish coverage by major journals and Alexa top ten thousand sites of an epidemic of racism—which is not actually real—has produced a predictable result. Very many Blacks and white liberal "allies" of the Black community *truly and sincerely believe* that the United States in 2018 is a wicked and negative society and that little has changed since Dr. Martin Luther King Jr. last marched across the Edmund Pettus Bridge in Selma. This perception has several empirically measurable effects. First and least important, many African Americans are feverishly alert for racism almost everywhere, having been trained to see the most minor and least offensive slights as evidence of a bigotry that "is everywhere," but rarely manifests itself. A fascinating and well-intentioned little piece called "Working While Black" provides an excellent illustration of this.

According to the author, who wrote under the name Rboylorn for Crunk Feminist Collective, working as a Black person always "carries with it the weight of blatant or casual racism." One example of this racism would be an executive being asked to talk about her own experiences as a minority: "You are expected to speak for and on behalf of people of color everywhere." However, another example would be *not* being asked to speak about life as a minority. It is apparently inappropriate for a Black manager to be encouraged "not to think of [her]self as Black" in an integrated meeting. Being perceived as bringing diversity to the team—obviously the key value-add of minority employees hired under affirmative action standards of performance—is also racist: "Your

Blackness makes it easy to see that a diversity quota has been met." Perhaps most entertainingly, the author bemoans the fact that—for *no* reason at *all*, of course—minority employees like her are regularly seen as hostile, aggressive, and "difficult." To Rboylorn, standard exhortations from management such as "be more friendly"[30] are loaded with racist subtext, and she claims to mockingly "practice a fake ass smile in the mirror" during mornings to get ready for the workday. To this serious businessperson writing for another major website, simply heading into the office is a traumatic process that can be difficult to endure. She describes Black employees as being "invisible" and "hypervisible" at the same time, trapped under the unwinking eye of Sauron ... or IBM.

The Continuing Oppression Narrative, as I call it, has consequences that go well beyond senior executives feeling a bit uneasy in their heated corner offices. According to the *Washington Post*, hardly a bastion of conservatism, a near-majority of African Americans believe the United States government is trying to genocidally exterminate them. A major study from Oregon State University and the Rand Corporation, evaluated in depth by the ink-stained wretches at the *Post*, concludes that "a significant proportion of African Americans" believe in the conspiracy theory that "government scientists created" HIV/AIDS to wipe out Black communities. More specifically, roughly half of the five hundred Black Americans anonymously surveyed by the OSU research team said that AIDS is a man-made disease created entirely by humans. *More* than one quarter of Black respondents stated that the disease was produced in a government laboratory, 12 percent believed it was created and spread by the CIA, and 15 percent described AIDS specifically as a form of genocide against Black—and not, say, gay—people.[31]

While the "soft bigotry of low expectations" often prevents American whites from publicly critiquing such beliefs, it is worth taking a paragraph to point out exactly how insane this one is. If the U.S. government were, in fact, using bioengineered diseases to wipe out a historically oppressed sector of its own country's population, this would be one of the greatest acts of evil in human history—arguably dwarfing the Holocaust.[32] If this were the case, as I noted in a previous book, I myself would currently be in armed rebellion against the U.S.A. But this is *not* true. HIV began, in fact, as a disease almost entirely confined to majority-Caucasian gay communities. It was darkly nicknamed "the gay plague" during the Reagan administration. Even today, to quote the *Post*'s Darryl Fears, well under "50 percent of new HIV infections in the nation" involve Blacks.

According to Michael Fumento's 1990 bestseller *The Myth of Heterosexual AIDS*, the chance of a middle-class white or Black heterosexual man contracting HIV/AIDS in his lifetime is about one in five hundred. Most of the damage done by beliefs such as the "they-coming-for-us-all" narrative around AIDS is done to the small minority of Blacks who do engage in high-risk behaviors. According to Phill Wilson, executive director of the highly praised Black AIDS Institute in Los Angeles, "It's a huge barrier to HIV prevention in Black communities. There's an issue around conspiracy theory and urban myths. Thus, we have an epidemic raging out of control."[33] A wholly avoidable epidemic, caused by a wholly false narrative.

And there is damage done even beyond that. One of the most important and least discussed side effects of the Continuing Oppression Narrative is that ordinary white Americans are becoming disgusted with the "POC" left, and not infrequently sliding into a dislike of Blacks or minorities overall. The alt-lite blog Iron Legion provides us with a good, if disturbing, example of this trend. Written by Simon Wolfe, the piece is headlined "Nothing We Do Is Good Enough for Blacks So Stop Trying." Opening with a review of some anti-white comments from Black rapper Azealia Banks, the article goes on to argue, "No matter how much white people do for Blacks, it will never be enough. They will always feel aggrieved. They will always want more from you."[34]

Allegedly, progressive political programs, such as affirmative action and welfare, "have not just failed to appease Blacks," but have created a racialized culture of dependency that has worsened race relations even further. While society implores whites to care about Blacks, "they don't even care about themselves and the issues that really affect them." The solutions proposed to this problem by the authors are striking: "Nothing is ever good enough for Blacks, but nothing ever seems to [actually help them] either.... We must separate." Behind and buoyed up by the chants of #BLM and reflected in the flames of each lovely little store burned for absurd and nonsensical reasons, the alt-right lurks.

However, there is a rather obvious third way here. Rather than picking between two racialist sides and fighting for one or the other, American citizens can simply begin telling the truth about race relations. There is no race war going on in the U.S.A., and there certainly is no epidemic of white-on-Black crime. In fact, interracial crimes on an annual basis have been consistently 75–85 percent Black-on-white for the past thirty years. More importantly, there is no horrifying epidemic of interracial crimes of any variety because 84 percent of white murder victims and 93 percent of Black murder victims are killed by a mundane member of their own race. We see constant media coverage of BBQ Becky, Permit Patty, Coupon Carl, and George Zimmerman not because these people are everywhere, but because the corporate media have an agenda to push. We should stop taking this agenda seriously—today.

CHAPTER 3

Taboo Obvious Fact #3: Different Groups Perform Differently

L et us broaden our lens of analysis. One Taboo Obvious meta-point has come up repeatedly, if in passing, during the last two chapters: different groups of human beings, varying in terms of such important variables as race and sex, will *also* vary in terms of virtually every other metric which can be used to judge people. For example, as chapter one pointed out, the African American violent crime rate is roughly 2.5 times the white rate (Department of Justice, 2012). In contrast, the Asian American violent crime rate is generally only 25–30 percent of the white rate. Gender gaps in terms of crime rate are even larger than racial ones, with men committing a range of crimes—including shooting/gunfire, robbery, and, unsurprisingly, rape—at more than ten times the rate of women. Other important characteristics, such as IQ and SAT scores, also vary widely among groups—although, as will be demonstrated at exhaustive length later on, this variation is primarily cultural rather than genetic.

According to National Assessment of Educational Progress figures from 2006, the mean white American IQ is just under 100, while the mean Black IQ in a typical large state (here, New Jersey) is 93. However much American whites and Blacks might bicker back and forth about these figures, both are 10–15 points higher than the mean IQs in a large number of Central African *and* Caucasian Eastern European nations. Globally, according to the archives of the apolitical international testing firm Brainstats (available at https://iq-research.info), scores vary from a high of 107 for Hong Kong down to a low of 59 for Equatorial Guinea —a finding which would appear to bear directly on U.S. immigration policy. While differences in group "dependent variables" such as income are almost always attributed to racism or other bigotry in U.S. upper-middle-class discourse, the next two chapters of *Taboo* contend that variables such as those just discussed above influence outcomes far more than either prejudice or ethnic conflict. This chapter focuses on the existence of group differences, while the next analyzes their impact from an empirical, quantitative perspective.

Crime rate is one of the most obvious examples of a variable that varies dramatically among groups of people and which predicts everything from low likelihood of economic success to high likelihood of experiencing "racist" behavior (such as motorists locking car doors). The definitive *Oxford Handbook of Ethnicity, Crime, and Immigration* notes that "there is general agreement in the literature" that African Americans, and most other minority groups, have higher crime rates within Western societies than whites do. According to the U.S. Department of Justice's Bureau of Justice Statistics, Blacks accounted for 39.4 percent of the prison and jail population during the most recent year on record, despite making up just 13 percent of the population. The equivalent percentage figures were 32.4 percent (62 percent) for non-Hispanic whites and 20.6 percent (16 percent) for Hispanics/Latinos. As a direct result, according to the BJS and the U.S. Census, the Black incarceration rate in state and federal prisons is 3,161 persons per 100,000, while the white incarceration rate is stable at 487 persons per 100,000.

These arrest and incarceration figures for Black Americans are not simply an artifact—the result of, say, police racism. The main technique used by government social scientists to collect crime data is not merely self-reporting by police officers, and it has not been for decades. Instead, every year since 1972, the Bureau of Justice Statistics has conducted the magisterial National Crime Victimization Survey (NCVS), a national survey of more than 150,000 representative and randomly selected American households. During the NCVS, citizen respondents are asked questions about their experiences with crime, including "the frequency of crime victimization and the characteristics and consequences of victimization." The survey collects reliable data on a broad range of crimes, including rape, assault, robbery, burglary, personal and household larceny, and motor vehicle theft. Simply put, if (1) the respondent pool for the NCVS "looks like America," and (2) the rate of crimes anonymously reported by victims to NCVS interviewers as having been committed against them by whites or Blacks (or any other group) matches the pool of whites or Blacks arrested for the same crime nationally in percentage terms, we can be fairly sure that widespread racial bias does not infest the American criminal justice system.

At least for the past few decades, exactly that has been the case. According to NCVS data from 1992–2010, analyzed by the social scientists Timothy Hart and Callie Rennison, minority victims of crime are in fact more likely to report serious crimes—committed both by members of their own races and by the Caucasian majority—to the police than are whites. Across the set of all crimes, "Black (49 percent of whom reported crimes) and Native American (also 49 percent) victims reported most often, higher than whites (42 percent) and Asians (40 percent)." For serious violent crimes such as aggravated assault, Blacks (61 percent) and Native Americans (59 percent) again reported more frequently than whites (54 percent), and Asians (51 percent) again brought up the rear. As these numbers indicate, victims of all races are quite likely to report crimes to police, with 43 percent of all criminal acts and well over 50 percent of serious violent criminal acts reported to police during the study period.

Furthermore, police-reported arrest rates—by race and for a range of serious crimes—roughly mirror the rate at which citizens accused individuals of that race of committing that crime. Citing the NCVS and a number of soundly done studies, the lengthy Wikipedia article on crime and race states, "The probability of arrest given the commission of a crime is higher for whites than it is for Blacks for robbery, aggravated assault, and simple assault, whereas for rape the probability of arrest is approximately equal across offender race." On the other hand, Blacks were slightly but significantly more likely to be arrested for at least two to three other crimes. This rough parity in arrests for real, serious crimes suggests that "Overrepresentation of Blacks in the criminal justice system is not consistent with the interpretation that Black criminals are more likely to be targeted for arrest."[1]

Homicide data also support the proposition that arrest and incarceration rates by race reflect crime rates by race. While police departments, frankly speaking, probably can "play games" in terms of who they choose to arrest for misdemeanor marijuana possession or driving under the influence, there is not one cop shop in a city with an elected mayor that could ignore corpses lying in the streets, or arrest African Americans for witnessed murders committed by Italian mobsters. And police homicide figures again indicate vast Black overrepresentation among perpetrators of violent crime.

According to Department of Justice data for 2013, a representative year which *preceded* the post–"Black Lives Matter" surge in urban murders, the full population of those formally charged with murder during the year included 4,379 African Americans (51.3 percent), 2,681 non-Hispanic whites (32.1 percent), 1,096 Hispanics (12.8 percent), 98 American Indians or Native Alaskans (1.14 percent), and 101 Asian Americans (1.18 percent). Somewhat remarkably, the total number of Black defendants prosecuted for homicide—almost 4,400—was 423 greater than the *combined* total number of whites, Hispanics, Native Americans, Alaskans, and Asians prosecuted for murder, despite the population of non-Black Americans being roughly seven times as large as the population of Black Americans.

As an interesting side note, it is critically important to be honestly critical of Black crime, but crime rate data provide almost no support for "alt-right" theories of white genetic superiority. First, adjusting for basic income and fatherhood variables eliminates almost all differences in Black and white rates of offending. An excellent 1996 study by Lauren Krivo and Ruth D. Peterson found that "racial differences in structural disadvantage" account for essentially all Black-white differences in crime across communities.[2] In plainer words, poor, fatherless young men commit virtually all blue-collar crime, and simply adjusting for the percentage of such men in the population across different communities eliminates most of the gaps in crime rate which are glibly attributed to race. Even more notably, many non-white American groups, including both Asian Americans and African immigrants, appear to have lower crime rates than whites do.

As noted above, only about 100 murders annually involve an Asian American perpetrator, as opposed to the 2,681 that involve a white perp. There are more whites than Asians in the U.S.A., but—assuming that non-Hispanic whites make up around 60 percent of the U.S. population and Asians around 6 percent—the white murder rate is still almost three times the Asian rate. As a direct result, the percentage of whites arrested for murder in a typical year is .0014 percent, while the percentage of Asians arrested for murder is roughly one-third of that rate, or .0005 percent.

According to the NationMaster web resource, low Asian rates of criminality are a global constant. Japan has 127,000,000 people and several huge cities, but a lower serious-crime rate than any other countries—except the miniature Monaco and Palau. "Street crime is almost unheard of." This appears, once again, to be primarily cultural rather than genetic. Quoting a Japanese friend, author Havard Bergo points out that "going to prison would be an unimaginable social stigma" for most people in the hierarchical and image-conscious nation to such an extent that there is a widespread Japanese "perception that crimes are mostly committed by foreigners." Japanese suspects, who obviously do in fact make up the majority of criminals in Japan, "face enormous pressure" to cooperate with respected police and prosecutors. Most do, leading to a remarkable conviction rate of over 99 percent.

Not only do American whites have higher crime rates than Asians essentially anywhere in the world, but they also dominate many categories of negative and antisocial behavior here in the U.S.A. It would be no exaggeration to say that many of these troubling Caucasian behavioral trends are downplayed in modern "discourse" because of an almost complete lack of concern from the academic and media left about what happens to poor white "deplorables." For example, and most notably, working-class white males absolutely dominate suicide rates in America.

According to a 2016 report from the Centers for Disease Control and Prevention (CDC), which was covered extensively and fairly by Britain's BBC, suicides in the U.S. increased from 10.5 per 100,000 people annually in 2000 to 13.0 per 100,000 in 2014. Suicide figures were even worse among men. The group-specific suicide rate reached 20.7 per 100,000 among all males and was considerably higher than that among white males without college degrees. According to the CDC's data, "middle-aged" working-income white people now account for a full third of all U.S. suicides. White male suicide does not appear to be an exclusively American problem. According to the Canadian Mental Health Association (CMHA), Canadian men die from suicide at four times the rate of women. In Ontario over the past ten years, "more men died from suicide than car crashes." Summing up the CDC and CMHA data, a writer for the plucky right-wing website Louder with Crowder remarked, "There's an alarming rate of suicide among white men. So alarming, the *New York Times* admitted it exists and is a problem."

A number of authors, dating back over decades, have pointed out how concentrated the North American suicide problem is among white males. Back in 1982, Joseph Williams noted in the *Times* that late-1970s figures from the National Center for Health Statistics showed a remarkable 40.8 suicides for every 100,000 older white men as opposed to 12.1 per 100,000 for older non-white men. All men were, and are, far more prone to self-harm than women, with the equivalent suicide rates for females being 7.9 per 100,000 for whites and 3.1 per 100,000 for non-whites. Interestingly, the collapse of white nuclear families was directly cited as a cause of at least the racial disparities under discussion. Among older African Americans, extended family structures spanning several generations provided most seniors with a good deal of "participation and meaningful activity."[3] In contrast, according to article source Dr. Richard Seiden, generally wealthier and more dispersed white families "ship their parents off to the dubious virtues of retirement ghettos," where dwells loneliness.

In addition to making up the large absolute majority of suicides, whites also dominate the annual DUI and car wreck tolls. According to a comprehensive twenty-two-page report compiled by the National Highway Traffic Safety Administration (NHTSA) in 2006, non-Hispanic whites made up both the actual and proportional majority of motor vehicle wreck deaths in the most recent year then on record (2002). Out of 43,918 automobile crash deaths, 31,326 (71.33 percent) involved whites, while 5,267 (11.99 percent) involved Blacks, 5,503 involved Hispanics, and less than 1,000 apiece involved Asians (977) or Native Americans (845). It is worth noting that auto wrecks, like suicides, are overwhelmingly concentrated among men. According to the NHTSA report, only 27 percent of white and Asian drivers, 24 percent of Black motorists, and 17 percent of Hispanic drivers killed in 2002 were females of any age.

It is also noteworthy that this white-dominated area of societal misbehavior, like suicide, kills far more people annually than the violent street homicides that so mesmerize the news media. The annual death toll from car wrecks has been remarkably consistent, generally in the mid-to-high five figures, for decades. *Fortune* magazine pegged it at 40,000 persons in 2016, almost exactly ten years after the NHTSA released the 43,000 figure in 2006. The overall number of crashes, furthermore, has actually been rising in recent years—jumping from 5,338,000 in 2011 to 6,296,000 in 2015, according to Ohio's Brannon Law Firm. In contrast, the total number of gun homicides is less than 12,000 in a typical year.

Drugs—especially opiates like heroin and fentanyl—also kill more Americans on an annual basis than guns do, and the users and dealers of these poisons *du jour* are again overwhelmingly working-class white males. In a bluntly worded article titled "Drug Overdoses Now Kill More Americans Than Guns," the Associated Press reported that "[m]ore than 50,000 Americans died from drug overdoses last year—the most ever." In 2015, heroin overdose deaths alone rose 23 percent to 12,989—"slightly higher than the [total] number of gun homicides."[4] The vast majority of the drug users to die from such overdoses are non-Hispanic whites. In 2016, a year demographically very similar to 2015, a total of 33,450 of 42,249 overdose victims (79 percent) were non-Hispanic whites, while exactly 4,374 were Black and only 3,440 were Hispanic or of Latin descent.

The astonishing recent increase in rates of suicide and drug overdose has actually impacted the overall life expectancy figures for young and lower-income white Americans. According to *New York Times* reporters Gina Kolata and Sarah Cohen, drug overdoses are pushing up the mortality rate for young white adults "to levels not seen since the end of the AIDS epidemic more than two decades ago."[5] Hard numbers support this claim: In 2014, the overdose death rate for whites between the ages of 25 and 34 was "five times its level in 1999," while the "rate for 35- to 44-year-old whites tripled." Although the death rate among young whites rose for every age and income group over the five-year period before 2014, it rose fastest among poorly educated, working-class Caucasians— by almost 25 percent for those without a high school education, as opposed to 4 percent for those with at least a baccalaureate degree. In contrast to all of this, death rates for young Black Americans are actually falling. As a result, a once-large gap between mortality rates for Blacks and whites has shrunk by 66 percent. Without "any further progress in AIDs mortality," death rates for whites and Blacks "will be equal in nine years," according to one medical source for the *Times* article.

So the alt-right is wrong. Whites—"Arctic Alliance" elites, to quote the dissident right-wing writer John Derbyshire—seem no more genetically inured from social pathologies than anyone else. Indeed, Caucasians dominate a whole range of socially problematic behaviors ranging from suicide to car wrecks to opiate abuse. But just as we should frankly discuss pathology in poor white communities, honesty compels us to admit that the extent to which American racial minorities dominate certain categories of crime is truly striking. This is overwhelmingly true in the case of what might be the most terrifying and widely despised of all crimes: random urban gun violence.

In my hometown of Chicago, the extent of this minority overrepresentation is staggering. As Devin Foley noted in a major 2016 article for Intellectual Takeout, 75 percent of those murdered in Chicago are Black, and so are 71 percent of their murderers. During the fairly typical year analyzed by Foley (2011), there were 433 recorded Chicago homicides.[6] Out of this pool of well over 400 victims, 326 were Black, 82 were Hispanic (a broad category including many Afro-Latinos), exactly 20 (4.6 percent) were white, and only 5 were "other"—with this latter category including all Asian, Pacific Islander, South Asian, and Native American ethnic groups combined. Essentially none of these murders of Blacks and Hispanics was the result of hate crimes committed *by* whites against oppressed minorities. Of the 171 offenders arrested, tried, and convicted in connection with the pool of murders just discussed, 122 (71.3 percent) were Black, 42 (24.6 percent) were Hispanic, *six* (3.5 percent) were white, and *one* (.6 percent) was Asian American.

The implications of this data are rather remarkable. As "shooters" in the gang scene tend to kill more than once in a typical year, it seems very likely that fewer than ten white criminals were responsible for every one of the Chicago murders committed by Caucasians in 2011. Even more striking, in the context of a city divided roughly equally between whites, Blacks, and Hispanics, we can estimate that an all-white Chicago would average perhaps sixty to sixty-five murders annually rather than four hundred to five hundred. Foley pulls few punches in his article, strongly—and correctly—implying that statistics such as these affect public perception of Blacks and openly saying, "It's hard to believe that racism is at the root of [this]." He concedes that some might argue "systemic racism" traps Blacks in poverty, but he points out that this fails to explain why Blacks target other Blacks for violence far more often than members of any other race, including "enemy" whites. The phenomenon Foley describes is not unique to Chicago. In 2016, the year he wrote his article, there were 15,070 murder victims in the U.S.A. Of these, 7,881 cases involved a Black victim and 6,576 cases involved a white or Hispanic victim.

As staggering as Black overrepresentation among murder defendants is, this statistic pales in comparison to Black overrepresentation among active shooters. Although—after literally thousands of targeted pieces from the media—most Americans see the archetypal active shooter as a crazy white boy in a trench coat, the actual act of "discharging a firearm in a settled or populated place" is almost entirely dominated by urban minority men. According to the 2016 report *Crime and Enforcement Activity in New York City*, Blacks made up 67.5 percent of all arrests for non-fatal shootings, Hispanics made up 29.2 percent of arrests for this crime, and whites and Asians combined made up 2.3 percent of arrests. For purposes of comparison, the Big Apple is 32.1 percent white, 29.1 percent Hispanic, and 22 percent Black. Similarly, in Philadelphia, 85.6 percent of identified non-fatal shooting offenders were Black, 11 percent were Hispanic, and roughly 2 percent were white. Philadelphia is 44.2 percent Black, 34.9 percent white, and 14.4 percent Latino. And so on.

After reading through reams of data such as that just presented, reporter Lois Beckett of the U.K.'s *Guardian* ran a piece headlined "Most Victims of U.S. Mass Shootings"—in other words, individuals shot with a firearm along with three or more other persons—"Are Black." According to the left-wing British paper's data analysis, a review of 358 recent mass shootings found that 75 percent of the victims whose race could be definitely identified were Black. Almost a third of mass shootings, when examined in detail, proved to be "drive-by shootings" or were otherwise specifically identified by LEOs as gang-related. Another third of the mass shootings were "sparked by arguments ... among people who were drunk or high." The hood is the locus for such almost absurd incidents of violence; Beckett pointed out that one Cincinnati neighborhood saw three multiple-casualty shootings within one square mile area during one year.[7]

The nearly universal stereotype of a mass shooter as a troubled, young, white conservative man is entirely a creation of the mass media. And troublingly, the combination of relatively little attention being paid to minority mass shooting cases and the "Stop Snitching" culture so prevalent in poor communities (of whatever race) means that relatively few mass shootings of Black victims are ever solved. Beckett noted that of the full pool of mass-victim shootings she investigated—which would include the suburban white cases—"only about half" were ever solved. In many urban centers, the numbers were much lower. By the close of Beckett's study period, Chicago had made arrests in only two of sixteen mass shootings, while Baltimore had eleven cases in 2015 "and had not solved one."

Racial differences in crime rate, just explored honestly for both Blacks and whites, do not stand alone. Virtually any critical statistic in which we might express interest varies among national, racial, and class groups. Furthermore, understanding variations in such critical variables is a necessary precondition to understanding the extent, if any, to which differences in group performance can be attributed to racism or bigotry. Although it is taboo even to utter these words, IQ provides probably the classic example of a group-variant trait.

The website brainstats.com provides a public service of sorts by listing the most recently available IQ data for almost every country in the world. The scores are, quite literally, all over the map. Hong Kong finishes in first place, with an average tested IQ of 108, followed by a bloc of other Asian tigers—Singapore (108), South Korea (106), Japan (105), and China (105). However, far down the list, the genetically similar populations of Thailand, Nepal, and Bhutan respectively post scores of 91, 78, and 80. Italy, perhaps surprisingly, is the highest-IQ "white" country, with a tested mean IQ of 102. Iceland comes in next (101), and the good ol' U.S.A. ranks in a tie for ninth in the world with a 98.

Eastern Europe places substantially behind the West, with the old Roman and Holy Roman Empire borders serving as a useful dividing line. France, Switzerland, the U.K., and the Netherlands post a 98, a 101, and a pair of solid 100s—while Lithuania, Albania, and Bosnia come in at 91, 90, and 90. Some states with an Africa-descended population do quite well, with Sierra Leone placing sixteenth in the world, Suriname eighteenth, and Guyana twentieth, while others like Benin (70) bring up the very tail end of the list. The pro-Black website African American Homeland uses a separate set of contemporary studies to compile a comparable list and similarly notes wide global variance in tested IQ. The average IQ scores they provide include the following: Greece (92), Malaysia (92), Croatia (90), Turkey (90), Indonesia (89), Brazil (87), Mexico (87), Philippines (86), India (81), Iran (84), Egypt (83), Ecuador (80), and Saudi Arabia (80). The finding that tested—if not potential—IQs vary widely among nation-states and population groups is indisputable.

It is important to note, contrary to the standard racialist position, that these differences do not seem to be primarily genetic in nature. The most powerful evidence for this point is the fact that IQ scores for the same genetic group frequently change dramatically over time. In his magisterial *Race and Culture*, conservative giant Thomas Sowell pointed out that the tested IQ scores for most oppressed white groups—such as the Irish—were far below the national average of 95–100 for hundreds of years. As late as the "Army Alpha" tests given to literally "all potential servicemen" prior to World Wars I and II, this remained the case. Similarly, on very large-N civilian tests of mental competence administered during this era and reviewed by Sowell, "Americans of Italian, Slovak, Greek, Portuguese, Polish, Croatian, Spanish, and Lithuanian ancestry all averaged in the 80s."

Sowell found that "Black Americans' average IQ was in the same range as ... and above some of these European groups." Southern whites generally scored worse than northern Blacks during the early modern era, with white military recruits from states like Mississippi and Alabama falling as many as five points behind Black troops from richer northern states like Pennsylvania and New York. Today, freed of "peasant" social culture and a bigotry often almost as severe as that experienced by Blacks, all or most of the white groups just listed test around the national IQ average. There is no purely genetic explanation for how this could have happened.

Blacks, too, experienced a surge in IQ scores following the civil rights movement. While the Black IQ was pegged at 78 by Arthur Jensen in the late 1970s and has often been given as "80–85" in the years since, these low scores appear not to have been the actual norm for at least a decade. In fact, in a ridiculous example of irony, leftist objections to any research concerning race and IQ appear to have succeeded primarily in keeping positive news about Black IQ gains from the mainstream press. Over in the serious academic world, however, social scientists William Dickens and James Flynn analyzed data from "nine standardization samples for four major tests of cognitive ability" in 2006 and concluded that Blacks have gained as many as 7 IQ points on whites over the past thirty years.[8] Across a range of large-N Black populations ranging in age from four to fifteen, average IQ scores ranged from 88.8 to 95.5. The latter of the two scores just given falls well within the normal white range, despite significant ongoing white-to-Black ratio gaps in income, single parenthood, and living conditions.

Over on the edgy "dissident right" side of the scientific race debate, blogger Audacious Epigone has, perhaps reluctantly, come to similar conclusions. According to his figures, the median Black IQ crossed the 90 mark more than a decade ago, back in 2006. Using the same National Assessment of Educational Progress estimates of average IQ that were employed by Dickens and Flynn and breaking them down by state, Epigone recorded mean Black IQs of 93.9 for Delaware, 92.9 for New Jersey, 92.1 for New York, 91.1 for Michigan, 93.6 for Virginia, and 94.5 for Washington. I am not listing atypical outlier estimates here; the state of Louisiana, a southern state twenty-eight spots down the list, posted a mean Black IQ over 90. The very lowest Black IQ recorded—87.8 for

Alabama—was ten points higher than the most common Black IQ estimate employed on the alt-right, and not too terribly far behind the
modern mean IQ for white Alabamians.[9] Again, there is no purely or
primarily genetic way that the median Black IQ could have jumped from
80 to (say) 92.5 within a window of no more than thirty years.

Although white racialists prefer not to discuss this, a great deal of
further evidence of the malleable and culturally determined nature of
IQ exists. The Eyferth study and similar "military brats" studies provide another piece of evidence for the culturalist camp. In the 1950s,
German psychologist Klaus Eyferth speculated that Black children
raised apart from both the racism and ghetto culture that were then
unfortunately prevalent in Black America could be expected to perform
intellectually on par with whites. To test this thesis, he administered a
German-language version of the standard Wechsler Intelligence Scale
for Children (WISC) test to hundreds of children fathered by American
servicemen with German mothers. Eighty-three of the children were
white, and ninety-eight were mixed-race: the daughters and sons of
Black GIs and white German girls. As a culturalist would predict, the
children had almost identical SAT scores. The white boys beat the
Black/mixed boys by four points—101 to 97—but the mixed-race girls
whipped the white girls 96 to 93.

The Eyferth study is a powerful piece of evidence. While medium "N"
in size, the sample tested included hundreds of people. The children tested
were not "malleable" infants and toddlers, but all at least eight and with
ages ranging up to thirteen; the average age of participants was around
eleven. Some might object that selection by the U.S. Army of only soldiers
within a certain IQ range slanted the results of the test, but we know from
the work of Sowell and others that the IQ averages of different racial
groups within the U.S. Armed Forces have ranged between 80 and 105,
and generally reflect the IQ distributions in our larger society. The most
accurate conclusion here seems to be the obvious one: white and mixed-
race kids raised in almost identical conditions, away from both the ghetto
and any racism whatsoever, will have almost identical IQs.

Perhaps most importantly from a scientific perspective, the key Eyferth study findings about the malleability of IQ and the high performance of multiracial adolescents were recently repeated outside the specific context of secured military bases overseas. According to a 2017 Brookings Institution report by Jonathan Rothwell, data from the 2015 National Assessment of Educational Progress (NAEP) show that there is "no [longer] any test score gap between white and multiracial high school students."[10] In reading and reading analysis, in fact, "multiracial students outperform other groups, including Asians" by a statistically significant margin.

This high performance was not due to any uniquely high level of socioeconomic status enjoyed by biracial teens; the average multiracial high school student comes from a family making $72,000, as opposed to $118,107 for whites and about $60,000 for Blacks.[11] Nor are multiracial children an "exotic" population, resulting mainly from marriages between small high-performing groups like Asians and Jews. Most are just Black and white. According to Rothwell, "[n]early half of multiracial students aged fifteen to eighteen report having Black ancestry, and Black-white combinations are the most frequent interracial origin of multiracial children." The sample used for analysis was huge; roughly fifty thousand kids take the NAEP annually and one thousand or more of them are multiracial. This finding, like Eyferth's, seems very likely to stand for decades.

In their useful resource *The Black-White Test Score Gap*, authors Chris Jencks and Meredith Phillips note another intriguing detail about (generally high) multiracial IQ performance. They point out, citing work by Lee Willerman, that mixed-race children raised by a Caucasian mother score a full eleven points higher on standard IQ boards than multiracial children raised by a Black mother. As the Black-white IQ gap has been pegged at fifteen points for much of the modern era, this finding indicates that virtually the entire gap can be traced directly to "family related factors," such as the amount of intensive study time spent with children, number of books in the home, and neighborhood safety. More simply put, adjusting for the one factor of "custodial parent race" eliminated 80–90 percent of the gap. While perhaps easy to misinterpret, this is again a purely culturalist result. There is no feasible genetic explanation for why almost all Black children raised in Situation X (that is, "attentive white mom") would pick up specific skills, use them to boost their average IQ by one standard deviation, and pass most of them on to their own children, while a genetically identical population of Black children raised in Situation Y ("the hood") would not do so.

Another powerful piece of evidence for the thesis that racial differences in IQ are largely culturally or socially determined is the fact that Black women do much better than Black men on all standard intelligence tests. Sowell has studied this phenomenon as well, noting in a 2002 *Jewish World Review* piece that "females predominate among high-IQ Blacks. One study of Blacks whose IQs were 140 and up found that there were more than five times as many females as males at these levels." This disparity is reflected, perhaps unavoidably, in contemporary higher education. The Summer 2018 issue of the *Journal of Blacks in Higher Education* pointed out bluntly that Black women hold "a large lead over Black men" in almost every field of higher education.

As the *Journal* notes, Black women currently earn around 65 percent of all B.A. and B.S. degrees earned by African Americans, 70 percent of all master's degrees, and 60 percent of all Ph.D. degrees and other doctorates. Even with all of the male firemen and cops auditing a course or two thrown in, Black women also dominate university enrollment, making up 63.6 percent of all African American university enrollments. At no less than twenty-three of the twenty-six elite universities to respond to an itemized questionnaire from the *Journal*, Black women outnumbered Black men. The only exceptions were MIT, Notre Dame, and the Citadel military college. Again, there appears to be no genetic explanation for Black women far outscoring biologically identical Black men at 90 percent of the nation's elite universities.

More evidence for the non-biological nature of the Black-to-white IQ gap is provided by the performance of Black immigrants. As Chanda

Chisala noted in a heavily quantitative piece published by—of all places—the far-right Unz Review, Black immigrants to Western nations generally perform at roughly the same level as whites. In Britain, for example, the average verbal reasoning IQ score is 100.8 for Britons of mixed Black and West African descent, 98.6 for Britons of mixed Caribbean descent, 95 for immigrant Blacks ("Black other/overall"), and 93.5 for Caribbean people. In contrast, British whites overall post a 101, but Irish travelers score an average of 84.6, Roma "gypsies" come in at 86, and even plain old "whites: other" record a 99.

Black West Africans and Caribbean people are essentially genetically identical to Black Americans, almost all of whom descend from West African captives sold overseas as slaves. Thus, again, an eight-to-ten-point tested IQ gap between Black West Africans and Black Americans logically cannot be genetic. After suppressing a bit of a giggle here, let me note that high Black immigrant IQ is also not a result of uniquely rigorous immigration processes employed by the U.S.A. and modern Europe. The U.S.A.'s "chain migration" process—which prioritizes the spouses, parents, and siblings of anyone already here over most elite professionals—is rightly a whipping boy for conservatives, and the incendiary results of Europe's recent "mass influx" policies can be seen on the news every night. Solid IQ scores for Black immigrants and multiracial teens seem to reflect healthy habits almost all humans could learn, rather than the effects of some (nonexistent) winnowing process at the border or in the classroom. That plain fact combined with the test scores themselves means that most genetically determinist explanations for modern IQ gaps basically fail.

Whatever the reason for them, however, IQ gaps certainly do exist and have real-world consequences. While acknowledging that tested IQ is to some large extent culturally determined, author Daniel Seligman pointed out that virtually all of the top executive, professional, and managerial jobs in the U.S.A. require an IQ of "at least 115 or thereabouts," and that major gaps in group representation across elite fields would thus appear in the absence of any racial bias whatsoever in society.

Using longitudinal 1992 IQ data, Seligman estimated that less than 3 percent of Blacks and not much more than 10 percent of whites would be qualified at a baseline level for these jobs. As we have seen, both white and Black IQs seem to have increased since Seligman wrote—a positive finding! However, his point about the logical fallacy of simply assuming that proportional representation will always exist in the absence of bigotry remains valid.

In a 2017 quantitative piece for Inside Higher Ed, Scott Jaschik made this point remarkably frankly, pointing out that scores on standard "success tests" like the SAT, all of which are basically IQ tests, vary among racial and regional groups in the U.S.A. to a surprising degree, which is rarely discussed in public. In 2017, the average Black SAT test-taker posted a verbal exam score of 479 and a mathematics score of 462, for a combined total of 941. American Indians did marginally better (963), as did Hawaiians and other Pacific Islanders (986) and Hispanics (987).

Whites scored more than 150 points higher than Blacks with an average verbal score of 565 and mean quantitative score of 553 for a total of 1118. Asians blew everyone else out of the water with an average combined score of almost 1200 (569 + 612). It should be noted that all of these scores are quite respectable and represent significant improvements over the baselines of "800 and mebbe 1000" which were invoked by educators as the Black and white average scores when I was a high school student in the 1990s. However, the plain empirical fact remains that the mean SAT score for Asians is 240 points higher than the mean SAT score for Blacks. There are only 1600 points on the test.

In the context of these very real performance gaps, only massive programs of preferential admissions can provide the level of visible "skin tone diversity" that elite universities and firms profess to want. As another unusually blunt piece in the *Journal of Blacks in Higher Education* pointed out, the number of non-Asian minorities that actually qualify for normal admission to highly selective institutions like Harvard and Yale is remarkably low. According to the author: "In 2005, 153,132 African Americans took the SAT test. They made up 10.4 percent of all

SAT test takers."[12] But only 1,132 African American college-bound students scored 700 or more on the math SAT, and only 1,205 scored at least 700 on the verbal SAT.

Increasing the cutoff score for analysis to a 750 on either test, which is usually about the cutoff for admission to the ten or so most selective colleges, "[w]e find that in the entire country 244 Blacks scored 750 or above."[13] In order to admit the tens of thousands of Blacks who actually make up 7 to 10 percent of virtually every entering Ivy League and Big Ten class, truly remarkable race-norming has to take place: Black (and Latino) students often receive admissions offers with test scores twenty or thirty percentage points lower than those of white or Asian applicants. At a typical top-50 educational institution, the "affirmative action edge" for minority applicants appears to be in the order of 300 test points.

An honest discussion of affirmative action at this level raises many interesting points and questions. First, it strikes me as remarkable that nationwide, institutional, and legally mandated affirmative action is so rarely invoked in response to claims of "white privilege." While lower-end white racism obviously still exists at the fringes of our society, the plain fact is that the middle-class white male applicant to any good college or Fortune 500 job does *not* actually enjoy massive white privilege. Instead, he is at a 250–310 SAT-point competitive disadvantage relative to an identically qualified Black or Hispanic opponent. It is also notable that those disadvantaged by contemporary affirmative action programs are no longer exclusively, or even primarily, Anglo-Saxon gentry sprigs. Instead, they tend disproportionately to be working-class Asian, Jewish, and immigrant kids—representatives of the groups that actually do best on today's meritocratic SAT. As David French has noted in *National Review*, pro-minority affirmative action today is "an enhanced-opportunity program for favored rich kids," which often disadvantages immigrant and ethnic white students slightly *worse* off than the Blacks who benefit.[14]

At any rate, for better or worse, the programs continue. And they have predictable effects. Gaps in tested IQ and standardized test scores, which exist between white and Asian students on the one hand and essentially all non-Asian minority (NAM) students on the other, are almost mirrored in gaps between white and NAM graduation rates. According to an in-depth review of racial graduation gaps by education reporter Lauren Camera, the *six-year* graduation rate for Black scholars at reputable (accredited, four-year, public) universities was 38.2 percent in 2003, and 40.3 percent in 2013. Despite a marginal increase of 2.1 percent in the Black graduation rate over the decade, the Black-to-white graduation gap actually increased due to a ten-year surge in the white rate from 55.4 percent to 60.7 percent (up 5.3 percent). These graduation gaps are not caused by the behavior of a few potentially retrograde outlier institutions—like the flagship state universities of the Deep South—but instead seem to characterize most or all major universities and top colleges.

A July 2018 *Journal of Blacks in Higher Education* article makes this point in some detail, stating accurately that the Black graduation rate for the University of Michigan is 67 percent as opposed to a white rate of 88 percent, and providing similar data for MIT (94/81), UCLA (88/73), Carleton College (90/69), Berkeley (86/70), and so forth.[15] Some leftist scholars, of course, attribute this pattern—and everything else—to "racism" rather than to the under-preparation of many minority students. However, there seems as usual to be literally no evidence for this thesis. The effect in question is as prevalent at northern schools as it is at southern ones, extends into the many historically black colleges and universities which are now integrated, and is often most pronounced at politically radical institutions such as California-Berkeley—which, as noted above, "boasts" a 16–17 percent Black-to-white graduation gap. Furthermore, as the social scientists Richard Sander and Stuart Taylor Jr. noted in their 2012 work *Mismatch*, college entrance exam scores predict academic success and timely graduation for Black students almost exactly as much as they do for white ones. The relevant scores simply *differ* between those two groups.

To a very real extent, that one sentence sums up this chapter. All manner of performance metrics, from crime rates to IQ scores, vary significantly among racial and regional groups. Furthermore, this variance often—usually—has little or nothing to do with trendy factors like "oppression" or "patriarchy." South Asians are, I suspect, far more "oppressed" than whites in post-9/11 America, but they nevertheless manage to score seventy points higher than Anglo-Saxons on the SAT. Most Blacks are descended from slaves (albeit from warriors before that), and we still experience some racism today. However, this has not prevented us from making up 60–70 percent of the world-famous centimillionaires in professional athletic leagues like the National Basketball Association. The reason for this is not that the Jewish-American and Irish-American businessmen that own teams in these leagues hate their own kind, but simply that Black people are—for whatever reason, and at the median rather than universally, and with all due respect to the Hick from French Lick—better at basketball.

CHAPTER 4

Taboo Obvious Fact #4: Performance—Not "Prejudice" —Mostly Predicts Success

Now to begin the next chapter in one sentence: not only do group differences have very little to do with racism or ethnic conflict, but they have much more to do with group *success* than bigotry does. Not only do "cultural performance differences" exist between racial, ethnic, sexual, and regional groups, but these factors predict success for different groups in different fields. This simple sentence seems logically indisputable, but it is in fact controversial to the extreme. Brave outliers like Thomas Sowell challenge this frame, but the debate about racial performance in the United States is largely divided between "Sharptonites" and "Jensonites." Sharptonites argue that essentially all differences in performance between (say) Blacks and whites, such as the SAT test–score gap, are driven by racism or by subtle variations on that theme like "stereotype threat" or "white privilege." Jensonites, well-reviewed in the journals although unmentionable in upper-middle-class public life, argue alternatively that genetic variations in traits such as potential IQ predict these dichotomies.

Both groups are wrong. This familiar dichotomy is a completely false one. Quantitative scholars using modern techniques like linear and logistic regression analysis—including me—regularly find that adjusting for the impact of one or two cultural differences in behavior completely eliminates most large intergroup gaps, which are normally attributed either to continuing racism or unchanging genes.

The existence of the Sharpton/Jenson dichotomy itself is essentially undisputed. In contemporary media and softer sciences such as sociology, the Sharptonite perspective is remarkably dominant. It is no exaggeration to say that almost every imaginable cultural quirk or simple failure in minority communities has been attributed to racism by a well-known liberal in the not-too-distant past. Participants in a recent Quora discussion headlined "What Are the Root Causes of the Problems That Black People in America Face Today[?]," which included many graduate students and junior scholars, were almost unanimous in saying that the answer was "racism." One user wrote, "Transatlantic slavery was the real beginning of the root causes of the problems Black people face in America." Nor has the racist abuse ever really ended. The next commenter down argued that Black folks today still face rowdy and underfunded schools, job discrimination, "risky subprime mortgages," and so on. This sort of prejudice—is my mortgage really as well-capitalized as my white neighbor's? Can I be sure?—is often argued to be both subtle and everywhere, nearly impossible to measure. Citing it, a third debater claimed, "Many white people are unaware of the benefits of being born white and have little understanding of what it is to be Black in this country."[1] And so on.

This sort of thing is not confined to grad school students on the internet. *The Atlantic* recently published a major, multi-page article titled "How Racism Is Bad for Our Bodies," which attributed most health problems in Black communities to You Guessed It. Citing social scientist Kathryn Freeman Anderson, author Jason Silverstein noted that 18.2 percent of Black participants in a recent large-scale study had experienced emotional stress, and 9.8 percent had experienced physical stress. The numbers for white participants were significantly lower—"only 3.5 and 1.6 percent of whites experienced emotional and physical stress, respectively."[2] He and Anderson attribute this disparity in stress to racism (not, say, poverty or Black gun crime), and Silverstein went on to argue that this stress leads to poorer physical and mental health: "When we feel stressed, we may want a drink, and, if we want a drink, we may also want a cigarette."

In many cases, apparently, no actual experience of racism is even required to trigger—and to justify—these unhealthy behaviors. The author writes that "[j]ust the fear of racism alone should switch on the body's stress-response systems." So far as I can tell, neither Silverstein nor Anderson ever actually demonstrated that slightly higher rates of stress among Blacks are due primarily to racism and not to crime. However, the piece went on to confidently conclude, "Race may be a social construct, but racism materializes in poor health." Ergo, policing strategies such as racial profiling should be discontinued on public health grounds.

Innovative stuff. Moving right along, Black unemployment is also due to racism. In a lengthy and numerically dense piece for the Center for Economic and Policy Research, Nick Buffie cited "racial inequality" before presenting a whole range of depressing statistics. From October 2014 to September 2015, according to Buffie, the unemployment rate was 4.7 percent for whites and 10 percent for Blacks. African Americans also had it worse when it came to how long they remained unemployed. "Data from the Bureau of Labor Statistics show that for Black Americans, the average duration of unemployment is 35.3 weeks and the median duration is 16.6 weeks," while the equivalent figures for whites were 28.5 weeks and 11.2 weeks.[3]

Furthermore, over in the McJobs sector, "involuntary part-time employment"—for example, flipping Filet-O-Fish sandwiches with the Peter Pan hat on—is more common for Blacks (6 percent) than for whites (4 percent). To his credit, Buffie did note that adjusting for such factors as gender, age, and level of education affects these ratios—and I would love to see what adjusting for more sophisticated variables like criminal history, access to a vehicle, and English proficiency does to them.

However, the general interpretation by the academic left of data like Buffie's is extraordinarily simple: "RACISM is on the loose!"

Some liberal thinkers even—dead seriously—blame white racism for urban Black crime. During the 2016 Philadelphia district attorney's race, leading candidate Joe Kahn, who went on to finish second, described one of the major underlying causes of crime in his city as "systemic racism … that came about long before any of us were born." One of his opponents in the Democratic primary, a noted white female judge, said that her very first task as DA would be to hire more Black assistant prosecutors to help counter "institutional racism" within the prosecutor's office.

As it happens, neither of the candidates just quoted virtue-signaled hard enough to win the election. The DA eventually elected—who also cited white racism as a major reason for his city's crime problems—was Larry Krasner, an activist defense lawyer best known as a defense attorney for the Black Lives Matter movement. Interestingly, none of these candidates bothered to offer an explanation for historically through-the-roof rates of *white* crime in Philly, a traditionally blue-collar city famous as the headquarters for the Philadelphia/South Jersey Mafia and the setting for gritty movies like *Rocky* and *Dressed to Kill*. Surely not oppression, also?

Along the same lines, HuffPost recently argued that Black people make up a disproportionate share of the prison population because "numbers aren't neutral." Author Kim Farbota argued that Blacks are three to four times as likely as whites to be arrested for common minor crimes such as marijuana possession and are at least slightly more likely to be convicted and incarcerated than whites charged with the same offenses.[4] Although it is well-argued, Farbota's article notably fails to explain why patterns of criminal offenses by race—as reflected in the Bureau of Justice Statistics' National Crime Victimization Survey—almost exactly match the rates of criminal arrests by race, as recorded by the FBI and most if not all of the country's major police departments.

In response to some of the absurdities of the Sharptonite school—and more broadly of what I have previously dubbed the Continuing Oppression Narrative—a "Jensonite" school of scholars appears to be growing in influence. Many prominent figures on the so-called alt-right, such as Jared Taylor, John Derbyshire, Vox Day, and Paul Kersey, openly argue that differences in performance among groups are due to differences in maximum genetic potential, particularly regarding IQ. The Yale-educated Jared Taylor, for example, has argued that the suboptimal response of Louisiana and Mississippi to Hurricane Katrina was due not to poor disaster relief planning, but to the fact that we have "Africa in our midst."

Making his case, Taylor detailed a long list of post-hurricane atrocities—most of which New Orleans and Louisiana authorities have plausibly argued did not happen. After Katrina, he claimed, "[l]ooted firearms spilled into the street. Some Blacks fired on any symbol of authority, blazing away at rescue helicopters and Coast Guard vessels." In the Superdome, used as a temporary hurricane shelter, "[t]he stadium reverted to the jungle. Young men robbed and raped with impunity. Occasional gunshots panicked the crowd." Things were, allegedly, even worse in the New Orleans Convention Center, where "degeneracy struck almost immediately," with criminals committing rapes, robberies, and murders. "Terrible shrieking tore through the night, but no one could see, or dared to move."[5]

Left-wing figures confronted by the chaos of Katrina, such as Kanye West and Randall Robinson, almost invariably blamed racism. But by 2005—when Taylor's piece was first published—the alt-right had the malign confidence to offer its own explanation. Doing so, Taylor first approvingly cited Jamaican writer Leighton Levy, who said, "I ... believe that Black people, no matter where they are in the world, are cursed with a genetic predisposition to steal, murder, and create mayhem." Taylor went on to argue, "[W]e have Africa in our midst, that utterly alien Africa of road-side corpses, cruelty, and anarchy that [we] thought could never wash up on these shores." Even more bluntly: "When Blacks are left entirely to their own devices, Western civilization—any kind of civilization—disappears." That stark sentence—without the white man, civilization falls—is the thesis statement of the alt-right.

Mr. Taylor does not write alone. On the same website, American Renaissance, Black female writer Zora Wheatley recently penned a widely recirculated column simply titled "What I Don't Like about Blacks." She wrote that Black problems "have less to do with white people, slavery, or capitalism than they do with genetics, evolution, and IQ," and went on from there to critique virtually every element of Black culture. Black English takes a few hits: the distinctive Southern-influenced dialect used mostly by African Americans is "so dumb and vulgar that ... clicks and grunts will be making a comeback." Black men are—I was surprised to hear—poor lovers, because "personality type, future plans, [and] courtship" are alien to us. In the end, Wheatley wrote, genes are the proximate and primary cause of all these defects, and this must be made absolutely clear: "The average Black person needs a clear way to understand why Blacks are, on average, exceptional basketball players, sprinters, and crooners, but not Rhodes Scholars." Between the two of them, Taylor and Wheatley did a solid job of summing up the genetic argument for the origins of racial differences.

Two things strike me as fascinating about the ongoing debate between Sharptonite cultural Marxists and Jensonite racialists. First, it has been going on essentially unchanged for at least fifty or sixty years. Second, the core arguments of both sides are clearly wrong, or at least simplistic. Professional quants in the social sciences have known for decades that (1) cultural variables predict group success or failure far better than either "racism" (that is, measured ethnic conflict) or genes alone and (2) adjusting for cultural variables such as "father in the home" or "hours of scholastic study per day" often eliminates very large performance gaps between races or ethnic groups. For whatever reason, these points have failed to have much impact on popular middlebrow discourse. However, they have been made often and effectively by a number of professional scholars—most notably by Thomas Sowell.

In a speech titled "Race, Culture, and Equality," Sowell provided literally dozens of examples of massive, culturally driven performance differences between peoples who are genetically identical, or nearly so. During most of the early twentieth century, for example, white immigrants to the U.S.A. from Eastern and Southern Europe differed so dramatically from British and Scandinavian immigrants in terms of formal education and tested IQ that the first group made only 15 percent as much annual income as the second. So far as I have been able to tell, the first group of immigrants—which included, for example, Sicilians and Russian Jews—also earned less than Blacks. This state of affairs—which went on for decades, if not a century—reflected realities back on the European continent. There, "real per capita income in the Balkans was about one-third that in Britain."[6] Even greater disparities between white groups existed on the true margins. With perhaps a touch of amusement, the Black and upper-class Sowell reported that when modern Europeans invaded the Canary Islands, they found a spear-chucking Caucasian population "living at a stone age level."[7]

Disparities such as these have not historically been confined to white or Western populations. Sowell pointed out that in the nation of Malaysia, during the entire decade of the 1960s, the Chinese minority earned more than one hundred times as many engineering degrees as their fellow Asians in the Malay majority. Halfway around the world in Nigeria and a decade or so later, the 55 percent or so of Nigerians living in the nation's agrarian northern provinces made up less than 10 percent of the students attending the fairly elite University of Ibadan and just 2 percent of the sizable group of wealthy Nigerians attending colleges abroad. Much-cited gaps between American population groups, such as a 6–7 percent spread in tested IQ scores between white and Black Americans, pale in comparison to these gaps between people of essentially the same race. Without ever denying that there may be some small genetic differences between ethnic groups—why *are* there so few Black swimmers?—Sowell made the obvious point that the family structures, study habits, and business customs a group has developed over time will generally affect its success, or lack thereof, more than anything else. In Eastern Europe halfway through the last century, he pointed out, Jews made up 6 percent of the population and half of the lawyers.

Nor are disparities like this confined to the past. In his *National Review* article "The Fallacy of White Privilege," conservative pundit Dennis Prager demonstrated that a number of cultural variables predict individual success far more than simply being white does. Poignantly, he pointed out that probably the most important of these is "two-parent privilege." Black Americans living in two-parent traditional family homes have a poverty rate of only 7 percent, as opposed to 22 percent for *whites* raised in single-parent homes. After bluntly discussing this 314 percent advantage in favor of Blacks, Prager declared the two-parent family the most important "privilege" in our society today. He also argued that the competitive, scholastically focused culture of Asian Americans constitutes such an advantage that it could be described as still another privilege—"Asian privilege." Asians benefiting from this cultural package, he pointed out, do better than white Americans according to almost all positive social metrics—from grades and test scores to average credit rating.[8]

Adjusting for sociocultural variables such as the presence of a father simply eliminates most of the group performance gaps that so enthrall the American left, and which the alt-right now attempts to explain in genetic terms. For example, back in 1995, the conservative social analyst Dinesh D'Souza, citing and drawing on the work of government economist June O' Neill, applied modern quantitative analysis to the wage gap between white and Black professional men. The results were striking. To quote at length: "Overall, Black men earned 82.9 percent of the white wage. Adjusting for Black-white differences in geographic region, schooling, and age raises the ratio to 87.7 percent; adding differences in [standardized] test scores ... raises the ratio to 95.5 percent, and adding differences in years of work experience raises the ratio to 99.1 percent."[9] At least in the modern era, less than 1 percent of the wage gap between Black and white males appears directly attributable to racism. Even assuming that subtle bigotry might have some impact on the "years of work experience" variable, *at least 95* percent of the variance in Black incomes is due to individual qualities and to cultural characteristics like valuing education. This truly remarkable finding appears to have been intentionally ignored by both sides of today's race debate.

Importantly, using similar stochastic analysis to adjust for variables other than genetic race also almost totally explains the crime gap between white and Black neighborhoods. In 1996, Ohio State sociologists Lauren Krivo and Ruth Peterson examined what factors predict crime in Columbus, Ohio—a large Midwestern city with a roughly equivalent number of poor white and Black neighborhoods. The authors found that whatever their racial composition, (1) almost all extremely disadvantaged neighborhoods "have unusually high rates of crime" and (2) poverty, chaos, fatherlessness, and other measures of "structural and economic disadvantage" predict crime about equally across Black and white neighborhoods. More specifically, the authors found strong and statistically significant correlations, across both white and Black neighborhoods, between crime and the following variables: poverty, high levels of joblessness, high rates of female-headed households/ low rates of present fathers, low rates of professionals in the community, percentage of vacant buildings in the area, and percentage of rental units in the area.

Essentially all of these factors had a higher impact on the crime rate than the percentage of a neighborhood that was Black, and adjusting for them almost totally eliminates the perceived relationship between Blackness and crime. In short, if this needs to be said, there seems to be no inherent genetic predisposition of Blacks to commit crimes. Densely packed inner-city neighborhoods with high rates of single parenthood and rental occupancy are likely to be violent places, whether their residents are African Americans, Italian Americans, Irishmen, Hispanics, or purple Oompa Loompas. The same will be true for sprawling and decaying trailer parks. And, to flip the script, these authors' findings also make it obvious that urban crime, which exists at similar levels among groups of all races in collapsing neighborhoods, is obviously not primar-ily a reaction to white racism.

All of this empirical work showing the primacy of cultural variables in predicting group success does not mean that there is no racism in the U.S.A today. Although its practical effects are largely countered by mas-sive affirmative action programs and laws such as the Civil Rights Act, racism obviously does exist. Indeed, a cynic might argue that no human society will ever truly be able to get rid of it. Fairly open bigotry appears to be prevalent in some sectors of the entry-level job market. In 2002, Northwestern University sociologist Devah Pager attempted to test employers' potential biases against job applicants by dividing a large pool of student volunteers into four groups: those who presented themselves to employers as whites with no criminal records, those who presented themselves as Blacks with no criminal records, those who presented themselves as whites with criminal records, and those who presented themselves as Blacks with criminal records. All students involved in the experiment were young people of similar age and appearance, who turned in essentially identical resumes and applications when applying for locally advertised jobs.

Strikingly, while 34 percent of whites "without a criminal record" were called back by employers for a job interview, only 5 percent of Blacks "with a criminal record" were called back. Even more notably, the percent-age of Blacks without a criminal record to be called back (14 percent) was lower than the percentage of whites with a criminal record (17 percent) to get callbacks. Pager, quite logically, attributed her results to the continued existence of subtle but pervasive racism. Several other studies have come to similar conclusions, with one major recent piece from the National Bureau of Economic Research ("Are Emily and Greg More Employable Than Lakisha and Jamal?") even concluding that job applicants with stereotypical Black names ("Sharkeisha") receive 33 percent fewer employer callbacks than those with white-sounding names.[10]

Even traditional "old-school" racism is not yet a thing of the past. According to Mic correspondent Zainab Akande, who cited generally undisputed 2010 Gallup data, 13 percent of Americans continue to disapprove of all interracial marriages. All groups contain some anti-swirl bigots, with roughly 5 percent of Blacks, 15 percent of whites, and intermediate percentages of Asians and Hispanics opposing mixed marriages. Another poll recently found that while 43 percent of Americans think the ongoing rise in interracial and multiethnic marriages is "good for our society," at least one citizen in ten sees it as "a change for the worse." These sorts of attitudes extend well beyond the chapel and the bedroom. According to journalist Frank Newport, who cited additional contemporary polling data, at least 7 percent of Americans would not vote for a fully qualified Black man running as their party's presidential candidate, 8 percent would never vote for a Hispanic, and a whopping 38 percent would never vote for a "generally well-qualified" Arab or other Muslim born in the U.S.A.

Unfortunate stuff. However, the simple reality that racism still exists does not challenge the empirical, mathematical point that cultural variables are a bigger predictor of group success than experiences with bigotry. Although this is almost never done in popular press coverage of these findings, it is worth taking a look at the weaknesses of the well-done but limited studies I just discussed. Perhaps most notably, in those experiments I cited that were designed to measure levels of workplace discrimination, *everybody of all races GOT a job.* In the National Bureau of Economic Research study looking at the impact of Black names on hiring decisions, whites got one callback per ten applications, while Blacks received one callback per fourteen to fifteen applications. However, the researchers responded to well over 1,300 want ads using relatively small sets of "white" and "Black" resumes. In the Pager study, 350 employers were contacted, and the widely cited 14 percent response rate implies that the primary Black group of student volunteers received more than forty callbacks for final interviews.

It is also worth noting that studies like these are almost invariably confined to the "entry-level non–affirmative action service job sector," and to white-owned employers in that sector. There is nothing unethical

about this; I am not the variety of scholar to attempt to insult high achiev-
ers like Pager to boost my own name. But a cynic certainly might notice
that this could very well be literally the only sector of the economy where
a qualified middle-class Black person would ever find herself at a hiring
disadvantage. In the era of institutional affirmative action and managing
diversity, people of color applying for colleges—or indeed faculty slots—
or any job with a Fortune 500 company are almost invariably bumped
to the top of the list.

    That claim is not hyperbole. Multiple serious studies of affirmative
action, such as *Mismatch* by Richard Sander and Stuart Taylor Jr. (2012),
find that a Black candidate for opportunities like those just mentioned is
generally 300–400 percent more likely to be brought on board than an
equally qualified white.[11] It is also hard to believe that minorities would
not have an advantage when applying to most of the successful minority-
owned businesses in the U.S.A.—Asians for middle-management jobs with
Panda Express or P. F. Chang's, or Blacks at the corporate offices of *Ebony,
Jet,* or the Charlotte Bobcats. Studies get published when they find evidence
of whatever it is that the author happens to be looking for, and—perhaps
coincidentally—studies of workplace discrimination focus almost entirely
on those niche areas where it still exists.

    Finally, it must be noted that, while real, the effect of modern discrimi-
nation appears remarkably minor. The widely cited hiring gap between
"innocent" Blacks and whites with a single, minor criminal count on their
record was exactly 3 percent. The rates of political and romantic discrimination against Blacks and other minorities discussed earlier are even less
fear-inducing. While it is shameful that 7 percent of Americans would not
vote for a qualified Black member of their political party for president, my
immediate reaction to that statistic was that at least the same level of prejudice must exist against many *white* groups. Fifteen minutes of research
verified that this is in fact the case. According to 2015 data, 6 percent of
Americans would not vote for a (presumably white) Catholic President, 8
percent would not vote for a woman of any race, 7 percent would not vote
for a Jew, 8 percent would not vote for a Mormon, and 24 percent would

not vote for a gay person. It is almost offensive to argue that this level of discrimination, which we literally all face, could stop a driven Black or Hispanic American—or an Irish Mormon, for that matter—from succeeding. For minorities and others, culture predicts success far more than outside prejudice of this kind; it "matters."

An especially important cultural variable, discussed by several of the studies mentioned so far, is the presence of a father in a child's life. This single cultural variable, in my professional opinion, is the cause of *most* of the contemporary problems in Black and poor white communities. The National Center for Fathering states the plain facts bluntly: "Children from fatherless homes are more likely to be poor, become involved in drug and alcohol abuse, drop out of school, and suffer from health and emotional problems. Boys are more likely to be involved in crime, and girls are more likely to become pregnant as teens."

Data on the link between widespread fatherlessness, which is a purely cultural variable almost unknown among most racial populations until recently, and poverty are remarkably clear. According to 2011–2012 census data reported by the National Center for Fathering, children in father-absent homes are 400 percent more likely to be poor than children in two-parent households. In 2011, only 12 percent of all kids in married-couple families lived in poverty—and recall the 7 percent figure for two-parent Black families—as opposed to 47.6 percent of children in female-headed families with no male spouse present. Poverty itself has dire effects on many other variables. Fatherless children have more problems in school, scoring as much as one full standard deviation below children from two-parent families on tests of mathematical ability, reading skills, and cognition. They are more likely to be truant when enrolled in school, more likely to drop out of school by age sixteen, and less likely to attain virtually all "academic and professional qualifications" as adults. Seventy-one percent of high school dropouts are fatherless. And there are worse things than not having money: the children of unmarried single moms are more than twice as likely as other children to attempt suicide or actually kill themselves.

In a society both plagued by and deeply sick of crime, the relationship between fatherlessness and youth violence is at least as notable as that between fatherlessness and low income. According to the social scientists Chris Knoester and Dana Hayne, there is a direct and statistically significant relationship between father absence and gang violence, as well as other youth violence: "If the number of fathers is low in a neighborhood, then there is an increase in acts of teen violence ... a 1 percent increase in the proportion of single-parent families in a neighborhood is associated with a 3 percent increase in an adolescent's level of violence."[12] Simply put, strong men keep the wild young boys who live near them peaceful by offering work opportunities, athletic coaching, math tutoring—and the occasional whack with a belt. In the absence of these men, no such discipline occurs. To a very real extent, what the left insists on calling "toxic masculinity" is simply untrained or even feminized masculinity: the fist-fighting and woman-chasing and dueling with guns that males naturally engage in without a dad or mentor to teach them better.

This data on the effect of fatherlessness, analyzed as a cultural variable, matters because illegitimacy has become an epidemic in the U.S.A. within the last forty years. The problem is especially severe for Black Americans. In an article titled, accurately enough, "The True Black Tragedy," economist Walter Williams noted that the native-born African American illegitimacy rate recently hit 75 percent. Williams pointed out that this is not part of the "legacy of slavery," but rather something entirely new in Black history: "As early as the 1880s," he argued correctly, three-quarters of Black families were two-parent families. Even among *slaves*, one well-known nineteenth-century study found that "in ... three-fourths of the families, all the children had the same mother and father."[13]

The reasons for this modern move away from the traditional Black family can be debated (Williams, a libertarian conservative, blames the growth of pay-per-child welfare), but its effects are clear. To quote Williams: "The fact is that most of the social pathology seen in poor Black neighborhoods is entirely new." It is no exaggeration to say, as both he and I have, that perhaps 60 percent of contemporary income, IQ, and incarceration gaps between Blacks and whites are due solely to the contemporary surge in father-absent families.

It must be emphasized that illegitimacy is not solely—or even primarily, speaking in numerical terms—a Black problem. It is becoming an American problem. Back in 2010, the website Thinking Housewife—an internet resource targeted at homemakers that is quite well-written, but not known for in-depth discussion of the issues of the day—noted with concern that births to unmarried mothers had climbed above 40 percent for all American births. Such births were remarkably common among all races, making up 28.6 percent of the total for non-Hispanic whites, 52.5 percent for all Hispanics (including white Hispanics), and 72.3 percent for Blacks.[14]

The site's writers noted that these "desolating" numbers represent a truly remarkable jump from almost any point in the past. Before 1960, the Black illegitimacy rate was usually not far above 10 percent. It "went up to 20 percent" near the end of that pre-modern period, but no higher. As late as 1970, the white illegitimacy rate was 6 percent. All of these illegitimacy rates and the trend lines surrounding them have gotten worse since the Housewives wrote. Less than two years later, a popular conservative website concluded that more than half of all births to American women under thirty were out-of-wedlock births. The illegitimacy rate, in fact, was rising fastest among whites in their twenties.

Importantly, the anti-success effects of illegitimacy—and most notably of being raised by a young single mother—seem to be exactly the same for whites, Hispanics, and Blacks. Some of these effects have already been discussed, although not necessarily from this angle, in the portions of this book dealing with record levels of suicide, drug use, overdoses, and car wrecks among working-class whites. An even more remarkable piece of evidence was recently uncovered by MTO News, an Afro-centric website with a large Black middle-class audience. In 2016, staffers for the site broke down FBI data on murder and violent crimes by city size and found something truly astonishing.

As of 2016, the most violent city in the country was Oceana, West Virginia, a formerly booming coal town hit hard by the opiate epidemic, where 4,175.99 violent crimes per 100,000 residents are reported in a typical year. On a per capita basis, the place was twice as violent as Detroit, which averages "only" 1,988.63 violent crimes per 100,000 persons per year. Indeed, the entire list of the most violent (small) cities was dominated by what I would have thought of as very pleasant places— formerly bucolic white or middle-class Black towns known for things like furniture sales: Wellston, Missouri; Cairo, Illinois; Lithonia, Georgia; West Wendover, Nevada; Mount Oliver, Pennsylvania; and Fruitport, Michigan. The modern problems of family and cultural collapse produce the same chaos in Mayberry that they do in Chicago.[15]

To sum up this chapter in a few sentences: racism and ethnic conflict certainly exist, and, for that matter, some tiny genetic differences between groups may exist as well. But differences in individual and group-wide culture and training predict success, measurably and empirically, far more than either of those other two factors. Adjusting for a very few variables—such as fatherlessness and drug use—is enough to move a typical U.S. community from "Oceana then" to "Oceana now," and Oceana is not unique. Culture matters.

CHAPTER 5

Taboo Obvious Fact #5: Racism Didn't Cause the New Problems of Today

The main points of the last two chapters were that cultural differences between groups (1) exist and (2) predict success. A corollary to these points is that, when all cultural differences are *adjusted* for, *contemporary* racism has almost nothing to do with the major problems faced by minority Americans today. This is, of course, a wildly provocative statement. The idea that the United States today is an "institutionally" or "structurally" prejudiced society is a cornerstone of modern liberal thought. The Black Lives Matter movement alone has staged 2,406 major marches against racism during the past few years. However, any serious claim that contemporary or recent bigotry is the cause of phenomena such as the 75 percent Black illegitimacy rate founders on three rocks. First, these problems did not exist among Blacks (or anyone else) when racism was much worse, (2) these problems do not exist for successful, dark-skinned African and Asian immigrants to the U.S.A., and (3) many or most such problems do exist among poor whites—perhaps the most genuinely neglected group in America—to roughly the same extent that they do among Blacks.

As was briefly discussed in the last chapter, the idea that prejudice is the cause of virtually all poor group performances, at least among minorities, remains the foundation of the contemporary activist movement. That movement is as vigorous today as it has ever been. Rather remarkably, civil rights activism against perceived oppression—*not counting the gay rights movement*—seems to be *more widespread today than it was in the 1960s*. Leanna Garfield's recent list of the largest protest marches in U.S. history opens with the 2017 protest of Donald Trump's inauguration and goes on to include Louis Farrakhan's Million Man March (1995), a 1993 march on Washington targeted at eliminating racism and (primarily) at achieving civil rights for gay Americans, the "Million Woman" pro-Black march (1997), the 2003 protests against the Bush administration, and the feminist March for Women's Lives (2004). Astonishingly, Martin Luther King's March on Washington was more poorly attended than any of the later marches on the list, drawing only 250,000 attendees as opposed to "anywhere from 500,000 to two million people" for the Million Woman March 34 years later. A cynic might suggest that King's followers, Black and white, were more likely to have jobs they could not leave at will than the Antifa fighters and BLM radicals who came after them.[1]

Garfield's list would probably have been swelled by at least a few additional rallies if compiled at this point in the Trump presidency. The seven-page Wikipedia article headlined "Protests against Donald Trump," which is an actual thing that exists, lists (as of July 25, 2018) 32 major American or international anti-Trump protests, including: the Women's March, the Day Without Immigrants, "Not My President's Day," the Charlottesville rally, and the recurring and no doubt delightful "Resist Trump Tuesdays." Quite a few of these attracted at least a few hundred thousand participants; Wikipedia provides a figure of 100,000 "plus" for the inaugural protest and lists the Women's March attendance at 2–4 million participants in the U.S.A. and 4–5 million worldwide. At least a few were more lively than the organizers probably expected; the casualty toll across anti-Trump events so far is four dead,[2] eighty-one injured, and 1,040 persons arrested.

With perhaps two or three exceptions, almost every march listed so far included opposition to "racism" or "prejudice" among its core principles. In recent years, "mass mobilization" events like these have been supplemented by specifically pro-Black protests organized by the Black Lives Matter movement. Almost 3,000 of these have taken place in the past 5 years. A report from Elephrame, a data archive website, lists 2,406 major BLM rallies ("protests and other ... demonstrations") over a period of 1,467 days. The list of these includes the various Trayvon Martin demonstrations and riots, the Ferguson Freedom Ride, the Ferguson riots, and the massive protests following the deaths of (among others) Walter Scott, Tamir Rice, Sandra Bland, and Philando Castile. This is to some extent speculation, but the hard numbers indicate that there are probably more civil rights marches per year today than there were in 1960!

Not a few of today's major marches are literally held at the locations where historic rallies took place during the original civil rights movement, either to commemorate the old leaders or to commiserate about how "nothing has changed." On March 8, 2015, a memorial of the "Bloody Sunday" marches and police attacks in Selma, Alabama, made national news, with the *Washington Post* reporting that tens of thousands of "marchers, government officials, and other public figures gathered Sunday"—for the second or third day in a row—"to commemorate the 50th anniversary of a brutal police assault on civil rights demonstrators." By mid-afternoon, area police reported, apparently with some trepidation, that "at least 15,000 to 20,000 people had joined the crush on and around the bridge."[3]

Eric Holder, then-President Barack Obama's attorney general, showed up and gave a speech denouncing ... you'll never guess it ... racism. Holder argued that the U.S.A. has perhaps improved since the 1960s, but that conservatives on the Supreme Court were attempting to use "profoundly flawed" decisions to "weaken the federal government's voting rights enforcement powers." He closed by saying that, as in the days of one-hundred-dollar-poll taxes, "Fair and free access to the franchise is still, in some areas, under siege." Holder also compared today's scuffles between BLM fighters and city cops to the civil rights movement, drawing applause when he noted that murdered civil rights workers such as Jimmie Lee Jackson were "unarmed Black men."

The problem with the idea that racism has declined ("gone underground") little, if at all, and that the minority problems of today are caused by racism—just as those of the past may have been—is threefold. First, most contemporary Black problems were less serious when racism was much worse. Few Black teenagers had babies out of wedlock in 1960, and almost no middle-class Black men went to jail, although the Black crime rate was still frankly a bit higher than the white crime rate. Second, most of these contemporary problems do not exist today for visibly non-white immigrants from Africa, South Asia, and the West Indies, who often outperform both American whites and Blacks. Finally, most of these issues, along with other terrible problems like opiate addiction, do exist for the working-class *whites* who live alongside poor Blacks. All of this indicates that internal American cultural collapse is the root cause of the problems we as a society face today.

While we have already discussed the Black illegitimacy rate as a cultural variable which negatively impacts Black success, it is also worthwhile to illustrate that the breakdown of the Black family has not itself been caused by racism. While it has been popular since the 1960s to say that broken Black families are "the legacy of slavery," this is empirically untrue to a rather remarkable degree. If anything, broken Black families are the legacy of white liberal do-gooding. As Walter Williams pointed out, during a typical mid-twentieth-century year (1938), only "11 percent of Black children ... were born to unwed mothers."[4] Even by the early 1960s, the nation's overall illegitimacy rate stood at only 7.7 percent, with Blacks slightly but not wildly overrepresented among the parents of illegitimate children. Then came pay-per-child welfare, no-fault divorce, and the normalization of illegitimacy. The nation's out-of-wedlock birth rate "began a rapid and relentless climb across all demographic lines," a trend which would continue apace until 1994, "when the Welfare Reform Act helped put the brakes on." However, Bill Clinton and Newt Gingrich's shared good work may have come too late. By that year, illegitimacy rates had stabilized very near where they stand today—at 29.1 percent for non-Hispanic whites, 40.7 percent for all Americans, 55 percent for Hispanics (including white Hispanics), and 72 percent for Blacks. The effects of this seismic cultural shift have been all too predictable. According to the most contemporary figures which I have been able to find, "[fe]male headed Black families earn only 36 percent as much as two-parent Black families, and female-headed white families earn only 46 percent as much as two-parent white families."

The collapse of the family has been so rapid and entire that it is edifying to compare illegitimacy numbers which caused panic in the past with those about which we are almost blasé today. In 1963, Senator Daniel Patrick Moynihan was so shocked by a "surge" in the Black illegitimacy rate—from 18 percent to 23 percent—that he felt compelled to produce his famous Moynihan Report, advocating fiercely for traditional "family structure" and decrying pathological inner-city behavior. The backlash to the senator's brief was enormous, with Moynihan's claims of an illegitimacy rate over 20 percent often called exaggerated and preposterous. As Rich Lowry noted in *National Review*, "The Left savaged [the report], accusing Moynihan (incorrectly) of analytic errors, blaming the victim, and racism." Even the pugnacious Lyndon B. Johnson administration "began to pretend it had never heard of Moynihan or his handiwork."[5]

Today, of course, the Black families and neighborhoods described by Moynihan should sound like Mayberry to all of us. The Black illegitimacy rate bemoaned by the senator as a harbinger of social collapse *falls significantly below the illegitimacy rate for every single non-Asian group in the U.S.A. today*, with whites surpassing it by 6.1 percent, Americans as a whole by 17.7 percent, Caucasian and mestizo Hispanics by 30 or more percentage points, and Blacks by roughly 39 points. We have become—in the literal, technical sense of this term—a nation of bastards.

The recent surge in illegitimacy rates is simply one aspect of a broader pattern of family and social collapse that has affected all races in the postmodern era. As Douglas Besharov and Andrew West noted in a section of their monograph on African American marriage patterns titled "The Decline of Marriage," "[o]ver the past fifty years, for all Americans, marriage rates have declined while divorce rates and out-of-wedlock births have climbed." In 1950, 67 percent of white women and 64 percent of African American women (over age fifteen) were "currently married" when surveyed by the census. However, by 1998, the percentage of currently married women had dropped 13 percent for whites and at least 40 percent for African Americans; Hispanic marriage rates also experienced a 13–15 percent decline.[6]

The same pattern was visible among men, with 12 percent fewer white men and more than 30 percent fewer Black men married in 1998 than in 1950. Unsurprisingly, given these figures, the divorce rate doubled for Hispanic women, tripled for white women, and quadrupled for Black women between 1970 and 1998. Obviously, all of these troubling trends—indicating both greater incidence of divorce among all races and growing white-to-Black gaps in divorce and non-marriage rates—took place in the modern post–civil rights era. Furthermore, the pattern of family collapse was most pronounced in the integrated urban North.

Crime, too, has not been some unchanging universal within postbellum Black culture. Once almost nonexistent outside large urban centers and a few notorious rural "hollers," rates of serious violent crime such as gangland killings also skyrocketed during the 1960s. This cultural shift was so dramatic that the thinker Steven Pinker has referred to what became the new normal for crime as a process of "decivilization." Quoth he: "After a three-decade free fall that spanned the Great Depression, World War II, and the Cold War, Americans multiplied their homicide rate by more than two and a half." To be more specific, homicides per 100,000 American citizens rose from a low of 4.0 in 1957 to a high of 10.2 by the 1980s.[7]

This upsweep in mayhem affected virtually every other category of major "index" crime, including murder, "rape, assault, robbery, and theft," and it lasted for more than thirty years. As Pinker noted, crime reshaped the entire American zeitgeist; "[m]ugger jokes became a staple of comedians," and the deadbolted door with 8–10 brass locks on it became a symbol of urban living. As with the previously presented data on illegitimacy and divorce rates, the 1960s collapse of social order hit African Americans—who tend to be concentrated in large, "cutting-edge" cities—the hardest, although it affected essentially all American population groups. By the mid-1980s, the homicide rate among young Black males had shot up to 72 per 100,000, roughly equivalent to the murder rate in urban El Salvador today. Again, none of this had much of anything to do with racism. The most violent city throughout most of the 1970s and 1980s was integrated New York—where Puerto Rican, Italian American, and other youths posted remarkable crime totals right alongside Blacks—and that town's Central Park gained international recognition as a "well-known death trap."

Conservative authors like Mona Charen have argued convincingly that the real cause of the post-1960 surge in crime, illegitimacy, and virtually every other negative social metric was well-intentioned but misguided liberal social policy. In her 2005 bestseller *Do-Gooders*, Charen pointed out a series of unmistakable correlations ("The graph looks like a ski slope!") between rising crime and liberalizing changes to the criminal justice system, such as the *Gideon v. Wainwright* case mandating a free public defender for criminal defendants, the introduction of mandatory Miranda warnings for accused criminals, the *Escobedo v. Illinois* case further extending the Miranda rule, and the "fruit of the poisoned tree" doctrine requiring LEOs to completely toss out any evidence acquired using any improper policing techniques (rather than sanctioning themselves for acquiring it).

Following all of these innovations, Charen correctly noted, the median expected punishment for a murderer dropped from 2.3 years in 1950 to 1.7 years in 1970. The same felon's chance of facing the death penalty dropped from 1 in 67 to 1 in 246. These last two metrics, summing up the risk analysis a criminal would engage in prior to committing a major crime, continued to worsen until 1993. Only after the mid-1990s election of a series of Republican and conservative Democratic officials—most notably New York's Rudy Giuliani, who implemented "broken windows" policing reforms suggested by criminologists—did America's larger cities begin to calm down.

Obviously, aspects of Charen's thesis can be debated. Many arguments have been made about the exact composition of the set of factor variables leading to the post-1960s crime surge. Steven Pinker, for example, has pointed out that young men simply made up a much larger share of the population of the "baby boom" generation than is normally the case—and young men are more naturally violent. There is probably some truth to that. However, substantial support for Charen's major claims is provided by the fact that crime seems to surge every time traditional policing strategies are sidelined in favor of liberal ones. An unforgettable 2016 headline on Chicago's DNAinfo website read, "Chicago Police Stops Down By 90 Percent As Gun Violence Skyrockets." Taking a more national focus, the conservative news site Breitbart recently went with this: "Crime Surges as Feds Restrain Police, Relax Sentences, Revive 1970s."

Bombastic headlines aside, Katie McHugh's article detailing the "Ferguson effect" for Breitbart was loaded with facts. McHugh pointed out that as of October 2015, Chicago was experiencing its deadliest season in thirteen years, "with shootings increasing 50 percent since last September." The same trend was increasingly visible nationwide. Since the Freddie Gray riots in April 2015, McHugh noted, Baltimore "homicides spiked 39 percent while non-fatal shootings doubled."[8] In Milwaukee, 2015 murder tolls were up an astonishing 76 percent from the year before (going from 59 to 104), while the equivalent figures for St. Louis, Washington, D.C., and New Orleans were 60 percent (85 to 136), 44 percent (73 to 105), and 22 percent (98 to 120). McHugh attributed this carnage to the "Ferguson effect": the retreat of street-level officers from aggressive policing following the Black Lives Matter movement. McHugh quoted Georgetown law professor Bill Otis, who argued, "The country [is] losing its nerve in the face of this very anti-police attitude that arose in Ferguson and accelerated in Baltimore."

Many leftist social programs—no-fault divorce, the normalization of illegitimacy, ineffective "community" policing, the (admittedly bipartisan) outsourcing of good blue-collar jobs—contributed to the American social collapse that occurred near the end of the last century. However, the elephant in the burning room was almost certainly the explosive rise of pay-per-child welfare, which reached epidemic levels before the mid-1990s Clinton/Gingrich reforms and is still far more widespread than most citizens realize. It is difficult to overstate the social impact of large-scale "public dole" programs such as those currently operating in the U.S.A. and Western Europe. Throughout almost all of recorded history, everyone's father's favorite cliché was quite literally true: those who did not work, or at least steal from those who did, did not eat. Young children who could not work required hardworking parents in order to live to adulthood—and, in almost every case, two parents were better than one.

Large-scale giveaway programs, the post-1960 standard throughout the Western world, completely changed that ancient equation. As the Heritage Foundation pointed out in a dense quantitative report headlined "How Welfare Undermines Marriage," the means-tested welfare system tends to discourage the formation of traditional two-parent families by actively penalizing parents who choose to marry. According to senior research fellow Robert Rector, the typical welfare recipient, "a single mother with two children who earns $15,000 per year" through part-time work, would generally receive $11,000 in a public housing subsidy and $5,000–6,000 annually in food stamps from the state. However, if she were to marry a man earning roughly the same amount, her food stamps would be cut to nothing and her housing allowance would be sliced in half. This would represent a loss of well over $10,000—and surely of a degree of independence—in exchange for a gain of perhaps $15,000 *before* the various marriage tax penalties kick in.[9]

Furthermore, my calculations and Rector's have so far taken only two welfare programs into account. There are literally dozens of them, even following the mid-1990s swing of the budget axe specifically at Aid to Families with Dependent Children (AFDC) cash handouts. Today these include "the Earned Income Tax Credit (EITC), Temporary Assistance for Needy Families (TANF), the Women, Infants, and Children (WIC) food program, Supplemental Security Income (SSI)," child nutrition programs, and Medicaid. With eligibility for most of this assortment of goodies at stake every time a man kneels down holding a ring, it is no great surprise that the poor are no longer marrying. Rector stated bluntly that the collapse of marriage in America "began with the War on Poverty and the proliferation of means-tested welfare programs that it fostered." Largely as a result of this collapse, "The USA is steadily separating into a two-caste system with marriage and education as the dividing line."[10] On one side of that line, in the middle and upper-middle classes, children of all races are raised by two married parents with at least a community college education. On the other, children—including far too many urban Blacks and poor rural whites—are raised almost invariably by single parents with a high school education or less.

There is virtually nothing uncontroversial in the social sciences, and a cottage industry of articulate liberals defending the dole has sprung up in recent years. In October 2015, for example, Eduardo Porter penned a widely praised feature for the *New York Times* headlined "The Myth of Welfare's Corrupting Influence on the Poor." Citing some genuinely innovative recent work done by Abhijit Banerjee of MIT, Porter argued that a recent meta-analysis of seven means-tested welfare programs located in environments as diverse as Morocco, Mexico, Honduras, Nicaragua, the Philippines, and Indonesia found "no systematic evidence that cash transfer programs discourage work."[11]

Banerjee is a top-tier scholar, but there are major problems with using his study's results to conclude that welfare does not have far-reaching, negative effects. Not all of his conclusions are particularly impressive or remarkable.[12] Citing World Bank data, for example, he remarks that transfer cash was not *always* "squandered" by recipients on alcohol, tobacco, and fun times. A rebuttal of ugly stereotypes, to be sure, but a damn low empirical bar to meet. More importantly, it is very questionable how well an analysis of small-scale assistance programs in genuinely poor countries like Morocco translates to the U.S.A., a global superpower where genuine privation is rare and the biggest health problem for most poor people is obesity.

Finally, and most notably for our purposes, Banerjee's focus is on the relationship between welfare and work rather than the largely undisputed relationship between welfare and illegitimacy. Also, remarkably, Porter seemed to torpedo the work of his main source a little further down in his article, writing, "There is little doubt that welfare can discourage employment, particularly when recipients lose benefits quickly as their earnings from work rise." Overall, some strong counterclaims aside, it seems indisputable that the 500 percent growth of the welfare state over the past five decades has had a significant, negative impact on metrics like fatherlessness and crime among Blacks and other Americans—and has certainly had more of an impact on these things than "racism" or "transphobia."

In addition to the fact that many of these issues did not exist when racism was much worse, further evidence that most problems in contemporary minority communities are not due to ethnic conflict or white prejudice comes from the fact that minority immigrants rarely have these problems. According to a 2014 U.S. Census Bureau graphic so pleasantly surprising that it became a trending online meme, the highest income group in the United States is not WASPs, but Indian Americans, with a median household income of $100,295. In order, the next three groups were Taiwanese Americans ($85,500), Filipino immigrants ($82,389), and Americans of Japanese heritage ($70,261). All told, at least eighteen groups—including Lebanese Arabs ($69,586), Iranians or "Persians" ($66,186), Nigerians ($61,289), and Syrians ($61,151)—finished ahead of "whites" when whites were analyzed together as a group. Foreign Blacks specifically did quite well in income terms. Nigerians were joined on the top-twenty list by both Black and "white" immigrants from the polyglot African nation of Egypt ($60,543) and by the Guyanese ($60,234). All available data also indicate that Black West Indians—Jamaicans, Bahamians, and so forth—finished not far behind whites.

This is important stuff. Nigerians and Black Guyanese look essentially identical to Black Americans, the huge majority of whose ancestors came from West Africa. The same is obviously true of West Indians. Nor, except perhaps for slight traces of an accent, do these high-performing Black immigrants generally display cultural or linguistic characteristics which would allow white Americans to rapidly distinguish them from potentially less favored native Blacks. The national language of both Guyana and most West Indian states—Bermuda, the Bahamas, Jamaica—is English, and the national anthem of Bermuda is the hardly exotic "God Save the Queen." American bigots are entirely unlikely to set aside their prejudices when they meet these new citizens, who are essentially well-off, dark-skinned Black guys from the islands who speak English and wear blue jeans. For that matter, there is little reason to suppose they would do so in the case of non-Black minority immigrants from countries with whom America has fought bloody wars, such as Vietnamese (whose median household income is $59,405), Korean ($58,573), and Japanese ($70,261) Americans. These Black and Asian minority immigrants are so successful not because they never experience racism, but rather because they intelligently exploit American opportunities such as the free market, public education, and affirmative action while also working and studying hard. There is a lesson here for native-born Yanks of all colors.

Nigerian Americans perform especially well on the "studying hard" front, a fact obviously correlated with their high average income (and virtually 0 percent rates of teenage illegitimacy and hard drug addiction). As far back as 2008, the *Houston Chronicle* had enough data to run a major article headlined "Nigerians the Most Educated in the U.S." According to the *Chronicle*, "a whopping 17 percent of all Nigerians in this country" hold M.A. or M.S. degrees, while at least 4 percent have a completed doctorate in hand. Fully 37 percent of Nigerian Americans have a bachelor's degree. In contrast, only 19 percent of whites hold bachelor's degrees, 8 percent have a master's degree, and 1 percent earned a doctorate.[13]

One Rice University sociologist summed up the Nigerian performance metrics simply: "These are higher levels of educational attainment than were found in any other community." And although Nigerians already fall among the twenty highest-earning ethnic groups in the United States, it is interesting to speculate about how much they might make if so many leading community members did *not* earn doctorates and choose to become penurious academics! West Indian immigrants also display similar characteristics, as described by University of Massachusetts Amherst's Suzanne Model in her excellent new book *West Indian Immigrants: A Black Success Story?*

Away from the pointless shouting of the politically correct, the very visible success of so many Black and Asian immigrant groups—earned despite real obstacles such as language barriers and theoretical ones such as undying racism—has inspired some serious theory. In a widely discussed 2014 *New York Times* piece, social scientists Amy Chua and Jed Rubenfeld pointed out the obvious: groups perform at different levels, and a great many immigrant populations outperform supposedly more privileged white Americans on virtually every metric, including IQ scores, test scores, grades, income, and rates of crime and addiction. Using data very similar to that which I have just cited, they point out that "Indian-Americans earn almost double the national figure" for household income, outperforming the U.S. median by $40,000.[14]

These authors, too, note the achievements of Black West Africans: "Nigerians make up less than 1 percent" even of the Black population of the United States, but make up roughly one quarter of all Black students at Harvard Business School. Some underprivileged Caucasian groups have also obviously experienced spectacular success over the years. Entering potentially fraught territory, the pair discretely analyzed the success of Jewish Americans, noting that Jews "make up only about

2 percent of the United States' adult population," but account for one member in three of the current Supreme Court, about two-thirds of Tony Award winners, and roughly one third of American Nobel laureates.

Chua and Rubenfeld crunched some data and concluded that, "for all their diversity," virtually all successful minority (and white!) immigrant groups in the U.S.A. share three distinct success-boosting traits. The first of these is a "superiority complex," a deep-seated belief that one is basically good, skilled, and can make it by working hard. The second might be called "hunger," or a feeling that whatever you have done so far, at least prior to ultimate success, is not yet good enough. The third is "impulse control," a willingness to work hard and long to grind out results, even in the absence of immediate gratification. The presence or absence of these traits, rather than "racism" or "reverse racism" or "late capitalism," is the primary factor which predicts success for individuals of all races. Furthermore, strong, stable families seem to provide the best greenhouses for developing the three key traits. Chua's best-known body of work deals with the "tiger mothers" and hard-working dads of the Asian immigrant community. I could not agree more with essentially all of her thesis.

Just as the remarkable success of dark-skinned Black and Asian immigrants indicates that the problems of "the hood" are not primarily due to contemporary racism, so also does the fact that working-class and poor whites experience these problems at roughly the same levels as Blacks. Interestingly, Chua and Rubenfeld noted this phenomenon in passing when discussing immigrant success, noting that below the most elite levels of society, white American parents today are "more focused on building children's social skills and self-esteem" than on actually teaching their kids business skills or the traditional moral virtues. This trend—combined with social phenomena like pay-per-child welfare, no-fault divorce, and the outsourcing of millions of blue-collar jobs—has had a significant effect on the quality of life among the white majority population of the U.S.A.

As has been noted—never say beaten to death—throughout this chapter and the previous one, the white "illegitimate" birth rate has been rising as fast as the Black rate. According to author Jesse Powell, who combined non-Hispanic whites with white Hispanics to obtain his figures, the white illegitimacy rate was 20 percent in 1990, 25 percent in 1995, and 32 percent in 2005. It has no doubt climbed higher since. Among many regional and lower-income white groups, today's illegitimacy rates top 50 percent. Because whites still make up the large national majority in the United States—about 75 percent of the population with Caucasian Hispanics included—this surge in family collapse among the legacy population has begun to actually affect national demographics. In 1980, 18.4 percent of all U.S. births were to unmarried women. In 2000, that figure was 33.2 percent, and by 2010, it was 40.2 percent. Across all racial groups, 88 percent of births to teenagers and a similar percentage of births to women of "prime marriage age" (healthy twenty-to-twenty-four-year-olds) were illegitimate. In an amusing note, by 2013, the Associated Press had responded to this remarkable demographic shift by advising journalists never to use the potentially offensive term "illegitimate child."

Illegitimacy and family collapse correlate with crime and poverty among whites just as they do among Blacks. I see this relationship on a daily basis in central Kentucky, albeit from the "privileged" standpoint of a well-paid and armed Black male living in a state capital city. Appalachia is one of the most economically deprived regions of the country by any legitimate standard, and contemporary social trends have worsened many of the area's problems. The Appalachian Regional Commission (ARC) stated that from 2010–2014, "Poverty rates across the US [averaged] 15.6 percent compared to 19.7 percent in the combined Appalachian regions of Alabama, Kentucky, Tennessee, Virginia, and West Virginia."[15] This gap becomes still more notable when statistical techniques are used to analyze the Appalachian *region* of each state separately from the rest of it. In Virginia, the statewide poverty rate is 11.5 percent, versus 18.8 percent for the Appalachian region of the state. In Kentucky, the state as a whole is dealing with an 18.9 percent rate of poverty, but the percentage of poor Kentuckians in the Appalachian region is a staggering 25.4 percent.

On an almost amusing note, the highly technical ARC report noted that much of the problem of Appalachian poverty stems from the fact that people within the region have and make "significantly lower amounts of money" than other Americans. By George, is *that* how being broke happens? However, the actual financial numbers involved are not funny at all. In 2014, the per capita income for residents of Appalachian Kentucky was less than $31,000, while the same figure for all Americans was $46,049. In fact, for at least a decade, *most* of the twenty poorest counties throughout the U.S.A.—almost all of which boast higher-than-average rates of (1) unemployment tied to outsourcing or job loss and (2) out-of-wedlock childbirth—have been majority-white rural locations rather than inner-city slum districts. This year's list includes locales like Wheeler County, Georgia ($19,220 median per capita income); Crowley County, Colorado ($19,443); Union County, Florida ($20,396); and Elliot County, Kentucky ($22,111).

With lost jobs and broken families come the bottle and the needle. Unsurprisingly, addictive drug use is a long-standing and growing problem among poor whites. We have already mentioned the opiate epidemic, but it is worth doing so again here. A recent report by Dan Nolan and Chris Amico at PBS's *Frontline* bluntly called the epidemic "the worst drug crisis in American history," with the authors pointing out that overdoses from heroin and other opioids now kill "more than 27,000 people per year" and death rates from drug overdoses "now rival those of AIDS during the 1990s." Hard drugs currently kill more Americans annually than car wrecks do. In 1999, nearly twice as many citizens died in motor vehicle accidents as from drug overdoses, but by 2014 those figures had flipped. In the latter year, 29,230 people died in auto accidents, but 47,055 perished as a result of hard drug use.[16]

Almost all of these needle-marked corpses are white. According to Nolan and Amico's statistics, the rate of fatal heroin overdoses for Caucasians is 4.4 per 100,000. For Blacks, the same figure is 2.5 per 100,000. The Hispanic rate is only 1.9 per 100,000, and for all Asians combined the overdose rate is a minuscule .03 persons per 100,000. The rates of opioid overdose combined for all groups are a bit higher, but follow the same pattern: 7.9 per 100,000 for whites, 3.3 for Blacks, 2.2 for Latinos, and .7 for Asians. The regional Tennessee newspaper *Commercial Appeal* made the same point as Nolan and Amico, but in considerably more agonized tones. Reporter Kevin McKenzie pointed out, "Of all deaths from opioid and heroin overdoses in Tennessee and nationwide, about 90 percent of the people were white."[17]

Black folks accounted for less than 6 percent of all opioid overdose deaths in Tennessee and less than 8 percent of all such deaths nationally, according to the U.S. Centers for Disease Control and Prevention. The *Appeal* concluded that as a result of the opiate epidemic, annual rates of death among young working-class white Americans have been rising at rates "comparable to the onset of the nation's AIDS epidemic" or those in Russia following the sudden collapse of the Soviet Union. In contrast, premature death rates for Blacks, Hispanics, and Asian Americans have been declining for years.

To sum this chapter up, the claim that contemporary Black problems such as illegitimacy, crime, and drug use can be excused by citing "racism" or "the legacy of slavery" fails almost totally. First, many or most such problems were much less severe when ethnic conflict in the United States was much worse; the Black illegitimacy rate was well under 25 percent just a few decades after slavery ended. Second, these issues are almost nonexistent for today's well-off Black and Asian immigrants to the United States, most of whom outperform whites. Finally and most poignantly, they certainly do exist for our poor Caucasian countrymen, who somehow seem to rarely catch the eye of all those liberal professionals paid to "care." We must all work together as Americans to solve problems like these wherever they happen to appear in America—rather than childishly quarreling over who exactly is to blame for what.

CHAPTER 6

Taboo Obvious Fact #6: Anyone Can Be Racist (and "Racist" Has a Real Meaning)

After spending a chapter arguing empirically that racism is not the primary cause of contemporary problems for minorities, it is worth taking a look at what racism actually is. In recent years, liberal debaters have spent a great deal of time arguing straight-facedly that almost anything can be racist. Treating Blacks especially well is "well-meaning racism," employing racial stereotypes (for example, of Italian or Black criminals) in the movies is "representational racism," neutral tests like the SAT (which produce slightly disparate results across racial groups) are part of "institutional racism," and so on. Furthermore, some claim, all of these varieties of racism are exclusively white provinces—only whites can ever be racist, due to the structure of contemporary American power relations. In a sentence, all of this is nonsensical garbage. Racism remains what it has always been: the vice of disliking members of other groups for genetic reasons. And importantly, by this or any other reasonable standard, many of the POC activists on the modern left are among the most racist members of our society.

The idea that racism, traditionally defined as simple skin-color bias, is some complex and all-enveloping miasmatic phenomenon has been prevalent on the political left for decades. In a widely cited 2018 essay, scholar Dr. Nicki Lisa Cole defined racism as any system of "practices, beliefs, social relations, [or] phenomena" that works in any way to produce a racial hierarchy, or that yields "superiority, power, and privilege for some … and oppression for others."[1] Cole stated openly that this idea of racism goes far beyond any mundane theory of race-based prejudice, and it frankly seems that her definition of the concept could encompass almost anything. The SAT exam, for example, "produces a racial hierarchy" because Asians usually do better than whites, whites finish one hundred or more points ahead of Blacks, Blacks often surpass Native Americans and recent Hispanic immigrants, and so forth. Is math racist?

Cole might well say so. She actually listed at least seven forms of complex racism that are to be avoided at all costs by right-thinkers. "Representational racism," according to Cole, is the presentation of racial stereotypes in essentially any context, such as depicting people of color as disproportionately likely to be criminals or Native American Indians as skilled and brutal warriors in a film. The related concept of "ideological racism" refers to the individual belief in any racial stereotypes whatsoever, such as the idea that Latin or Italian women are fiery or passionate lovers. "Discursive racism" refers to the use of terms which a liberal or sensitive person might see as racially loaded, such as "ghetto" for a decaying neighborhood. "Institutional racism" refers to laws and other policies that disproportionately affect people of color, such as educational tracking policies that move children into specific classes on the basis of tested IQ. And so on, through "interactional racism," "structural racism," "systemic racism," "subtle racism" (which I would argue should be applied to all of the above), and "racism in sum."

In a similar piece, cultural critic Nadra Kareem Nittle focused on unpacking just one of Cole's categories of prejudice: institutional racism. "This is defined"—by Nittle, so far as I can tell—as "racism perpetrated by government entities such as schools, the courts, or the military." Nittle sees this form of racism as a more serious issue than any individual bigotry: "Unlike the racism perpetrated by individuals, institutional racism has the power to negatively affect the bulk of people belonging to a racial group." Some of the examples of institutional racism described by Nittle, such as race-based slavery, are indisputable. Others, such as alleged racial profiling by LEOs in high-crime minority areas, seem less valid.

Notably, like most leftists, Nittle seems to feel that *the simple existence of disparities in group performance*, or in public attitudes toward particular groups, is by itself de facto evidence of racial discrimination. Thus, she points to the facts that "Black and Latino men" are disproportionately stopped by police in inner-city New York, that Middle Easterners of fighting age are often searched at airports, and that Hispanics are thought of as unusually likely to be illegal immigrants in U.S. border states such as Arizona as some of the more glaring examples of institutional racism on record. To Nittle, apparently, all of this is bias and all of it must end.

Popular consultant Robin Hughes outdoes even Nittle and Cole in her analysis of institutional racism, coming up with no less than ten signs of the practice. Her piece was published on the generally quite serious Diverse Education website. Her take on what constitutes racism is unsurprisingly broad. For example, in a corporate setting, "When pictures of presidents, board members, award-winning whomevers are hung, and they do not depict a demography that matches that of the state ... then your organization might have an institutional racism problem."[2] Your move, NAACP of Iowa! Similarly, executives should take a hard look at "who receives highly honored awards in [their] organizations." An institution such as a research university or a sales floor may "have an institutionalized racism problem if there are few or no folks of color in the pool."

Obviously to Hughes, hiring exclusively whites into a firm is evidence of institutional racism—something I would probably agree with. But, apparently, so are most hirings of minorities: if a department has hired several highly qualified people of color and now believes that baseline diversity goals have been met, "you still have a problem." Even if there are quite a few employees of color, when the administration can easily name two or three minority high performers regularly asked to sit on in-house committees, racism remains. And so on, through the other seven rules.

A key idea for all of the authors cited so far is that numerical disparities by themselves are generally or always evidence of racism. Cole says this very bluntly. If more children of color are "tracked" into remedial classes, for example, what could this be but racism? In reality, this thesis—while expressed well and sincerely by Cole—is very questionable, if not out-and-out wrong. As we have noted throughout this book, cultural characteristics like crime rates, (tested) IQ scores, and rates of drug use and self-harm vary wildly among ethnic groups. Most American college students do fairly well by world standards on tests of intelligence and scholastic excellence. But on a hypothetical college campus where SAT scores averaged 950 for Blacks and Native Americans, 960 for Hispanics, 1100 for whites, and 1180 for Asians, there would be no logical reason to assume proportional representation of all four groups across both honors and remedial classes.

Despite this rather simple logic, however, the principle known to attorneys as "disparate impact" has found its way into formal American law over the past several decades. Simply put, it is essentially illegal for a completely neutral rule implemented by an employer (for example, firemen being required to take strength and IQ tests) "to affect one group of people ... more than another." More technically speaking, a business or union policy is defined as having a disparate or "adverse" impact if it causes "a substantially different rate of selection in hiring, promotion, or other employment decision which works to the disadvantage of members of a race, sex, or ethnic group." The legal language "a substantially different [caused] rate of selection" is generally interpreted to mean that in any situation where the percentage of Blacks—or female Italians, or whatever—within a specific business or workforce is less than 80 percent of what would be expected given the population demographics of the region surrounding that employer, a prima facie case for discrimination exists and individuals within the affected group can sue.

In other words, simply showing that people of one race or sex are underrepresented within a firm or any one major sector of that firm's business is often sufficient to spark a lawsuit. Demonstrating that there exists any specific policy (for example, an IQ test), whether intentionally racist or not, that has caused this state of affairs usually suffices to win the case: "A violation of the 1964 Civil Rights Act may be proven by showing that an employment practice or policy has a disproportionately adverse effect on members of the protected class." Importantly, *no* discovery of actual racism or animus on the part of any actual human being is needed in order for widespread practices such as tests of physical fitness or driving skills to be invalidated across entire industries.

This is silly. In a sentence, the basic problem with the institutional racism argument is that *disparate outcomes do not prove, or in most cases even imply, discrimination.* As has been discussed extensively over the past few chapters, different groups tend to do and enjoy—and thus excel in—different things, for a variety of social, cultural, economic, and (*gasps*) perhaps even genetic reasons. Thomas Sowell, who has made this point for a career, summed it up splendidly in the pages of *National Review*. Listing a whole range of group performance disparities that obviously have nothing to do with "racism" or contemporary ethnic conflict, Sowell opened by pointing out that for the twelve consecutive years from 2001–2012, every home-run leader in baseball's American League was Hispanic.[3]

Hispanics are hardly alone in totally dominating a specific area of American or world enterprise. Indian Americans have won the Scripps National Spelling Bee for seven consecutive years. Literally all of the world's bestselling brands of beer—including China's Tsingtao—were first brewed by Germans or people of recent German heritage. Sixty-eight of the one hundred top-ranked marathon runners in the world (as of 2012–2013) are Kenyans. In many or most cases, adjusting for differences between groups in terms of specific skills or training—how many

Germans drink beer, or East Africans run daily to school, or Blacks play basketball?—totally eliminates the performance differences attributed by the left to oppression. In his typically blunt style, Sowell stated, "This [assumption] of equal outcomes requires not one speck of evidence, and defies mountains of evidence to the contrary."

Whatever its logical validity, the idea of unmeasurable institutional racism will likely be with us for some time. In terms of contemporary attempts to redefine the basic meaning of "racism," it hardly stands alone. Another mainstream, serious idea on the contemporary left is that only white people are capable of racism. Mikala Everett recently made this case in the pages of a major collegiate newspaper, the *University Star*. Her opening sentences are blunt enough: "Minorities cannot be racist. I'll say it louder for the people in the back who did not hear me— minorities cannot be racist."

While admitting that a sensible traditional definition of racism is the belief that some races are "inferior or superior" to others—we'll get back to that venerable idea later—Everett went on to reject that idea and instead argued, "To carry out acts of racism, a race must have power and privilege." She concluded that there has never been a time in American history when a substantial number of non-whites have been in positions of power or privilege over whites. Barack Obama, president of the United States when Everett wrote, could not be reached for comment. Nor could Eric Holder, his attorney general, or General Colin Powell, who was secretary of state during the previous Bush administration.

Jokes aside, the claim that racism is "prejudice plus power," and thus is possible only for members of dominant groups, is not confined to campus radicals and other fringe-dwellers. Incredibly popular, it influences the behavior of massive businesses. In late 2016, for example, a major tech blog pointed out that Google appears to be tailoring its search results in order to promote the claim that ethnic minorities can never be racist toward whites. According to writer Jasper Hamill, the tech titan's search results "appear to foreground left-leaning answers to this highly controversial question."[4]

For example, when Hamill and a team of staffers searched Google using queries such as "Is it possible to be racist to a white person," the first answer, which appeared to be taken verbatim from HuffPost, was: "WRONG no [you] can't racism requires power and prejudice. White people have power to oppress Black people because they control the system and economic structure in society."[5] Another top search result stated flatly that any "usage of the word racist relative to a hate speech by Blacks ... is incorrect." Blacks, apparently, can be individually "prejudicial" [sic] but not racist. A third search result stated simply, "Racism is ... a system that acts against people of colour in this country."

The top online debate-and-bantz sites, many of which appear among Google's top search results, continue the same pattern. Over at Medium, writer Ariel Pontes concluded that minorities sometimes can be racist: "Reverse racism is real and immoral." However, as irritating as this "reverse racism" may be, it is almost never as dangerous or problematic as "regular racism." Pontes flatly mocked those on the right who allege that racism against "oppressed minorities" is no worse than racism against presumably privileged members of majority groups, and therefore criticize "the very categorization of racism into 'reverse racism' and 'regular racism.'"[6] All people are equal to liberals, but some are a bit more equal than others.

The first and most basic issue with these inventive modern definitions of racism—which state that any system producing disparate outcomes is racist, that racism is a thing only possible for whites, and so on—is simple: they do not gel with the actual and correct definition of the word. The major dictionaries, encyclopedias, and quantitative guides to the sciences are amazingly consistent in defining racism as (1) an ideology of racial hatred that is usually or always (2) based around perceptions of biological inferiority. The first actual *definition* of racism to pop up after an internet search, from the venerable Oxford English Dictionary, is: "prejudice, discrimination, or antagonism directed against someone of a different race based on the belief that one's own race is superior." The OED's first sub-definition of racism focuses on genetic bias: "the belief that all members of each race possess characteristics or abilities specific to that race ... so as to distinguish it as inferior or superior to another race." Individual prejudice, which liberals often attempt to disentangle from the concept of racism, is also noted by the dictionary to be an almost exact synonym.

The OED does not stand alone in choosing to continue using a sensible and traditional definition of racism. She is joined in doing so by almost all other real reference works. The Merriam-Webster definition, generally considered the American standard, is almost identical. The first component of that definition is: "a belief that race is the primary determinant of human traits and capacities and that racial differences produce an inherent superiority of a particular race." The third part of the definition, again, describes racism simply as any "racial prejudice or discrimination" on the part of any individual.

Even honest liberals generally do not disagree. The online Free Dictionary calls racism "the belief that race accounts for differences in human character or ability, or that a particular race is superior to others." A solid alternative definition, once again, is any "discrimination or prejudice based on race." The Anti-Defamation League (ADL) concurs, defining racism as "the belief that a particular race is superior or inferior to another," and/or that "a person's social and moral traits are predetermined by ... inborn biological characteristics." Both the ADL and the allied Southern Poverty Law Center (SPLC) list multiple minority-led organizations, such as the Nation of Islam, as racist hate groups. Sane quantitative social scientists tend to pretty much agree with definitions like the ADL's, with D'Souza (1995) calling racism "an ideology of bio-genetic inferiority" and professors Paul Sniderman and Edward Carmines describing it as "the strong dislike of (X group)," often based in genetics.

Whew—that was a lot of sources, and often boring ones at that. But they were cited for a reason. All of this *matters*. The traditional definition of racism—intense, genetically based dislike for another race—is not better than the rising leftist definitions simply because I, a chubby center-right writer from Chicago, say it is. Rather, the trendy leftist definitions can be called wrong because the huge majority of serious dictionaries, encyclopedias, and empirical resources disagree with them. And they disagree for a reason. The traditional definition has endured for over one hundred years because it has multiple real advantages over the major alternatives. Perhaps most importantly, taking the leftist definition seriously would require scholars to ignore the probable majority of serious acts of racism by redefining racist acts committed by minorities such as Blacks and Asians as simply ineffective outbursts of individual prejudice. This is not a small matter, given that the FBI (among other entities) recently concluded that African Americans are *more* likely to commit racist hate crimes than any other group in the U.S. population.

According to an article by Brian Anderson, 24.3 percent of all hate crime offenders during the year 2013 were Black, almost double the percentage of the Black population. For all the unending media frenzy about "Nazis," only 52.4 percent of hate criminals were white, even though non-Hispanic whites make up 63.7 percent of the population. Ratios of percentage of the population to percentage of offenders were about equal for most other major groups—Native Americans made up 1 percent of both the population and the offender pool, Samoans and other Pacific Islanders made up .2 percent of the population and a bit more than .1 percent of the hate offenders, and Asians made up a minuscule .7 percent of hate criminals despite constituting 4.8 percent of the population. Anderson noted bluntly, "The only race that exceeds their population percentage in hate crime offenders are ... Blacks."[7]

Data from multiple additional years appear to confirm the point Anderson made using only 2013 data. A 2012 breakdown of hate crime statistics, which I obtained directly from the FBI, reiterates that there are indeed plenty of white asshats in America. Of 3,467 racially motivated hate crimes during that fairly representative year, 66 percent were the result of "anti-Black bias," generally on the part of a white offender. However, fully 22 percent were the result of an offender's anti-*white* bias. Most of these attacks were committed by African Americans, as were a

substantial chunk of the 1,340 incidents motivated by anti-Jewish prejudice and by "sexual orientation bias" against gay individuals. There
seems to be no logical reason to define these literal violent hate crimes
as something less than acts of racism, based only on the skin color of the
felon holding the bat or the noose.

Globally, the idea that members of a temporarily non-dominant
group cannot be racist but can be ineffectively prejudiced at the individual level would lead to still more absurd conclusions. The *Daily Mail*
in Britain, for example, recently ran a major article on South Africa's
terrifying Afrikaner Resistance Movement (AWB). According to staff
pen Simon Tomlinson, racialist leaders within South Africa's white Boer
community are "brainwashing teenagers to rise up in defiance of Nelson
Mandela's hard-fought dream of a Rainbow Nation." By day, young
members of the group, referred to as war-fighters and "soldiers," are
"pushed to their physical limits with assault courses and self-defense
lessons," all the while being told that a war with their country's Black
majority is imminent and inevitable. By night, they get to rest—but
receive extensive *Mein Kampf*–style political indoctrination via films
and pamphlets.[8]

Within the piece, AWB boot-camper Dion Bernard described the
results of all this. He seems, unfortunately, to have become a classic
biogenetic racist. When asked how he would react to a Black teammate
or former school chum seeking a conversation, he replied, "You cannot
mix nations. I don't have Black friends. If they come to my side and ask
to speak to me, I will say no. Or I will turn my back on them and walk
away." The Bible, apparently in the form of a passage I have yet to read,
is invoked to support this view: "It says Black people must live with Black
people and white people must live with white people." Scary stuff. However, at present, Boer whites make up only 7 percent of the South African
population and are being stripped of their dominant economic position
by the Black-led African National Congress, which recently voted to
nationalize large, white-owned farms. Using the logic of social justice,[9]
the fact that they do not hold "institutional power" would mean that

white Boers—literally the ethnic group responsible for apartheid—cannot properly be called racist.

The African nation of Burundi provides an even better test case for this bizarre principle. The country is largely ruled by the Tutsi ethnic group, members of which have traded atrocities with their Hutu neighbors inside Burundi and in neighboring Rwanda for decades. "Bouts of ethnic cleansing" have historically been frequent, and two bloody civil wars were fought between Tutsi and Hutu factions during the 1970s and early 1990s. In 2015, conflict broke out again. The country witnessed large-scale political conflict as then-president Pierre Nkurunziza attempted to run for an unprecedented third term, and a violent coup attempt against him was mounted and failed. In short, all groups inside the country have fought one another violently for decades, and the currently dominant group makes up only 14 percent of the national population.

Does this lack of a stable power position mean that the literal genocides initiated by the Tutsis cannot technically be described as acts of racism? Or, to reverse the question: As the Hutu make up the majority of the Burundian population, but are out of power, should Hutu attacks in today's climate be considered merely examples of "ineffective personal prejudice?" If the answer is "yes," will that change the minute the Hutu next take back power through the ballot or the bullet? The very idea seems absurd, writing as both a political scientist and a human being. A dead man killed by either side in the wars would be damned unlikely to have cared what some collegiate seminar in Feminist Debate said about the power position of his murderer.

Perhaps the strongest argument against the idea that only members of majority groups can be racist because "only they have power" is that in America and most of the Western world, this would require a completely unified all-white ruling class. The logic here is fairly direct. In order for (say) a homeless white coal miner but not Barack Obama to be "privileged" and capable of true effective racism, the United States would (1) need to have a single dominant group to which all whites and no non-whites belonged, and (2) all whites within that group would need to share racist opinions against non-whites. In this context, it actually could be logically assumed that minorities would have almost no ability to resist or harm whites. A solitary Klansman would be acting with the approval of most of America, while even the wisest or most physically powerful Black man could be only *vox clamantis in deserto*.[10]

However, the very nature of my example—President Barack Obama—shows how absurd this argument is. In fact, the American ruling class, like the national population it leads, is wildly diverse. The last president of the United States was a Black man. One of the most powerful entities in Congress is its raucous but highly effective Congressional Black Caucus. Over in the business sector, Jews, East Asians, South Asians, and Nigerians all outearn whites by a substantial margin. Given these realities, arguing that minorities are incapable of racism seems to represent an incompetent (or intentional) confusion of the individual with the group level of analysis.

It may still be true that *all* whites combined still have more power than all POC combined. As an example of this, the average white woman makes 5–10 percent more money than the average Black woman ($24,892 to $22,690 in 2016). Gaps like this are magnified, in terms of overall group strength, by the obvious fact that there are more whites than Blacks. But this fact says almost literally nothing about day-to-day individual interactions. Judging from the data just given, probably 45 percent of Black people have more money or influence than the average white person and would be in a superior power position during a quarrel. Only during a civil war pitting all minorities against all whites, it seems, would this rather basic logic collapse.

Such a war of all against all seems extraordinarily unlikely, given that there is almost no unity of attitudes about race—or much of anything else—among whites or any other large American group. It is absurd that this even needs to be said, but most white people are not members of the Ku Klux Klan, and by and large do not agree with racist ideas. Author Anna Maria Barry-Jester recently made this point at some length in a major article for FiveThirtyEight headlined "Attitudes Toward Racism and Inequality Are Shifting." In the piece, Barry-Jester points out not only that most Americans are not racist, but also that attitudes toward race relations have been moving in a positive direction for decades.

For example, "[w]hile 31 percent of white Southerners favored seg-regated schools in 1972, by 1985, so few people shared that belief that the question was removed from the survey altogether." In 1972, 25 percent of whites and 48 percent of white Southerners said that they would not vote for a qualified Black president from their own political party. As we have seen, however, only 6–7 percent of whites clung to this opinion by 2010. Even final "barrier taboos" about living and eating together seem to have collapsed. By the 2010s, just 28 percent of South-ern whites believed they should even have the *legal right* to discriminate in any way when selling a home.[11]

Today, in the long shadow of social shifts like this, groups such as the Ku Klux Klan certainly do not represent mainstream white or con-servative thought. The plain fact is that they are marginal bands of bitter losers with far less institutional power than the mighty NAACP or National Urban League. After doing a bit of investigative journalism and vetting the figures put out by organizations such as the Southern Poverty Law Center, ATTN:'s Kyle Jaeger claimed in 2016 that there are currently 190 active KKK groups in the United States, with a total membership of perhaps 6,000 individuals.[12] In comparison, the Facebook fan page for one equivalently radical group on the extreme left, Arizona Antifa, boasts 30,000 active followers.[13]

Jaeger stated the obvious: "The KKK … isn't nearly as influential or brazen as it was at its peak in the 1920s (when it had 1.5 to 4 million members)." Cal-State San Bernardino's Brian Levin, director of the uni-versity's Center for the Study of Hate and Extremism, pointed out that the modern Klan's numbers are very small, and the activities of these fringe racist reactionaries have "primarily been limited to … leafleting." Today, the biggest threat posed by the sad remnants of the Klan is prob-ably a lone-wolf attack by a single nut—and even that would likely fail, given the rates of legal gun ownership in those states where the organiza-tion retains any significant presence.

In the current climate of anti-racism and extreme political correctness, even buying a Confederate flag—much less a KKK one—can be a bit of a challenge. Following 2015's horrific Dylann Roof massacre, a range of companies—including Walmart/Sam's Club, eBay, Sears, Target, Etsy, and Amazon—agreed to totally ban the online or in-house retail of any merchandise even depicting the ol' Stars and Bars. Walmart executive Brian Nick gave a semi-formal statement to CNN about the move, saying, "We never want to offend anyone with the products that we offer. We have taken steps to remove all objects promoting the Confederate flag from our assortment—whether in stores or on our web site. We have a process in place." Today, the leading Google search result for the phrase "buy a Confederate flag" is the niche online retailer rebelsupplies.com.

The actual voting behavior of whites provides further evidence of an ideologically diverse, generally anti-racist electorate—almost the literal opposite of the monolithic bigoted force envisioned by SJWs. The Center for American Progress (CAP) notes that the white vote is almost evenly split between the two major political parties, although the Republicans do maintain some advantage. According to CAP scholar Steve Phillips, the slight majority of whites voted for Republicans in "every election over the past 50 years," but a "meaningful minority of whites support the Democratic nominee every election."[14]

The Democratic vote share among whites fluctuates between 40–45 percent in a typical year, although the otherwise unaccomplished Walter Mondale hauled in a record-low 34 percent of white votes in 1984. During more typical election years, Jimmy Carter pulled in 48 percent of whites in 1976, Bill Clinton won 44 percent of the white vote in 1996, and even Michael Dukakis (tank photo and all) polled over 40 percent among whites in 1988. The first Black president, Barack Obama, did well among whites, securing 43 percent of the white vote and roughly 95 percent of the Black vote during his historic first election in 2008.

Unsurprisingly, given that young people tend to be more liberal than their elders, young whites test as even less conservative and more pro-diversity than their older peers. According to Salon's Sean McElwee, 43 percent of millennial whites and at least 54 percent of millennials overall believe that it is "the government's responsibility to provide health insurance for all," versus 46 percent of Generation X (36 percent of Gen-X whites) and only 42 percent of baby boomers. These sort of broad policy preferences translate into practical political activity. McElwee pointed out that almost 55 percent of white millennials supported Barack Obama's presidential bid, and that millennial college students—here not broken down by race—supported Obama by 35 percentage points over Mitt Romney in 2012. As a center-right voter from the business world, all of this news is hardly manna from heaven to me! But it certainly militates against the idea that the white population of the U.S.A. constitutes one monolithically conservative, viciously racist voting bloc. Counting white allies as part of the leftist coalition, in fact, the white and POC voting blocs in the United States are of almost identical strength.

Essentially every component of the activist left's take on racism is simply wrong. According to every major dictionary and encyclopedia in the world and many top quantitative works of social science, racism is one specific thing—belief in the genetic inferiority of another race, generally combined with dislike. Such a belief certainly can extend beyond individuals and be entrenched within institutions by law, as it was in Southern systems of governance and housing during the horrific Jim Crow era. In this one sense, "institutional racism" can be a meaningful term.

However, simple differences in performance among different groups ("There aren't many Filipinos in the NBA") are not proof or even evidence of institutional racism—or of racism at all—prior to some empirical test of how different groups do in terms of the characteristic being tested for ("How *tall* are Filipinos, usually?"). And furthermore, the entire idea that widespread "subtle, institutional" racism exists in the modern American context seems questionable, if not flat-out wrong, given (1) the remarkably diverse nature of the American ruling class and political scene, (2) the existence of explicitly pro-minority programs such as affirmative action, and (3) the fact that different groups do very differently on performance metrics such as the SAT, and that these variables are rarely adjusted for before comparing the performances of these different groups.

After dismissing these modern innovations in "racism studies" and returning to a sensible and longstanding definition of racism, two things become immediately apparent. First, people of any racial background can be racist. And unfortunately, quite a few people of all backgrounds still are. My own research indicates that at least one-tenth of whites and perhaps one-seventh of people of color test as traditional racial bigots. Second, as the numbers just given indicate, at least as much real racism seems to exist among minorities as among whites. Due to popular politically correct ideas about "white privilege" and racism being "prejudice plus power," quite extraordinarily racist organizations which exist in communities of color are given a leeway they would never receive if headed by whites.

The Nation of Islam (NOI) provides the best and most obvious example of this trend. Although often treated by the U.S. media as charismatic radicals well worth listening to, "Black Muslims" are in fact biogenetic racists who believe that Caucasians are quite literally a demonic, subhuman race bred from Blacks by mad scientists eons ago. According to official NOI theology, an evil Black genius named Yakub began the creation of the white race roughly 6,600 years ago.[15] A resident of the island of Patmos, Yakub devised a plan to create a new strain of human beings using a technique known as human grafting. Doing so, he thought, would test his skills and might result in a more predatory race of sapiens that "would rule the original Black man." Given that Yakub himself was Black, why he would want this result remains a mystery which has never been explained by the Nation. But, ah, well— religion is often a mysterious business.

At any rate, Yakub—accompanied by exactly 59,999 followers— moved to a remote region of Patmos, where he established a theocratic dictatorship and began breeding humans. After two hundred years of "breeding out ... Black traits" and killing the darker babies born to his followers, Yakub produced a brown race, generally considered by Black Muslims to have been ancestral to Hispanics or East Indians. Two hundred years later, "the red man" was bred out of the brown man, and Amerindians came to exist. Two hundred years after that, "the yellow man" or "Easterner" was bred out of the red. Yakub eventually died, hundreds of years old, but his followers continued his life's work. And, finally, two hundred more years down the road, the apex of human evil—THE WHITE MAN—was produced as a mutant offshoot of East Asian genetic stock.

According to NOI theology, as expressed in Elijah Muhammad's *Message to the Blackman in America*, whites are devilish, barely human predators: "Lie[s] were born into the very nature of the white baby, and, murder for the Black people was also born in them." Unsurprisingly, this new species clashed with the peaceful, civilized Blacks who had created them. After a variety of adventures, Yakub's new race found themselves exiled to cold Europe, where they lived naked in caves "eating raw meat" before being drawn out of the hillside by Moses (!), who taught them to wear clothes and use simple weapons. Even Moses eventually gave up on his troubled protégés, using dynamite (!!) to kill some three hundred of them during one clash. However, presumably after a gap of some years, the Caucasian former cavemen learned to use Black and Jewish technology, usurping power from the Black population and transporting the first slaves to the Americas. According to NOI doctrine, the white children of Yakub were destined to rule for six thousand years before the "original Black peoples of the world regained dominance." The Nation believes that this six-thousand-year period of Caucasian rule ended in 1914, with its conclusion perhaps signaled by the World Wars among majority-white nations.

In the NOI belief system, all this frank nonsense is canonical. The modern story of Yakub is first found in the writings of Wallace Fard Muhammad (also known as Wali Fard), who founded the Nation of Islam and included the story in his doctrinal leaflet *Lost-found Muslim Lesson #2*. His protégé, the "Honorable" Elijah Muhammad, who essentially created the modern Nation, included it almost verbatim in *Message to the Blackman*, devoting a whole chapter ("The Making of the Devil") to the alleged subterranean origins of whites. The Nation still fiercely defends the Yakub story today. In 2013, the "religion's" widely circulated *Final Call* newsletter included an article titled "National Geographic Proves Teaching on Mr. Yakub," in which the Nation of Islam research group drew some rather remarkable conclusions from a recent archaeological finding that "Europeans as a people are younger than we thought."[16]

Amusing as all of this may be, it should be noted that the Nation of Islam is no small band of random cranks and loonies. In 2007, the SPLC estimated the core membership of the Nation to be between twenty thousand and fifty thousand persons. As we have seen, this is between three and ten times the size of the membership of all American KKK groups combined. The group maintains dozens of mosques, a professional website (www.noi.org), an apparently accredited school (Muhammad University), and a trained fighting force of Black men known as the Fruit of Islam. In terms of the sheer power of its base, it is more than a bit edifying to compare the generally tolerated Nation, whose members sell bean pies on urban street corners and run well-reviewed downtown restaurants, with the universally reviled "alt-right."

A close rival to the NOI in the "widely tolerated racialist organization" game is the La Raza, or Aztlán, movement. Essentially, the La Raza or La Raza Unida movement is a collection of racially conscious Hispanic individuals and organizations who believe the United States should be replaced as the governing power in the American Southwest by force, if necessary. As former congressman Charlie Norwood noted in 2006, "[These groups] teach that Colorado, California, Arizona, Texas, Utah, New Mexico, Oregon, and parts of Washington State make up an area known as 'Aztlan.'" Within this area, which is a fictional national construct based upon the furthest theoretical expansion of the Aztec Empire, all land properly belongs to the followers of Hispanic nationalist movements. La Raza holds that "[t]hese are all areas America should surrender to La Raza once enough immigrants, legal or illegal, enter to claim a majority, as in Los Angeles." Pushed aside by this stronger and more deserving new nation, the current land borders of the U.S.A. will simply be wiped out.[17]

Many of the groups which believe this or something like it belong to "mainstream" political lobbying organizations like the National Council of La Raza (NCLR), now known as UnidosUS, which advocates for Latino causes such as bilingual education. Like the Nation of Islam, this is an empirically powerful, nationally influential organization. Staff writers at *The Hill* noted that the NCLR took in "over $15.2 million in federal grants ... alone" in 2005, with much of the money going to support get-out-the-vote drives for preferred La Raza political causes. Like most members of the Nation, and a surprising number of other minority activists, many advocates of Aztlán seem to be open biogenetic racists. MEChA, the Movimiento Estudiantil Chicanx de Aztlán, or Chicano Student Movement of Aztlán, openly stated, "Chicano is our identity; it defines who we are as a people. It rejects the notion that we ... should assimilate into the Anglo-American melting pot. Aztlan was the legendary homeland of the Aztecs!" The very term La Raza, it should be noted, literally means "the Hispanic race." The Anglo-Saxon equivalent of an organization called "La Raza Unida" would be one titled "Forward the Unified White Race."

Not only are minority racists at least as common as white bigots on the VDARE side of the aisle, but they also seem to be much more well-connected politically. In early 2018, for example, a brief burst of media attention followed the revelation that multiple members of the Congressional Black Caucus had been meeting at least occasionally with Nation of Islam boss man Louis Farrakhan. According to The Daily Caller's Peter Hasson, the entire Congressional Black Caucus "held a secret meeting with Farrakhan in 2005 but hid it from the public to avoid controversy."[18] At least two very prominent caucus members, Maxine Waters and Al Green, met with Farrakhan on other occasions. Both representatives were caught on tape embracing Farrakhan in 2006, a full year after the Congressional Black Caucus's secret meeting with the racialist leader.

Although twenty-one *current* members of Congress were at the first 2005 meeting between governmental leaders and Farrakhan, all of them have refused then and since to denigrate the "minister" on the record. Illinois representative Danny Davis may have been the most effusive of the lot, telling The Daily Caller that Farrakhan is an "outstanding human being" and that it would not be anything out of the ordinary for him to meet with the Nation of Islam leader personally. Davis was quoted in part as saying, "I personally know [Farrakhan], I've been to his home, done meetings, participated in events with him."

Even former president Obama apparently had a polite if infrequent working relationship with Farrakhan. In January 2018, around the same time the Congressional Black Caucus story broke, respected photojournalist Askia Muhammad released a photo depicting Obama together with the controversial Nation of Islam leader taken during Obama's tenure as an Illinois state senator. The two tall men are both smiling broadly, standing side by side. According to Muhammad, at least a few Congressional Black Caucus members not only had a friendly overall relationship with Farrakhan, but also specifically attempted to hide this picture of him and Obama—then considered a rising political star—altogether from the public. At least one Fox News account has quoted the photographer as saying the Congressional Black Caucus pressured him for a decade or more to keep the image hidden. According to statements made by Muhammad on *Tucker Carlson Tonight*, "A staff member from the Black Caucus called me and said, 'We have to have the picture back,' and I was kind of taken aback."

The Black Caucus's make-like-dad-and-keep-mum request to the nervous photographer was not a casual one-off request. After at least "a couple" of phone calls centered around negotiations, Muhammad agreed to give the picture (and presumably its negatives) to *"Minister Farrakhan's chief of staff"* (italics mine). In short, more than twenty very powerful congresspeople and the future president met with the head of the Nation of Islam—who presumably believes in the Yakub story—had the event photographed, and then pressured at least one of the photographers to give up images from it to avoid hurting the reputations of those in attendance. The Klan could never *dream* of such access, and rightly so!

Obviously, Barack Obama is not himself a Muslim radical, zany rumors over on the right wing of the American eagle aside. But examples of minority racism at this level—the president of the United States meeting with the leader of a Black hate group—serve to confirm a rather obvious point about racial prejudice. Racism is not some system of institutional behaviors that needs a team of sociologists just to define it, possible only for male members of temporarily powerful majority groups. By that standard, the white supremacist AWB of South Africa and the Tutsi of Rwanda and Burundi could never—no matter how genocidal they became—qualify as racist. Rather, racism is one of the simplest and oldest of all human vices: the dislike of our human brothers because of the color of their skin and the perceived content of their chromosomes. To reiterate a perspective on life's many mundane evils which has been consistent throughout this book: we are all capable of racism—and we all have a duty to fight it together.

Taboo Obvious Facts #7 and #8: Whiteness Isn't the Only "Privilege"—and "Cultural Appropriation" Is Not Real

While criticizing ideas of racism, it is worth taking a minute to critically examine the concepts of white privilege and cultural appropriation. In addition to arguing that both institutional racism and traditional individual racism are as real as ever, many leftists also contend that there exists a "subtle racism" made up of privileges whites enjoy simply as a result of being white. Most notably, white privilege is the ability to be seen as a welcome, wanted member of the ruling class simply as a result of one's white skin, while cultural appropriation is the ability to oppress members of minority groups simply by borrowing things from their cultures. In the affirmative action era, both of these ideas fail completely as logical constructs. Cultural appropriation, in particular, may be one of the silliest damn concepts ever embraced by smart people. But to be able to seriously engage an educated leftist, it is important that one understands these ideas.

White privilege is the easier of the two concepts to define. Simply put, white privilege (WP) is the idea that all people who are white—compared to equally situated people of color, if not to all POC—receive a series of benefits just because they are white. According to tolerance.org's widely cited article "On Racism and White Privilege," what the site's authors refer to as white skin privilege serves multiple functions. First, it provides Caucasians with perks "that [they] do not earn and that people of color do not enjoy." These perks include a range of mundane day-to-day positives: the ability to more easily find Band-Aids that match one's skin tone, being able to use the comped shampoo in fine hotels or quickly purchase hair care products at the drug store, and so on.

Second, white privilege "creates real advantages" for whites. The tolerance.org team claims flatly that white folks "are immune to a lot of challenges." For example, it is alleged that a white person's skin color would rarely work against them during a job or college admissions interview or at a police traffic stop. Finally, and perhaps most importantly, "white privilege shapes the world in which we live." Subtle advantages enjoyed by people of European descent determine the very way "we navigate and interact with one another and the world." For example, when white students are taught about the glories of the U.S.A. or ancient Rome, they are informed that the accomplishments of other white people made these grand civilizations possible.

The original article proposing the theory of white privilege, penned by Peggy McIntosh in 1989, lists even more benefits of whiteness. The full list of these—it runs fifty items—includes, "I can arrange ... to be in the company of people of my race most of the time," "I can be pretty sure my neighbors will be neutral or pleasant to me," "I can go shopping alone most of the time," "I can go into a music shop and count on finding the music of my race represented," "I do not have to educate my children to be aware of systemic racism, for their own daily physical protection," and—perhaps most remarkably—"If I want to, I can be pretty sure of finding a publisher for [my writing]."[1] The Wikipedia page for "white privilege," quoting McIntosh, sums up all of this as "an invisible package of unearned assets."

Some radical authors very specifically claim that white privilege outweighs class as a predictor of success, arguing that even the poorest of Appalachian white sharecroppers enjoy this privilege and that severe material deprivation does not greatly interfere with the operation of whiteness. In a piece titled "Explaining White Privilege to a Broke White Person," liberal author Gina Crosley-Corcoran described a genuinely hardscrabble childhood that I, also a former poor kid, sometimes found difficult to read about. Opening by saying, "I came from the kind of poor that people don't want to believe still exists in this country,"[2] she went on to describe surviving northern-Illinois winters without heat or running water and using a coffee maker to boil ramen noodles with water taken from public bathrooms, among other adventures. However, while admitting that some of McIntosh's fifty benefits of white privilege seem to relate more to class or individual character than to race, she insisted that she benefited strongly from others on the list ("I can turn on the television ... and see people of my race"), even as a hungry kid. Whether most people would trade such benefits for the right to live in a heated brick house and eat bacon and eggs for breakfast is never discussed by Crosley-Corcoran.

A concept connected to white privilege is cultural appropriation. According to leftist writer Nadra Kareem Nittle, cultural appropriation is "the adoption of ... elements from another culture without the consent of people who belong to that culture." This is, at least potentially, an astonishingly broad idea. Nittle employed the standard academic definition of culture: "the beliefs, ideas, traditions, speech, and material objects associated with a particular group of people."[3] So cultural appropriation is the unfair, unjust, illegal, and unwanted taking or borrowing of anything not historically associated with you or your people. Cultural appropriation can thus include "unauthorized" use of another culture's clothing, music, language (!), religion (!!), folklore, dance, cuisine, symbols, or ideas about medicine. As is usual in leftist writing, whites are presented as the worst offenders when it comes to cultural appropriation. Although all groups are capable of this egregious cross-fertilization, appropriation is most likely to be hurtful "when the source community is a minority group," which has, of course, probably been "oppressed."

In a separate piece, this one for the website Everyday Feminism, author Maisha Z. Johnson gets a bit more specific. She describes cultural appropriation as the specific "power dynamic" in which members of a dominant culture borrow from the cultures of people who have been oppressed at some point by that dominant group. An example might be American whites borrowing from American Blacks or American Indians. This is very, very, very bad, for many reasons, of which Johnson gives at least nine. First, such borrowing "trivializes violent historical oppression."[4] Naming a professional sports team the Washington Redskins might remind Native Americans that they were once defeated by whites in a series of bloody wars.[5] Cultural appropriation might also cause "gentrification." For example, Yelp reviewers seeking authentic Mexican food outside of poor immigrant neighborhoods might result in white-owned versions of ethnic restaurants springing up and outcompeting minority-owned enterprises, or even lead to population change pushing POC out of their homes.

And so on. In situations where barriers like classism, racism, and "xenophobia" may mean that authentic ghetto or *barrio* residents lack the tools to successfully market products such as salsa or yoga or *brujeria* witchcraft, Johnson argues, white people have the ability to "turn those same culturally specific tools into profit," thus hurting the very communities they were borrowed from. This is, presumably, why virtually all successful rap acts and cooks at good Chinese restaurants are white. At any rate, Johnson concludes that cultural appropriation is certainly a serious and Very Bad Thing, and not at all just a bunch of incoherent nonsense made up by purple-haired campus activists smoking pot in dorm rooms.

There are many rebuttals to the theories just discussed. The most basic—specifically to the idea of white privilege—is that the concept is remarkably crude and univariate. In reality, there are *many* "privileges" that exist in this world (class, region, age, sex, IQ, attractiveness, birth order), and using modern scientific techniques to *adjust* for some of them—we come again to this concept!—eliminates almost all of the financial and other gaps between whites and POC which are generally attributed to racism by leftists. The edgy blog Bit of Fun (www.bitoffun.com) does a good job of pointing out the obvious fact that many different things predict success: "White privilege is not the only type of privilege that exists. There are many other privileges, for example tall privilege. In the population, just over 14 percent of men are 6 foot tall [or] more, but 58 percent of CEOs of Fortune 500 companies are 6 foot tall or taller."

The authors also note that Jewish (or Asian) privilege could be coherently argued to exist. Of all racial and religious groups, Jews are quite arguably the most academically focused, and they represent "by far the highest earning demographic" in many major nations, certainly outperforming both gentile whites and middle-class Blacks in the U.S.A. Even physical attractiveness could logically be considered a form of privilege. The Bit of Fun authors cite some empirical data and point out that people considered to be attractive receive significantly more dating and employment opportunities than those who are not. Crudely but accurately, they point out that even breast cup size is something that measurably affects income: "Just ask any waitress whose income is based on tips."

In a much more buttoned-down piece published by *National Review*, Dennis Prager lists quite a few other empirically measurable privileges. Chief among these, as was noted in a previous chapter, is two-parent privilege or "traditional family privilege." Prager is worth quoting at length on this point: "If you are raised by a father and a mother, you enter adulthood with more privileges than anyone else in American society, irrespective of race, ethnicity, or sex. That's why the poverty rate among two-parent Black families is only 7 percent. Compare that to a 22 percent poverty rate among whites in single-parent homes." Clearly, being reared in a two-parent stable home is one of the "decisive privilege[s]" of our time.

Obviously, *the* most "decisive" power-granting privilege of our time—within the U.S.A. and virtually every other society—is social class. Indeed, this has probably always been the case. It is hard to imagine a historical Western nation where it would not have been preferable to be a dark-skinned nobleman, even one with average looks and marital issues (think Othello or Haile Selassie), than a majority-group peasant. The same rule applies today.

For a recent experiment of my own, I examined the effect of dependent variables—including race, sex, urban/rural status, self-rated appearance, religious tradition, sexual orientation, height, weight, and social class measured as income—on a one-hundred-unit empirical measure of privilege, which included checkbox items ranging from "I have never gone to bed hungry" to "I know what frequent-flier miles are." I found that multiple variables (male sex, Christian religion, non-LGBT status, urban versus rural background) had more influence on individual privilege than minority race, and that by far the most influential variable was social class. It is no exaggeration to say that probably 60–70 percent of the "privilege" one enjoys in life—whether measured in terms of income, happiness, or a ladder metric such as the one I used—is due directly to social status and how much *money* he or she makes.

The question "Is social class more important than race/ethnicity?" recently came up on debate.org, and the graduate school debater types on the site reached conclusions similar to mine. Fully 80 percent of all respondents to the question responded "yes" rather than "no" or "maybe." One commenter said bluntly, "A rich white person will grow up in privilege just like a [rich] Black person, and a poor white person will grow up with discrimination and hardship just like a poor Black person." Even the minority of debaters who disagreed with this claim, many of whom cited incorrect leftist articles of faith like the prevalence of police brutality against Blacks, freely conceded the significant impact of class privilege on life. One such writer outlined a compromise position: "Social class is extremely important [to] how a family behaves and its practices, but race is also important because of the social impact it has on the family. If anything, both are equally important."[6] This was recorded as a "no" answer to the question.

The Atlantic, somewhat surprisingly, would call even that gentleman wrong, and me essentially correct. Back in 2013, the center-left weekly ran a piece called "When Class Became More Important to a Child's Education Than Race." The theme of the article is simple: although the U.S.A. has not yet fulfilled Dr. King's dream that race will never limit a child's opportunities, how wealthy that hypothetical child's parents are is far more influential. According to quantitative social scientist Sean Reardon, the test-score gap between poor children (in the bottom decile of income) and wealthy kids (90th percentile and up) has expanded in recent years and is now more than 50 percent larger than the vaunted Black-white achievement gap.[7]

While Black students may trail white peers by two or three grade levels, poor children "now languish at achievement levels that are ... four years behind their wealthy peers." Furthermore, Reardon noted that the impact of social class on performance has actually become stronger in recent years; race is "about as good a predictor" as it was three decades ago, but "income has become a much stronger predictor of how well kids do in school." In Reardon's models, like mine, the impact of class privilege far outpaces that of race.

Along with pointing out the measurable impact of social class and other nonracial variables on life outcomes, another strong and obvious counterargument to claims of universal white privilege is simply noting the existence of massive, nationwide affirmative action programs designed to benefit minorities. Honest discussion of the practice has been lacking in the national conversation during recent years, but affirmative action, first legally instituted via the Philadelphia Plan in 1967, has never vanished from the national scene. Generally defined as the attempt to achieve proportional representation of underrepresented minorities via preferential admissions and hiring, affirmative action in fact confers an absolute, empirically measurable *advantage* on POC during virtually every collegiate or Fortune 500 application process. The Department of Labor notes on its website that any contractor or subcontractor seeking to do business with the massive federal government must take "affirmative action" to recruit and advance not only Blacks, but also "qualified minorities, women, persons with disabilities, and covered veterans."[8]

No passing fancies, these affirmative actions must include "training programs, outreach efforts," and multiple other aggressive steps, all written into each company's formal personnel policies. In order to explain this complex system in more depth, the DOL website provides links to at least three other websites—one for "the Office of Federal Contract Compliance Programs," the "Affirmative Action and People with Disabilities" main page, the "Executive Order 11246 Fact Sheet," and so forth. No fewer than six major laws and regulations are also cited, with in-depth links attached: the Rehabilitation Act of 1973, the Vietnam Era Veterans' Readjustment Assistance Act of 1974, the "Obligations of Contractors and Subcontractors" under 41 CFR, Part 60-1, and three more.

For all of the loose talk about "subtle racism" and "white skin privileges," massive pro-minority affirmative action exists in virtually every sector of commercial and industrial business. Even the merit-focused tech sector recently committed to meeting new diversity goals. Following a widely reported post by Tracy Chou on Medium in 2013, which challenged tech players to tell the world what percentage of their software engineers were women and minorities, Apple and others made their hiring statistics—broken down by race and gender—publicly available, while committing to hire more diverse employees. Pinterest, seeking "woke" market share, specifically positioned itself as the tech firm "working hard to hire more women, as well as Black and Latino workers." In 2015, the company published a set of hiring goals focused largely on diversity (rather than, say, competence in coding) and explicitly committed to make 30 percent of its engineering hires women over the next year.[9]

Because of the large empirical disparities in current group performance discussed earlier in this book, the practical advantage conferred by affirmative action on POC—not to mention women, the disabled, gay little people, and so on—is often empirically very sizable. We are not speaking here of a "quick hand up" given to the more disadvantaged, in racial or class terms, of two essentially qualified candidates, but instead of large racial preferences. This is especially true in the academic sector. As was noted in chapters three and four of this book, the mean combined math/verbal SAT scores in 2017 were 941 for Blacks, 963 for Natives, 987 for Latinos, 1118 for whites, and 1181 for Asian Americans.

All of these scores are actually quite solid, and it is encouraging to see that Blacks have crept within fifty or so points of the 1000 SAT score that was considered normal for whites when I attended high school (from 1995 to 1999). No longer do African Americans or Southern whites regularly post combined math/verbal SAT scores of 690 or 730. Well done. That said, however, the topic of this chapter is "privilege." In this context, it is extremely relevant to note that the SAT score gap between Blacks and whites is 177 points, and that the gap between Asians and Hispanics is 194 points. Achieving diverse, "properly balanced" entering classes thus obviously requires top colleges to spot minority entrants at least that many points on the test.

Or more. In a fascinating review of William Bowen and Derek Bok's book *The Shape of the River*, Alan Wolfe of the *New York Times* pointed out that scoring gaps between racial groups on the SAT and similar exams tend to be largest among the best students. As a result, at the highest-ranking American colleges and universities, "Efforts to diversify the student body translate into a 400-point bonus for minority students." This "bonus" is so large because of the minuscule number of Black and Hispanic students who score at truly elite levels on standardized exams. In 1995, for example, only 70 Black Americans scored over 700 on the verbal portion of the SAT, while just 221 more scored over 650.[10] The corresponding figures for the much larger and higher-scoring population of whites were 8,239 and 16,216. It is no exaggeration to say, as Wolfe does, that the ten or so most competitive American colleges are literally fighting over perhaps 400 Black and Hispanic teenagers with stratospheric test scores. One level down, among "solid high-average" test-takers with combined SAT scores of 1200–1300, a Black applicant is 3–4 times as likely to be accepted into a university as an equivalent white applicant. White privilege, indeed.

One remarkable effect of the scope and prevalence of affirmative action preferences is that the debate over affirmative action is no longer sharply divided between whites (opposed) and POC (in favor). Many high-performing minority groups, such as Asians and non-American Blacks, are beginning to notice that the policy of accepting only a certain preset number of applicants from each ethnic group hurts them as much as it does whites. In late 2017, an Asian American–headed group called Students for Fair Admissions filed a series of targeted lawsuits accusing selective schools like Harvard, the University of North Carolina, and the University of Texas-Austin of "rejecting qualified Asians … in favor of less-qualified Black and Latino students."

Our Asian brothers have a strong case. The Students for Fair Admissions plaintiffs contend that the percentage of Asian students at elite colleges has remained basically stable over the past several decades—despite the fact that the number of Asians represented among the most qualified college applicants has increased dramatically. Hard numbers back up this claim. During the late 1990s, 21 percent of all SAT test-takers who scored a 700 or better on the exam were students of Asian descent. But by 2012, Asian American scholars made up a third of that top group. However, the percentage of Asian American students admitted—to, for example, Harvard—has remained stable, at almost exactly 21 percent, for the entire twenty-first century. At present, Asian American students have to score roughly 150 points higher on the SAT than *white* students in order to enjoy the same chances of admission to several elite colleges. Lawsuits targeting the policies responsible for this, brought by the families of passionate and hardworking minority students, await what will no doubt be a highly entertaining resolution.

The benefits of affirmative action, combined with such other perks as obvious mainstream media and social media double standards regarding speech, are so significant that several conservative authors have begun to straight-facedly argue for the existence of "*black* privilege." William Levinson of American Thinker, admittedly a somewhat extreme voice, contrasted the public (if often phony) groundswell of outrage that typically follows an allegation of racism against a white public figure with the studied mainstream media silence around the past antics of Black leaders like Al Sharpton.

Levinson reminded readers that during a late-1980s exchange of pleasantries with the Arab American owner of famed New York store Freddy's Fashion Mart, Sharpton called Fred Harari a "white interloper," while one of his associates labeled the merchant a "cracker" and pledged "to see this cracker suffer." This argument was recorded on tape, and transcripts of it have been fully available to the media since it was recorded. Shortly *after* this exchange, Freddy's Fashion Mart was burned to the ground—specifically following an upsurge of violent street protests which Sharpton helped lead—and seven people were killed.[11]

Within a few years in either direction of the Fashion Mart fire, Sharpton (1) helped represent Tawana Brawley during her world-famous rape hoax, (2) was later successfully sued for slander by a New York district attorney he accused of participating in the rape, and (3) allegedly attempted to buy a large amount of pure cocaine from an undercover FBI agent. Yet years after all this, "the Reverend Al" currently hosts a show on MSNBC and tends to be treated as a sort of respected emeritus figure by the Democratic Party. In contrast, Levinson noted, it would be difficult to even add up the number of white public figures fired from elite jobs after casually or jokingly making mildly racist comments. He provided the example of Don Imus, dismissed from his post as a shock jock radio host after calling a team of women's basketball players "nappy-headed hos." That wasn't nice, to be sure, but no one died as they did in the Fashion Mart fire.

CNN also recently discussed the concept of Black privilege in a longer and considerably more mainstream piece by John Blake. While Blake clearly does not believe that Black privilege is a thing, he is a pro and lays out the arguments of those who do in a fair and nuanced fashion. Some of them make more than a bit of sense. For example, "Blacks can belong to clubs and organizations that cater specifically to their race," and often do. However, there can be no National Association for the Advancement of White People because such a group would immediately be deemed racist and intolerable.

Such pro-minority double standards allegedly extend to language. No one much cares when Black folks "call white people 'honky' and 'cracker,'" but whites simply "cannot use the N-word."[12] David Horowitz, quoted at length, provided still more examples: "College professors practicing 'affirmative grading' hold Black students to lower standards than others. Corporations offer programs and internships to Black workers but not to whites."[13] At least in part as a result of all this, a major 2011 study found that 55 percent of all whites said white Americans experience racial discrimination today, and many said that whites experience more racism than Blacks do.

Like Blake, I find the concept of "Black privilege" to be a bit of a stretch. It is more than a little absurd to see well-off white men in suits and ties practicing the posture of hands-out victimization that is already unbearably annoying when adopted by minority leftists. Simply put, it is hard to believe that any large group of people has it too terribly bad in 2019 America, and even harder to believe that white people are overall worse off than Blacks or Native Americans. As Blake noted, at least some advantages of whiteness remain today. For historical reasons, "The wealth of white households is 13 times the median wealth of Black households," for example. However, while Levinson and Horowitz's examples of "Black privilege" fail to convince me that minorities now have the whip hand in America, they certainly destroy the idea of unchallenged universal white privilege. We Americans are all in it together now, confronting a tough global economy and challenging world security picture.[14]

White privilege, while eminently debunkable as a concept, can at least be coherently argued to exist. Cultural appropriation, on the other hand, is an insanely stupid idea. First, using the common definition given above—which prioritizes minority claims but appears to define everyone as capable of appropriation—almost literally every element of human existence would qualify as "cultural appropriation." The use by members of society Y of things originally invented in society X is an absolute constant of civilized life.

To give just a few examples: the modern jet and rocket engines that power our machines here in America were largely developed by the Germans, our effective small cars and hibachi grills were first built by the Japanese, my favorite beer (Guinness Stout) was originally bottled in Ireland, and the food a dating couple might enjoy in a good South Asian restaurant traces its roots back to India or Pakistan. More broadly, farming was developed by Egyptians or Middle Easterners, while hunting and most weapons presumably, like our species itself, originated in Black Africa. Can no one outside the cultures which originally developed these tools and technologies use them? The idea sounds ridiculous because it is.

Even using a narrower definition of cultural appropriation—that it occurs only when members of a "dominant" group take from members of a group which they have a history of oppressing or successfully warring with—still bans perhaps half of all human exchange, if no longer all of it. Muslim Turks fought several victorious wars with the Greeks. Can citizens of modern Turkey eat gyros? The warlike Mongols conquered Russia. Can their descendants in central Asia drink vodka?

Within America's polyglot society, questions like these become even more complicated. White Americans have traditionally oppressed Blacks, of course—this is undisputed—but surely all legacy Americans outrank recent immigrants from the third world. Should African Americans, then, logically not be able to eat tacos or fajitas? And of course, oppressive power dynamics extend well beyond race. Today, few would deny that gays or the poor are more put-upon than Asian Americans or middle-class Black people. Can anyone outside these groups, then, guiltlessly enjoy the art forms they pretty indisputably invented: electronic dance music in the first case, and hip-hop and country music in the second?

Beyond these fun questions, there exist at least two other sweeping and powerful arguments against the idea of cultural appropriation. First, at least here in America, *no one* is fucking oppressed. Very arguably, no one has been oppressed for quite a while. We are a country so wealthy that the biggest health problem facing poor people is obesity. The U.S.A. does have a history of racism, and Blacks in particular have endured some agonizing time on the cross here in this land. However, it is also the case that racial segregation was banned by law back in 1954, and "discrimination in accommodations" based on virtually any major personal characteristic (race, sex, ethnicity, color, religion, and so forth) was made illegal via the Civil Rights Act back in 1964. Since the late 1960s, when the Philadelphia Plan was launched, formal programs of affirmative action/positive discrimination *in favor* of minorities have been mandated by law. Populations so oppressed that they really have no chance to use their own culture for gain, à la Black Delta blues musicians in the 1910s, simply do not exist in the modern United States.

This point is further strengthened by the fact that many of those shouting the loudest about "cultural appropriation" (of, for example, yoga) are not American Blacks or Native Americans, but rather immigrants from POC world powers like China and India. It is difficult to see how the U.S.A. has *ever* oppressed these mighty countries—who are nuclear powers, our global rivals, and often best us at the negotiating table—or why we owe much of anything to rich citizens from those places who voluntarily move here.

A second point against the idea of cultural appropriation is the biggest and most obvious of all: No such moral rule exists or has ever existed. Modern liberals just made it up. Not one Western, or Eastern, or West African moral philosopher until about twenty years ago ever argued that it is somehow unethical to learn from another free person if your group once won a war against his. Indeed, taking this argument seriously would completely destroy the value proposition for the "diversity" so beloved on the left. To ask a crude and tough question, but one that might be plausibly raised, what exactly is the benefit to white Americans of having Blacks around if the whites are forbidden to enjoy jazz, soul food, street ball, and urban fashion—simply the fear of crime? The same question applies in reverse, of course. If, using the broadest definition of cultural appropriation, Blacks and Asians are not supposed to eat Italian food or jam to hard rock or date cheerleaders, what do *we* get from our white countrymen—just the racism? Absent the ability to learn from one another and develop together, which in business we sometimes call *"managed* diversity," neighbors of a different race or ethnicity are just annoying foreigners you are likely to clash with.

In this context, it is no surprise that during the exact time frame during which the ideas of "white privilege" and "cultural appropriation" grew more prevalent, the United States has seen a massive resurgence of semi-official segregation within locales such as college campuses. As the College Fix noted back in 2016, Black collegians have recently begun demanding almost complete separation from their white peers, including "safe spaces" on campuses that can be used only by students of color. At the University of California, Los Angeles (UCLA), for example, something called the Afrikan Student Union is insisting on an "Afrikan Diaspora floor" and an "Afro-house" residence hall, both to be made available exclusively to Black students. In a sentence that makes one wonder exactly how many racially exclusive Black organizations exist at UCLA, student activists argue that "The Afrikan Diaspora floor is a way for us to connect more to other Black students, the Afrikan Student Union, and the Afro-Am department."[15]

Across the country at New York University (NYU), a diverse group of students demanded to be segregated from one another a year or so ago, claiming, "Within the NYU 2031 plan ... an entire floor of the mixed use building in the Southern Superblock plan [should] be entirely dedicated to Students of Color."[16] Segregation on that campus would extend to gay and bisexual students as well, with another entire dormitory floor set aside for, to use their terminology, the "queer students on campus." Back in California at around the same time, students at UC Berkeley demanded the creation of an African American Student Center, including both designated office space and residential housing, to be located centrally on campus and run by the school's African

American Development Office. And so on. Those readers with a strong stomach and trouble sleeping can check out a full list of demands like this, issued by students at seventy-six different four-year colleges, at www.thedemands.org.

The example of *the literal return of actual segregation* shows the real danger of such concepts as cultural appropriation and universal white privilege, which might initially seem lightweight and silly. These are not mere fancies, but rather tentative first steps down a very dangerous road. If we decide to again judge people not primarily as individuals, but rather as members of intractable and often squabbling tribes, it will become increasingly difficult to ever find common ground between them. Down that path lies balkanization and the clashes and even genocides that resulted from that in the Balkans themselves. Let us take a different road.

CHAPTER 8

Taboo Obvious Fact #9:
A Sane Immigration Policy Isn't
Racist (And We Need One!)

Although U.S. immigration policy is not the focus of this book, many of the topics discussed in *Taboo* are directly related to it. Very recent changes to U.S. immigration policy have, to a remarkable degree, caused both the glorious diversity of the modern United States and many of our uglier racial conflicts. To an extent rarely, if ever, before seen in the recent history of nations, the U.S.A. completely revamped national immigration policy during the social revolution of the 1960s. While I strongly support maintaining a basically anti-racist and welcoming policy of American legal immigration, some analysis and improvement of the current U.S. system would be very advisable.

Most casual observers of the U.S. political scene are unaware just how much, and how recently, America's immigration policy moved away from historical norms. To give a bit of a history lesson, current U.S. immigration policy dates back only to the Immigration and Naturalization Act of 1965, or the "Hart-Celler Act," which was backed by JFK and his brother Ted Kennedy, among others. According to a critical but scholarly review of the law, the Hart-Celler Act "abolished the national origins quota system" for immigrants that had been established in the

1920s in order to favor the citizens of allied nations and shifted the primary basis for the selection of immigrants "from an applicant's nation of birth to his or her family relationships." Simply put, the law eliminated almost all discrimination based on where an applicant for immigration was born.

This was a sea change. U.S. immigration policy up to this point, whether because of prejudice or logic (or both), had always favored immigrants from our traditional source nations within Europe, as well as the nearby Black-majority island states of the West Indies. The Hart-Celler Act removed these preferences and replaced them with large-scale admission of immigrants falling into preferred categories such as "relatives of U.S. citizens or permanent residents," individuals with skills or trades viewed as useful to the U.S.A., or "refugees of violence or unrest." Family unification was probably the primary goal of the law, and the new immigration framework was designed to "increasingly allow entire families to uproot themselves from other countries and reestablish their lives in the U.S."[1]

American politicians, especially those on the political left, downplayed the potential impact of Hart-Celler to a significant degree. Speaking on the floor of the Senate, liberal congressional lion Ted Kennedy said emphatically, "This bill will not flood our cities with immigrants. It will not upset the ethnic mix of our society." Attorney General Robert Kennedy, who reported directly to President John F. Kennedy,[2] was even more blunt and—if this is the appropriate word—optimistic. He predicted that because of cultural differences and past clashes, fewer than five thousand immigrants "from the entire Asia-Pacific Triangle" would ever enter the U.S.A., after which all immigration from that source region "would virtually disappear."

Statements like these were either extraordinarily flawed underestimations or out-and-out lies. The conservative news site Free Republic called the claims "clear[ly] untrue" and pointed out that the number of legal immigrants to the U.S.A. jumped to 400,000 within two years of the passage of Hart-Celler and to 800,000 persons by 1980. The annual inflow was well over 1 million persons as far back as the early 1990s, and it reached 1.2 million individuals per year by 2004 before finally stabilizing at around that level. None of these figures takes note of *illegal* immigrants at all, at least 300,000 of whom enter the United States annually, generally "to join legally admitted relatives."[3] Notably, the maximum number of legal immigrants allowed to enter the country each year is set by law and is thus totally unrelated to economic trends such as the American unemployment rate.

The ethnic composition of America's immigration pool has changed as dramatically as its size. Free Republic points out that over the last fifty years, immigration from western and northern Europe "shriveled to less than one-tenth" of the total flow of immigrants to the U.S.A. Over the last fifteen years, Latin America alone has accounted for over 40 percent of all legal immigration, with East Asia not far behind. A well-sourced piece by history.com makes this same point, noting that the policies instituted by Hart-Celler had "greatly changed the face of the American population" by the late twentieth century.[4]

Between 1965 and 2000, by far the largest number of immigrants to the United States (4.3 million) came from our southern neighbor Mexico, with the Philippines coming in second at 1.4 million. The Dominican Republic, Korea, India, Cuba, and Vietnam were also leading sources of immigrants during this period, with each country sending between 700,000 and 800,000 of its citizens to the U.S.A. Aided by natural population growth in our rich nation, the Mexican American population of the United States grew from less than 5 million in 1970, the first census year after Hart-Celler, to roughly 35 million today.

Conservative opponents have hardly been shy about attributing a broad range of negative effects to the 1965 legislation. Just over our northern border, Mark Dwyer of Canada Free Press claimed bluntly that the law "allowed chain immigration of underachievers and over-breeders … by awarding higher preference to the relatives of those already in America than to prospective immigrants with sought-after skills." As President Trump has been known to point out, the range of family members who qualify as "preferred" for immigration purposes is quite broad, including the spouses and children of permanent resident aliens (folks who are not citizens), and the brothers and sisters of any U.S. citizen. Not wholly unfairly, Dwyer asked, "How many Americans in 1965 *had* brothers and sisters who were not U.S. citizens?"[5]

Dwyer also argued that unceasing mass immigration over fifty years has had other effects. Perhaps most notably, "Virtually all U.S. population growth in the last four decades was due to post-1973 immigration and the higher-than-average fertility of post-1973 immigrants (legal and otherwise)." A quick glance at U.S. birth rate data indicates that this claim is probably accurate. The birth rates in most modern Western nations hover at or just below replacement levels, and the most recent birth rate recorded for American non-Hispanic whites was roughly 1.7 births per woman or per female-male pair. Without the post-1965 immigrant influx, we would have "no overpopulation explosion." More specifically, "our once well-functioning infrastructure would not be overwhelmed," "our public schools would not be crowded with ... needy Spanish-speaking kids," "our highways would not turn into huge parking lots" filled with novice immigrant drivers—and so on.

Dwyer is clearly a hard-right conservative, and some of these claims strike me as more than a bit of a stretch. To pick on perhaps the weakest of them, I personally find that Mexican Americans drive no worse than white country boys, big-city Black guys, or virtually anybody else! But one important and plainly accurate point the Canada Free Press piece does make is that mass immigration has caused substantial *political* demographic changes in the U.S.A. It is not at all uncommon for 90 percent of American Blacks and 75 percent of Latinos to vote for the Democratic Party in significant elections, and this holds nearly as true for foreign-born minority citizens as for native-born minorities.

Dwyer argued bluntly that "[c]reatures like Rep. Nancy Pelosi and Sen. Harry Reid" would have had virtually no chance at long and successful political careers in western U.S. states were it not for "the 1965 INA and the 'demographic shift' that it caused." Interestingly, it now appears that even these white liberal leaders may soon be replaced by the hard left, as indicated by the success of candidates like Alexandria Ocasio-Cortez and Ilhan Omar. It is frankly hard not to see amoral desire for more voters as the driving force behind at least some recent Democratic Party positions on immigration.

Whatever the validity of the more partisan right-wing claims about Hart-Celler in particular and U.S. immigration policy in general, there is little doubt that a massive population shift inside the United States followed the 1965 passage of the Immigration and Nationality Act and that this could have near-future political implications. From a stable peak of roughly 90 percent between 1920 and 1965, the U.S.A.'s white population percentage dropped to 81 percent by 2000 and stood at 74.76 percent around the time of the last decennial census. During the same period, the Black percentage of the American population increased to 12.36 percent, the Asian percentage rose to 4.38 percent, and the percentage of the population composed of multiracial or "other race" individuals reached 5.63 percent. Notably, the estimates just given do not take Hispanics into account. The Hispanic population was pegged at 34,814,000 individuals, or 12.6 percent of the overall population, in the 2000 census, and has since grown to 17 percent of the total. Counting all Hispanics and people of mixed or "other" race as non-white, it can be coherently argued that the U.S. population has shifted from 90 percent to 57 percent white over the last fifty years.

Even beyond analyses of politics and demography, the impact of mass immigration is currently being felt throughout society. To a rather striking extent, many statistical trends which are almost never associated with population change are revealed to be largely race (and class) stories when examined in greater depth. National average scores on the SAT and similar tests, for example, are frequently accused of increasing and decreasing almost at random. The higher education website Magoosh recently noted that although American SAT scores have been fairly solid in the recent past, the mean score in 2015 had fallen to 1490 (out of 2400). This average represented a decline of seven points from the previous year and was the lowest such mark since 2005. This finding was presented with considerable interest as something of a curiosity. However, in what may be a *Taboo* "exclusive," it appears possible to explain this pattern simply by adjusting for demographic change.

Remarkably, mean and median SAT scores for American whites seem to have remained roughly the same for almost fifty years.[6] In 1972, when 90 percent or more of all SAT test-takers would have been non-Hispanic Caucasians, the average combined math/verbal score on the exam was 1039 (509 + 530). The equivalent average scores for 1973 and 1974 were 1029 and 1026, respectively. For purposes of comparison, the mean *white* math/verbal scores in 2008, 2012, and 2015 were 1065, 1063, and 1061. The gap between the 1972 combined scores and the 2015 combined scores for whites was 22 points out of 1600, or 2.1 percentage points.

In contrast, the 2008, 2012, and 2015 mean test scores for Mexican or Mexican American students were 917, 913, and 911. For Puerto Ricans, the same figures were 909, 904, and 906.[7] Blacks scored a bit below Mexican Americans, and the average figures for all other Hispanics or Latinos were 916, 908, and 910. Whatever cultural or historical factors might explain these performances, the plain logical fact is that the expansion of these lower-scoring groups of students from 10 percent to perhaps 40 percent of the pool of SAT examinees logically has to be a primary reason for dropping or stabilizing scores, especially in the much-cited context of rising minority scores.

Furthermore, the fact that a rough stability has existed among U.S. SAT scores in recent years seems largely to be due to the high performance of other immigrant minority groups, such as East Asians, Indian Americans, and Jews. Asians posted mean scores of 1094, 1113, and 1121 during the three relevant years, scoring more than fifty points ahead of whites on average. Both of the trends just mentioned are essentially unchallenged, hard to miss once pointed out, and potentially relevant for U.S. immigration policy.

The current mainstream-left response to data of this kind seems to be calling for *more* mass immigration. Many scholar-activists argue that such problems would not exist in a majority-minority—and thus presumably less "racist"—America. One of the most rapidly growing movements in contemporary American politics, complete with its own Twitter and Facebook hashtag (#AbolishICE), is focused on the total elimination of the governmental agency Immigration and Customs Enforcement (ICE). *The Nation* ran a major article on this campaign in March 2018 headlined "It's Time to Abolish ICE."[8] According to prominent immigration lawyer Dan Canon, who was quoted throughout the piece, "A lot of people [don't] have any kind of direct experience with ICE, so they don't really know what they do or what they're about. If they did, they'd be appalled." To Canon, core ICE tasks such as deporting illegal aliens are unnecessary exercises in cruelty: "They scoop up people in their apartments or their workplaces and take them miles away from their spouses and children."[9]

Illegal immigrant rights groups seem to be jumping on the Abolish ICE bandwagon *en bloc*. Mary Small, policy director for Detention Watch Network, said that responsible politicians need "to be honest about the fact that the core of the agency is broken." Her group has repeatedly attempted to defund ICE via a campaign called #DefundHate, which seems to have predated #AbolishICE. For his part, Angel Padilla, policy director of the ironically named Indivisible Project, agreed, arguing, "ICE is terrorizing American communities right now.[10] They're ... separating children from parents every day. We are funding those activities, and we need to use all the leverage we have to stop it."

In typical activist fashion, *The Nation*, which obviously sympathizes with the Abolish ICE movement, attempted to describe the very process of enforcing the laws against illegal immigration as racist. Noting that one central operating assumption of ICE is that all undocumented immigrants are real or potential threats, *The Nation* claimed that this means "ICE's tactics are philosophically aligned with racist thinkers like Richard Spencer." How? Well, white nationalists like Spencer and Jared Taylor have in the past had the temerity to suggest that well-publicized raids on prominent but "non-criminal" illegal aliens would probably have a deterrent effect, in that the large majority of illegals would get their affairs in order and choose to leave the country of their own accord rather than waiting for ICE agents to pick the departure date for them. Apparently, ICE is Nazi-like because both ICE and "Nazis" want most illegal immigrants out of the country.

The #AbolishICE debate has crossed the pond in recent months. In June 2018, England's *The Guardian* ran a piece headlined "It Is Time to Abolish ICE. It Cannot Be Reformed." According to author Amy Gottlieb, there is no way to repair a government agency which was designed "to tear families and communities apart" with limited oversight. The core of Gottlieb's case is more personal and emotional than logical. She writes, "Every day I live with the terror that my husband Ravi will be taken away from me and permanently exiled from his home in the United States." There is, unsurprisingly, no evidence of any kind that ICE plans to deport Mr. Gottlieb, who is a legal permanent resident and taxpayer literally married to an American. But, his wife argues, the agency probably could; Ravi was once convicted of wire fraud twenty years ago. Whatever the actual risk, Gottlieb sees her situation as analogous to wartime: "What I am living through feels like a battle … we are in a fight for our lives."[11] This must end, and reform is alleged to be impossible for an organization premised on the idea that mass deportations of illegal aliens make us safer. Root and branch, she contends, ICE must be abolished.

To be fair, some advocates of eliminating ICE favor simply replacing it with a more humane structure along the lines of the Bush-era Immigration and Nationalization Service (INS), and Gottlieb herself mentions this possibility. However, most activists, including Gottlieb, seem at the very least to see traditional border security as nonessential for the nation. Gottlieb openly admits, "Some may question who will perform the duties of ICE if it is abolished." But, she asks, "Are those duties essential to sustaining strong communities?" The answer she gives is no. In her experience, stringent enforcement of immigration laws more often does the opposite. Rather than armed soldiers and police (she claims), what truly makes people safer are communities where everyone has access to "basic services, including education, healthcare, and jobs, and where loved ones can stay together" regardless of fripperies like paperwork.

In modern activist discourse, the idea that employing immigration cops is Hitleresque morphs almost seamlessly into the idea that having borders at all is a debatable, take-it-or-leave-it sort of proposition. HuffPost, because of course it did, recently released a list of no fewer than sixteen reasons "Why Opening Our Borders Makes More Sense than Militarizing Them" in a piece penned by author Roque Planas. The list opens with the blunt and provocative question, "What would happen if the United States suddenly stopped building walls and instead flung open its borders, not unlike the European Union?" The answer, according to Planas: good things! "For most of its history, the United States has had ... open borders," and he argues we should bring them back posthaste.[12]

Another major contemporary article in the libertarian *Reason* magazine carries a bit more intellectual heft but makes essentially the same argument: the U.S.A. should eliminate visas entirely among all the North American Free Trade Agreement (NAFTA) countries and at a minimum allow Canadians, Americans, and Mexicans to travel freely among those three nations for any reason, or none at all. Central Americans might, conceivably, receive the same benefits. And *why* do this? The answer seems to be, in large part, for the sake of the immigrants: such restrictions on border crossing as visas and even effective guest worker programs create "cruelties for the people" involved. The solution proposed is to treat all men, at least in our sun-dappled hemisphere, as brothers.[13]

Arguments for open borders have recently become common even on the "RINO" wing of the Republican Party. *Fortune* magazine's Rutger Bregman penned a fairly good one in 2016. Arguing that the problem for today's U.S.A. "isn't too much immigration, but too little," Bregmen attempted with some success to debunk standard arguments against immigration, pointing out that immigrants do take American jobs but also create new ones via consumption, and that immigrants overall have a slightly lower crime rate than native-born Americans. Perhaps most memorably, he argued that open borders make immigrants more likely to leave. In the 1960s, for example, prior to any serious militarization of the U.S.–Mexico border, "70 million Mexicans crossed it, but, in time, 85 percent returned home."[14]

There are obviously serious rebuttals to Bregman's arguments. To give just two, there is—first—a great deal of evidence that *illegal* immigration does boost crime and drive down wages. The policies described by Bregman would, by definition, almost entirely benefit illegal immigrants, because legal immigrants have already managed to enter the country without breaking the law. More broadly, it is probably true that allowing free movement of people and capital worldwide would boost global GDP. This is a major argument of Bregman's, who cited potential job gains in the U.S.A. and elsewhere and estimates a jump in GDP of 67 percent. However, that figure is for the *planet*. Wording this as politely as possible, there is little evidence indeed that allowing unlimited migration of poor third-world immigrants into the U.S.A. would boost GDP per capita *here*.

Even with all the arguments against them outlined, ideas like those contained in the *Fortune* and *Reason* articles have an inherent, atavistic appeal to most Americans. Probably the defining element of the U.S.A.'s national mythos is that we are a nation of immigrants, forged out of near-wilderness by steely-eyed settlers and pioneers. In a passionate letter to a relative about the process of immigrating to the U.S.A. that was widely reprinted, journalist Andrew Lam summed up this American ethos. He discussed how the dream of coming to this near-magical place where things *work* and all people are free can move the hearts of human beings all around the world, as well as their feet.

Lam wrote, "Didn't the American Dream, or rather the dream of coming to America, cause the movement of millions in our homeland, and stir the souls of many millions more?" From Lam's point of view, one of the worst effects of 9/11 on America was the partial rejection of the pro-immigrant ideal which followed the attacks—involving "hate speech," "hate crimes," and worst of all, "the nation of immigrants turning its back on immigrants once more." In a passage of lyrical beauty, Lam moved on to distinguish "the USA" from "America." The United States is merely a nation made up of men with amoral strategic interests who do things like wage wars on terrorism. But *America* is the magical place mentioned above.[15]

In America, everything can be found that a human soul might dream of: "transparency, freedom, democracy, opportunity, due process, fair play, and the promise of progress." The U.S.A. is the place to which an H-1B1 visa brings you to do business, but *America* is where any free citizen can work hard and keep what they earn and gain respect. To Lam, this exceptional nation must always extend to the world an open, ungauntleted hand. His essay ends with a poignant one-sentence message to future would-be immigrants: "Is the American Dream still alive? No, cousin, not really. Not without you."

Saying this sort of thing is almost mandatory when Americans discuss immigration. In an essay topped by a page-high picture of the Statue of Liberty holding her torch, liberal journalists Randi Weingarten and Maria Teresa Kumar made the same points as Lam, if more prosaically. Citing a few specific cases, these authors referred to the deportation of illegal aliens as generally immoral and unacceptable. Such immigrants and their families, legal or not, aspire only to do "what our parents and grandparents did when they came to America," helping to build "this great country into a beacon of freedom, hope, and opportunity in the world." Continued immigration is thus allegedly vital to the economic health of the U.S.A. Furthermore, our country has a moral duty to save many, if not all, refugees globally: "'Never again' must mean never again for everyone."[16] And so on.

Surprisingly, Weingarten and Kumar did not cite the famous Emma Lazarus poem, "The New Colossus," which is mounted to this day on a cast brass plaque inside the lower level of the Statue of Liberty. This makes them virtually unique among open-borders advocates. Lazarus

was a political and economic socialist, and her words succinctly sum-
marize the left-wing understanding of what immigration to America
should mean. To quote:

> Give me your tired, your poor,
> Your huddled masses yearning to breathe free,
> The wretched refuse of your teeming shore.
> Send these, the homeless, tempest-tost to me,
> I lift my lamp beside the golden door!

In reality, prose is rarely as beautiful as poetry, but it is generally
more useful—and Lazarus's golden words have always had rather little
to do with the reality of U.S. immigration laws. Immigration to the
U.S.A. has been a selective process since the nation's beginning, although
this fact is often downplayed. The left-leaning, highly respected Pew
Research Center says that the United States "began regulating immigration soon after it won independence from Great Britain."[17] By 1790, just
seven years after the successful conclusion of the American Revolution,
federal laws had been passed limiting citizenship to free white people of
sound moral character who had lived on American soil for at least two
years. By 1870, fewer than eighty years later, citizenship had of course
been extended to persons of African origin. However, between 1870 and
1875, further tough restrictions on immigration were implemented.
These included total bans on criminals, people with contagious diseases,
polygamists, any anarchists or similar political radicals, beggars, pros-
titutes, and pimps.

Many of these standards remain in effect, and even "softer" immigration laws like the 1965 Immigration and Nationality Act explicitly
established favored classes of immigrants, such as skilled craftsmen and
the family members of American citizens. The 1965 legislation also,
although rather theoretically, placed actual caps on rates of immigration
from the Western Hemisphere. At no point during American history has
immigration to the United States actually been an open-entry process.

Even legendarily welcoming Ellis Island rejected between 2 and 20 percent of all applicants in a typical year. The question regarding immigration has historically been not whether the U.S.A. should have any entry standards at all, but rather *which* immigration standards we wish to maintain and enforce.

At least one standard has struck most previous generations of Americans as essentially undebatable. Almost from the beginning, probably *the* key rule of U.S. immigration policy has been that no immigrant should be admitted who is likely to become a welfare recipient or other "public charge." The legal language of the public charge rule, found (should you be curious) at Section 212(a)(4) of the Immigration and Nationality Act (INA), is extremely straightforward. The rule states, "Any alien who ... is likely at any time to become a public charge is inadmissible." The logic underlying this one simple sentence has guided U.S. immigration policy for centuries.

As the Center for Immigration Studies (CIS) puts it, "Congress has long sought to ensure that aliens immigrating to the United States are able to support themselves."[18] The country's first fully general immigration law, dating back to the 1800s, included public charge language, and by 1903, Congress had made immigrants actually deportable if they became public charges at any point during the first two years (later increased to five years) after their entry. The CIS concedes that "both provisions have been modified ... over the years," but points out that their underlying spirit very much remains part even of today's Immigration and Nationality Act.

Although the pro-immigration left has, inevitably, begun to argue for the elimination of the public charge rule, the plain fact is that selective immigration policies have existed throughout the country's history and are more necessary than ever today. The reason is simple, if rarely said in public: today's United States is a semi-socialist welfare state containing more than three hundred million people and is no longer a brawling frontier republic in need of young men to kill bears and fight Comanche raiders. Screening out potential public charges should logically be more of a national goal than ever before. Frankly, the U.S.A. has done a very poor job of doing so in the recent past.

In 2015, the CIS, a right-wing but empirically focused organization which employs many top quantitative scholars, published a major study detailing the relationship between immigration and welfare dependency. According to the center's research team, 51 percent of households headed by an immigrant used at least one federal welfare program, defined as any government-provided cash, housing, food, or medical care, compared to slightly less than 30 percent of native households.[19] Jason Richwine, one of the study's authors, estimated that the average household headed by an immigrant represents a net cost to taxpayers of $6,234 annually in federal welfare benefits. This figure was 41 percent higher than the $4,431 in benefits received by members of the median native-headed household.[20]

High welfare use is an issue for both legal immigrants and illegal immigrants, with many members of the latter group able to collect welfare through their children. In 2015, illegal immigrant–headed households cost the government an average of $5,692, while legal immigrant households cost an average of $6,378. Recent immigrants from Mexico and Central America were the biggest welfare users, with households led by individuals in this category using $8,251 of benefits in a typical year.

It should certainly be pointed out that high rates of immigrant welfare dependency are not driven by laziness or malice. Few people *want* to be on welfare, and by some metrics immigrants work harder than native-born Americans. Richwine concluded that higher immigrant consumption of public aid dollars can be explained almost entirely by the fact that immigrants, *on average*, have a lower level of education and a much higher number of children than native-born Americans. Almost 25 percent of immigrant households are headed by someone with less than a twelfth-grade education, as opposed to 8 percent of native households. Thirteen percent of immigrant households have "three or more children," as opposed to roughly 5 percent of native households. Immigrants are quite likely to work, and to work hard. However, it seems that stereotypes about massive working-class Hispanic and Eastern European Catholic families, like most stereotypes, contain a substantial grain of truth.

While on this topic, it is worth quickly debunking a common misunderstanding about illegal immigrants and welfare. It is often said that "Illegals can't directly get welfare benefits." This is, in debater's parlance, a "true but worthless" point. Because of the U.S.A.'s controversial policy of birthright citizenship, any child born inside the borders of the country to two illegal immigrants automatically becomes an American citizen in the eyes of the law, and programs such as Medicaid and food stamps are open to all American citizens. Illegal-headed families can thus receive substantial welfare payouts in the names of their citizen children. Illegal immigrants are also at least as likely as other Americans to take advantage of fully available public services such as emergency medical care and free public education. Regardless of legal status, most people can find a way to benefit from a welfare state as large as the one that exists in contemporary America.

It is important to point out that these data from the CIS report are not stand-alone outliers from a right-leaning foundation. The general conclusion that more than half of all immigrants are on welfare is not seriously disputed. The utterly mainstream *USA Today* recently ran a feature piece called ... well ... "More Than Half of Immigrants on Welfare." On one occasion quoting the CIS, the article pointed out that about 50 percent of immigrant households receive at least one variety of welfare benefit, with the list of these including "Medicaid, food stamps, school lunches, and housing assistance." *USA Today* went a step further, pointing out that these numbers "increase for households with children, with 76 percent of immigrant-led households receiving welfare," versus 52 percent of native-led households with kids.[21]

Scholar Steven Camarota, quoted in the *USA Today* piece, made the obvious point that more selective immigration policies could fix this problem. To him, the primary issue is "a system that allows a lot of less-educated immigrants to settle in the country, who then earn modest wages and are eligible for a very generous welfare system." There exists specific empirical evidence for this claim: more educated "Old World" immigrants, who are generally admitted to the U.S.A. via H-1B or other skilled-worker visas, use welfare at very low rates—32 percent for East Asians, 26 percent for Europeans, and a remarkable 17 percent for Indians and other South Asians. The existence of a massive welfare safety net inside the modern United States is a strong argument for sane, selective immigration policy.

The social justice movement, albeit unintentionally, provides another strong argument for selective immigration. Not only is the United States of today a socialized welfare state rather than a coonskin-capped frontier land, but the open reluctance of many elites to defend and promote American ideals or mandate the assimilation of immigrants provides further reason to be skeptical about unchallenged mass immigration. According to at least one elite American university, the University of Minnesota, even mentioning the traditional "melting pot" is a bit racist. No, I am not kidding. A widely circulated list of the "racial microaggressions" which are discouraged or forbidden on that institution's campus includes the phrase "America is a melting pot." Among other phrases dismissed as racist or problematic by the anonymous author of the list were: "There is only one race, the human race," "Everyone can succeed in this society," "I do not see color," and—unbelievably but actually— "Where are you from?"[22]

Laughable as these examples may be, the Minnesota list reflects a "serious" trend in scholarly thought: the tendency to reject the melting pot ideal and dismiss cultural assimilation as somehow racist. Back in 2006, Mark Friedman became one of the first to publicly make this argument in his article called "The End of the Melting Pot." In the piece, he described the concept of an assimilationist melting pot as a sort of American creation myth. The idea of the melting pot here, of course, is that immigrants come to America and blend their unique cultural contributions into a "broth" that is the constantly developing American culture. Over time, the descendants of first-generation immigrants from (say) Italy shed their original cultural identity and become Americans—but they become part of an American culture that now includes Italian contributions ranging from pizza pies to decent pasta to quality opera. However, Friedman argued that this ideal probably never existed, and should not be pursued today even if it once did. According to him, "America is not a pot of melted cultures, but rather a place of coexisting cultures, each vitally alive and unmelted."[23] Next door to the unassimilated Somali, apparently, live the German *Junker* and Mexican peasant!

After a few perfunctory pieces of praise for the old American Dream, Friedman explained why he believes all of this and chooses to reject the melting pot. First, of course, the beloved old American stew was racist. The melting pot metaphor included the idea that immigrants might have to tolerate some racism and bias as part of "a temporary transition period" while working to become Americans. Unacceptable! Worse, Friedman contended, this prejudice never ended for members of many groups; history demonstrates that quite a few immigrant groups and cultural minorities have never been fully welcomed into the American mainstream. Although a great deal of evidence (for example, the German assimilation and the civil rights movement) would seem to militate against this claim, he doubled down on it in the very next sentence: "Racism and intolerance are not temporary, but rather chronic, conditions of American society." What we really need is not some bigoted, assimilationist ideal, but a permanently multicultural society.

A hipper, less scholastic critique of the melting pot ideal comes from Everyday Feminism's Maisha Z. Johnson. According to Johnson, the idea behind the melting pot sure *sounds* good: "[O]ur cultures are supposed to blend in harmony, rather than remaining separate, so that we all have equal opportunities." But, she continued, it is worth thinking about how an actual melting pot would work in practice. At a gathering such as a picnic, every dish present—"delectable chocolate cupcakes," fatty beef ribs, jalapeño peppers, corn on the cob—would all be dumped into a giant soup kettle at the same time and boiled into a shapeless brown mush. Then, "to top it all off," a foodie at the event might toss in a bottle of fish paste or sriracha ketchup, making the whole thing smell as though it is "bubbling up from the ocean through the sewer."[24] What a mess the whole thing would be! What a terrible idea!

What a remarkable argument for segregation! To a rather astonishing degree, Johnson's underlying belief seems to be identical to that held by the alt-right and neo-Nazis: that the different human "ingredients" which make up our society (Blacks, Irishmen, Italian Americans, legal immigrants) are completely incompatible and *should be kept separate as much as possible*. Obviously, tossing a bunch of *compatible* ingredients into the same bubbling pot produces a delicious meal. Beef, carrots, onions, potatoes, celery, salt, and pepper make a delicious stew when combined. To add a south-of-the-border spin to the same analogy, ground beef, beans, peppers, onions, garlic, tomatoes, and spice powder blend to give us chili. To those of us who continue to believe human beings come together far more often than we clash, the classic American metaphor remains fully viable. Rejecting the melting pot, it would seem, means rejecting the possibility of real integration.

Food metaphors aside, it can hardly be denied that the rejection of traditional theories of immigrant assimilation by many American elites and the reality of modern America as a welfare state are factors relevant to the immigration debate. Another set of relevant factors is purely political in nature and raises an important question. How far left do we wish to move as a country? The past fifty years of mass immigration have had truly profound electoral effects, to such an extent that at least a few "edgy" conservative commentators have openly argued that Democratic congressmen backed the 1965 Immigration and Nationality Act as an intentional political chess move. Ann Coulter, for example, flatly claimed, "Half a century ago, Democrats looked at the country and realized they were never going to convince Americans to agree with them. But they noticed that people in most other countries ... already agreed with them." The solution, she said, "was obvious."[25]

Some empirical evidence supports Coulter's argument that American leftists have not "won any arguments," but rather "changed the voters." She pointed out, probably accurately, that without tens of millions of post-1965 immigrants and their descendants voting *en bloc* for Democratic candidates, Barack Obama would never have been elected president in 2008. The numbers certainly indicate that Obama would not have won reelection against Mitt Romney in 2012 and would likely have been defeated in a landslide. During Obama's 2012 race, he won a solid 39 percent of the white vote, but also 70.6 percent of the Hispanic vote, a surprising 73.2 percent of the Asian American vote, and a truly remarkable 92.7 percent of the Black vote. Once votes for several fringe third-party candidates were subtracted from the mix, exactly 6.4 percent of Blacks, including foreign-born Blacks, turned out to have voted for the GOP candidate, a middle-of-the-road anti-racist from the financial sector.

The same trends were visible during the 2016 election, which pitted Donald Trump against Hillary Clinton. Immediately prior to the end of that race, in late September 2016, a Brookings Institute report noted that Trump was polling at 35 percent or better among young whites,[26] but below 10 percent among young Hispanics and about the same among African Americans. From my reading of the graphs in the piece, Trump—who *won* the election—polled at roughly 2 percent among several sizable groups of young Blacks, finishing behind not only Jill Stein of the Green Party, but also behind the options "other" and "undecided." If allowed to continue, such demographic trends could potentially doom the American Republican Party. The Pew Research Center has repeatedly projected that whites will be a 47 percent minority of the American population by 2050 (and conservatives by then a probable minority among whites), with Hispanics making up 29 percent of the population, Asians 9 percent, and Blacks 13–15 percent. At least absent major changes in minority voting behavior—which might occur depending on how immigrants are selected, but seem unlikely to under the current system—that could well translate to: GOP, RIP.

Regardless of whether Coulter's argument about intentionality is correct, it is indisputable that five decades of ongoing mass immigration have dramatically reshaped the face of America. Some of the effects of this change, such as improved food and sports, a growing GDP, and millions of brave and resourceful new citizens, are good. Other aspects of the phenomenon, such as a massively growing welfare state (empirically) and the decline of American conservatism (subjectively), are less so. My own opinion, formed after analyzing this topic in some depth for a major book, is that large-scale immigration to the U.S.A. should not be ended, but should be logically reframed with a focus on immigration policy benefiting legacy Americans of all races and creeds, as well as, and indeed prior to, benefiting immigrants. Four principles strike me as essential cornerstones of a saner immigration policy.

First, I propose an end to "chain migration." While often used in an incoherent or genuinely racist fashion, this term simply refers to the undisputed fact that under today's U.S. immigration policy, a single individual can sponsor the immigration of a sizable number of family members into the United States. Under current law (the 1965 Immigration and Nationality Act, as amended), any U.S. citizen or lawful resident may petition for immigration visas for any immediate relative, including all spouses, parents, children, and siblings. According to the text of Hart-Celler and to contemporary legal blogs like the American Immigration Lawyers Association's *Think Immigration*, there is no annual limit on the number of spouses, unmarried minor children, and parents of U.S. citizens who may enter the U.S.A. to reunite with their citizen relative. Furthermore, as of 2009, an additional 226,000 visas per year are granted to groups like "the unmarried fully adult children of citizens (23,400)," the spouses and children of noncitizen permanent residents (114,200), the *married* adult sons and daughters of citizens (24,000), the brothers and sisters of fully adult citizens (65,000), and so on.

If I were "King of America," I would end most of this. Obviously, we can and should all respect the desire of any human being to be surrounded by loving family members. But the brother's-wife's-father model of immigration literally allows the migration of entire Bosnian or Haitian villages to the U.S.A. with fairly little vetting inside a window of perhaps ten to fifteen years. Two of the specific relationships just mentioned, father and wife, fall into uncapped categories of individuals who are virtually guaranteed admission. I advise restricting preferred family-based immigration to the spouses and minor children of current natural-ized citizens. Such a policy would prioritize the immigration of stable, married-couple nuclear families, which God knows we need more of here! Furthermore, if extended to permanent residents of the United States, my "Reilly Policy" would also remedy a cruel current backlog in the immigration process—where the actual husbands and wives of people who might as well be citizens are forced to compete for a limited number of U.S. entry slots with the sisters and half-brothers of those who are.

While sitting on my golden throne, I would also almost certainly repeal the "anchor baby" rule of birthright citizenship. Due to some recent innovative interpretation by the Supreme Court of legislation originally intended to protect the rights of newly freed Black slaves, the current legal rule is that anyone born on U.S. soil—even if that person is the child of two illegal immigrants—is an American citizen. Techni-cally speaking, any baby born on a plane flying through undisputed U.S. airspace would probably be considered a natural-born American. While that is a unique and unusual scenario, "maternity tourism" to the United States has become a profitable midsize business over the past two decades, with tens of thousands of well-off Chinese and Mexican couples traveling to the U.S.A. specifically to deliver babies.

This is not right-wing speculation. CBS recently ran an in-depth article about the practice, identifying at least two busy "maternity hotels" in the Los Angeles area alone and describing nearby neighbors as very annoyed by the constant comings and goings of pregnant guests and their spouses or partners. "Anchor baby" may indeed be an insensitive term, but the rule that everyone born here is a full citizen of this country is, simply put, idiotic. Nations must have the right to choose who their citi-zens are, and the rule of birthright citizenship should be promptly ended by legislative or judicial fiat. Presumably, individuals born in the United States before the legal change could be grandfathered in as citizens.

In addition to streamlining family-based immigration policy and eliminating birthright citizenship, I would extend the vetting process for potential immigrants beyond the rather milquetoast requirements of today. While the bureaucratic process of immigrating to the U.S.A. can no doubt be long, costly, and dull, it is also the case that today's immigrants have to meet very few specific standards of performance in order to enter the country. According to the official website of Citizenship and Immigration Services (www.uscis.gov), prospective naturalized citizens of the United States must be at least eighteen years of age; be able to prove that they have resided in the U.S.A. for at least thirty months during the past five years; be able to communicate in basic English (by reading and writing one of three simple sentences correctly); have a basic understanding of U.S. history, government, and the Constitution; and be a person of solid "moral character" who will not definitely become a public charge. That is about it, and the "able-to-read-English" standard is currently being attacked as racist and coercive.

I would ... add a bit to that. In addition to retaining all of the conditions above, the United States should require, at a minimum, that all immigrants be sane, non-criminal, able-bodied and healthy enough to support themselves and not endanger others, and employable.[27] The first three requirements are not especially grueling, although some would be wildly controversial in today's climate. Criminal background checks are already part of the "green card" application process for permanent residency, should remain so, and should be repeated as part of any application for citizenship. "Sanity" as we understand it can be measured using any number of widely available tests, as well as via a check of records (where available) to determine whether an immigrant has ever been adjudicated as mentally ill. A requirement that immigrants be "physically sound" would obviously not prevent a British or Iraqi soldier who lost an eye fighting alongside our troops in the Gulf from immigrating, but frankly should bar most individuals suffering from long-term degenerative medical conditions, which are almost certain to prevent employment, or from contagious epidemic diseases such as AIDS.

At present, a review of the Center for HIV Law and Policy website reveals that HIV/AIDS has not been "a bar to entry into the United States for visitation or immigration purposes" since 2010. Indeed, HIV status "may be a basis for applying for asylum, a form of immigration protection in the United States," if an immigrant is able to show that they fear persecution or harassment back home because of their diseased condition. We live in a brave new world indeed. We Americans obviously do not wish to be the harsh stewards of a cruel country, and almost all laws contain a clause that allows them to be appealed in exceptional cases. Surely, this nation might choose to admit (say) the beloved wife of an exceptional scientist who fell ill while still living overseas. Overall, however, the rule that immigrants be able to work and contribute to society and be free of deadly plagues seems a reasonable one.

The requirement of immigrant employability is based on the same principle of "ability to contribute," and would probably be even more controversial. Simply put, I believe we should require all adult immigrants to the United States to show convincingly that they could find work here before granting them admission. There are several ways by which this might be done. H-1B visa holders and other skilled workers from overseas, by definition, almost always have an employer already lined up inside the U.S.A., and a job offer, contract, or similar document would of course serve as evidence of employability for any immigrant.

However, the simplest way to vet the employability of an individual in our technological economy would be simply to give them an IQ test. As this book has discussed at some length, the median IQs of all major racial groups in the U.S.A. are currently above 90, and an IQ of 85 is generally thought necessary to perform the complex functions associated with most modern jobs. There seems to be no reason not to condition entry to the U.S.A. on the ability to work here as measured by a score above (say) 88 on a modern, culture-fair, "matrices" test of IQ.

This policy might, again, be dismissed by some as harsh. However, it seems to me to be no great favor to bring people who might well have benefited their home societies into a potentially hostile foreign country where they will almost certainly be unable to earn a good living. The empirical evidence in favor of this argument is staggering. A recent article in Stockholm's The Local reported that by May 2016, fewer than 500 (494) of more than 163,000 Africans and Middle Easterners to migrate to Sweden during the past decade or so had managed to find jobs in that nation's first-world economy. Many of those who had not, often ambitious working-age men, were miserable. Britain's *Independent* ran a similar piece, noting that most migrants had found Sweden to be "less [than] a utopia," and that the disgusted Scandinavian nation has literally begun offering unemployed migrants 30,000 kroner (about $6,000) apiece simply to go home.[28]

A final harsh but real suggestion for immigration reform would simply be this: no welfare for immigrants. Although it might be difficult in practice to fully implement this rule, any sane immigration policy should not only stipulate that illegal immigrants can receive no means-tested welfare programs (AFDC-style cash payments, Section 8 housing, food stamps, and so forth), but also bar legal immigrants from doing so as well—at least for a trial period of perhaps a decade. This is, again, an arguably hard but undeniably sensible policy. Throughout history, the whole "Go West, young man" goal of immigration has been to earn success for oneself in a new land. It is insane for any society to allow foreigners to migrate there in order to go on the dole. While it would be morally and practically impossible to deny visitors to—or legal residents within—our country access to certain government services, such as emergency medical care or free school lunch programs, the general rule should be that people unable to successfully compete here should head back home and get to work developing their own countries.

In sum, my modest suggestion for a U.S. immigration policy is that we admit only high-performing people who want to come here and who are able to clear certain requirements in order to do so. At a bare minimum, immigrants should be sane, non-criminal, able-bodied and healthy enough to support themselves and not endanger others, and able to demonstrate employability via a mechanism such as a job offer or qualifying

IQ score. Such immigrants, when naturalized as citizens, should obviously be able to sponsor their wives, husbands, and minor children as future Americans—but not their entire families.

As a civilized and kindly nation, the United States should sometimes make exceptions to these rules for legitimate refugees and asylum seekers. However, the huge majority of illegal immigrants today—who hail from civilized-if-poor nations like Mexico and Poland—are not "asylum seekers." A generally recognized principle of international law is that individuals legitimately seeking asylum should—or must—seek refuge in the first safe third-party country in which they arrive. This would be Mexico in the case of virtually all Central and South Americans, and Canada in the case of many if not most Eastern Europeans or Asians. Additionally, race should not be a factor at all in U.S. immigration policy. I write in the year 2019, and POC such as Japanese and Nigerian Americans often significantly outperform legacy white Americans. However, skills, intelligence, and plain willingness to be a productive member of this society should be unmoving metrics used to judge immigrants of all colors. If these standards do not always produce perfect equity among all groups in terms of who receives a chance to enter this country, versus simply an equal opportunity to try and do so, that is not America's fault.

We Americans should welcome prospective citizens from all around the world, but we frankly deserve the best of them.

CHAPTER 9

Taboo Obvious Fact #10: The "Alt-Right" Has Nothing to Offer[1]

Thus far, much of this book has been devoted to criticizing identitarian movements on the minority left. The same toxic behavior is equally damaging when it is engaged in by the Caucasian right. One significant white reaction to both demographic change and the taboo nature of honestly discussing race—the rise of the white racialist "alt-right"—is significant, somewhat understandable, and absolutely wrong and misguided. Conservatives must understand the temptations of alt-right philosophy but reject it utterly. Although it is easy to see why working, poor white Americans feel neglected and abused by recent U.S. administrations, actual adoption of any major alt-right proposal (such as breaking up the U.S.A. into "ethnostates") would quite literally destroy the country. This cannot and should not be allowed. As Benjamin Franklin said centuries ago, we Americans must hang together, or we will surely all hang separately.

The basic fact that white Americans fear demographic change and are beginning to perceive increasing bigotry against them is indisputable. In recent years, large majorities of whites across several major studies have said that Caucasians face substantial discrimination in the United

States. According to one large-N poll released in October 2017 by the Robert Wood Johnson Foundation and Harvard University, more than half of all whites—roughly 55 percent—believe that "there is discrimination against white people in America today." Increasing percentages of whites said that they themselves had directly experienced discrimination, with 19 percent of all whites saying that they personally experienced discrimination when applying for jobs.[2]

Thirteen percent of whites felt they had been discriminated against at least once in terms of being paid equally to other coworkers or considered for promotions, while 11 percent were aware they had faced discrimination while applying to college.[3] A typical statement provided by a respondent on the qualitative portion of the survey came from sixty-eight-year-old Tim Hershman of Akron, Ohio, who said, "Basically … if you want any help from the government, if you're white, you don't get it. If you're Black, you get it."[4] The poll producing these data points was a large and well-conducted one; researchers surveyed a random sampling of 3,453 U.S. adults, which included nearly 1,000 whites.

In a different study, researchers from Harvard and Tufts found that many whites feel that they are *more* discriminated against than Blacks and other minorities. The scholars conducting this poll asked a large and evenly divided pool of whites and Blacks—209 whites and 208 African Americans—to rate levels of racism against both ethnic groups since the 1950s on a 1–10 scale. The results were fascinating. Both whites and Blacks correctly perceived that anti-Black bias has declined sharply since the 1950s, with whites perceiving a decline from about 9 to 3.5, and Blacks seeing a decline from 9.7 to 6.1. However, whites, citing such social policies as affirmative action and minority set-asides, believed that discrimination against Caucasians had increased from an average of 1.8 in the 1950s to 4.7 today. Blacks, in contrast, saw anti-white discrimination as more stable, ranking this as a 1.4 in the 1950s and 1.8 in the modern era.

Attitudes like this have significant political consequences. Perhaps most notably, whites who perceive significant discrimination against whites and strongly identify as white are much more likely to support tough-talking conservative political candidates. In a recent article for HuffPost, journalist Dominique Mosbergen used quantitative evidence to point out that white disaffection is one of the driving forces behind Donald Trump's political movement. According to a 2016 survey by HuffPost and YouGov, Trump supporters are significantly more likely than Americans overall to feel that whites face "a lot of discrimination," and less likely to think that Blacks and Hispanics are often discriminated against. Specifically, at least 45 percent of Trump supporters said that white Americans often experience discrimination, in comparison with 24 percent of all Americans. Rather remarkably, only 22 percent of Trump supporters said that *Black* Americans face "a lot" of bigotry.[5]

On the left side of the political aisle, many activist voices seem to have given up on the idea that white identity should be valued at all. Radical filmmaker Michael Moore recently told CNN's Jake Tapper that white Americans need to learn to welcome near-total demographic change. Scoffing at potential Democratic Party leaders such as Howard Dean or Martin O' Malley, he advocated for far-left Black Muslim Keith Ellison for head of the Democratic National Committee and a possible presidential candidate. To quote Moore: "Keith Ellison ... that is the future. The fear that I think a lot of white voters have is that they know the truth, which is that—as the Census Bureau says—before 2050, white people are gonna be in the minority in this country. For the last two Septembers now, the majority of kindergartners in schools in America are not white. That's the new America, and we need to have a party that's gonna represent the majority here."[6]

Swinging back to the right, where dwelleth the American majority, white fear of demographic change seems to affect Caucasians' views of a wide range of social programs, as well as of specific politicians. For example, Tom Jacobs of the *Pacific Standard* argued in 2018 that "fear of coming minority status drives white opposition to welfare." Using data from the social scientists Robb Willer and Rachel Wetts, Jacobs noted that the attitudes of whites and POC toward welfare diverged

dramatically in 2008, with the split coinciding with a rise in racial iden-
tification and racial resentment among whites.[7]

This divergence seems to be very specifically linked to dislike of
demographic change. In a thought experiment designed by Willer and
Wetts, white subjects who were told that whites will in fact remain the
national majority into the future and then asked what they would do
with the welfare budget proposed cutting an average of $28 million from
federal welfare spending. Whites who were told that Caucasians will
soon become a minority in the United States proposed cutting an average
of $51 million.[8] Members of the second group also reported significantly
higher levels of moral objection to welfare, and higher levels of dislike
and resentment toward members of other races. The two scientists, as
well as Jacobs, concluded that more policies eliminating or severely cur-
tailing welfare programs will likely be enacted in the years to come.

More broadly, such strong attitudes as those of the white subjects
analyzed in the survey tend to have far-reaching social consequences.
Over the past decade or so, a new social movement, the alt-right, has
arisen in response to feelings of disenfranchisement among young
working-class and middle-class whites, especially in the American
heartland. Precisely defining the alt-right can be tricky. White nationalist Richard Spencer seems to have coined the term in 2010, using it to
mean a contrarian conservative movement centered around the white
"Europa" identity.

Since then, however, the phrase has been used—often by liberal
opponents—to describe an ill-defined collection of white nationalists,
white racial supremacists, neo-Nazis, Confederate sympathizers, would-
be fascists, "and other far-right fringe groups." Over the past three or
four years, the reach of the concept has further been extended to cover
the most passionate American nationalists, paleoconservatives such as
Pat Buchanan, anarcho-capitalists, 4channers, men's rights advocates
such as Roosh V, neo-monarchists, and even many participants in the
2016 Donald Trump presidential campaign. Confusing stuff.

One fairly coherent definition of the alt-right comes from two well-known edgy writers on the heterodox right: Allum Bokhari and Milo Yiannopolous. Both wrote for Breitbart, and they divided the movement into a number of subcategories. These include intellectuals (serious if heretical thinkers like Jared Taylor and Vox Day); instinctive "throne-and-altar" traditional conservatives, many of whom felt homeless in the Mitt Romney GOP of 2008–2012; meme-loving internet trolls on sites such as 4chan and Reddit who take the hard-right's side against the Sarah Jeongs in the internet's freewheeling debate culture; and a small minority of genuine neo-Nazis and genetic racists.

My own definition, while substantially overlapping with theirs, differs somewhat from that given by Bokhari and Yiannopolous. To me, the easiest way to sum up the alt-right is to say that it is a collection of movements whose members strongly embrace white racial identity and more broadly wish that the 1960s cultural revolution—with its rejection of genetic racism, focus on enforced racial equality, globalism, and embrace of feminism and gay rights—had never occurred. Judging from at least one hundred read-throughs of the American Renaissance and VDARE websites, alt-right beliefs almost universally include (1) genetic racism rebranded as "race realism," (2) passionate American nationalism, (3) anti-feminism and glorification of the housewife, (4) a weakness for fascism and even monarchism (check out "God Emperor Trump" on Google sometime), and (5) a view of most gays and essentially all transgender people as odd perverts.

Whatever the exact composition of its ranks, the alt-right's strategy for recruiting new members is essentially unquestioned. The movement exploits feelings of anger among young whites by presenting itself as an honest teller of forbidden truths—especially truths relevant to white middle-American interests—in a dishonest era. The American Renaissance website, for example, consistently makes reference to social trends almost never reported in the mainstream media. The site prominently includes both a list of hate crimes targeting Trump supporters—more than one hundred in all, concentrated on the East and West Coasts—and a map identifying the locations of hoax hate crimes.

As my last book, *Hate Crime Hoax*, pointed out, a very large number of hate crime allegations—between 15 and 50 percent of prominent cases—turn out to be complete frauds. However, this is essentially never reported on in the mainstream media. It certainly is reported on by American Renaissance, which provides the names and personal details of more than one hundred hate hoaxers, a full description of each crime and its location, and a surprisingly sophisticated breakdown of statistical data allowing us to learn, for example, that American Muslims are 34.7 times as likely as whites to fake hate crimes.[9] Similarly, alt-right and conservative (and presumably other) contributors to Google Maps and several Google groups recently prepared an actual, detailed map of all the unreported attacks on whites which followed the 2012 shooting of Trayvon Martin by Hispanic neighborhood watchman George Zimmerman.

That list includes more than twenty individual incidents, reported under banner headlines like "Mob of 30 'Teens' Attacks Two White Reporters" and "Black Bank Robber Said He Robbed Bank in Revenge for Trayvon." The list has been viewed 619,113 times and counting—a rather remarkable achievement, given that *despite the fact that it is a Google map*, Google has apparently suppressed the list in search results. I was able to find it only by using rival search engine Bing. In the interest of free speech, the link to the list can be found in the endnotes.[10]

As examples like this illustrate, the appeal of the alt-right is at least partly understandable in the context of wildly dishonest national discourse dominated by left-leaning media, academia, and the NGO sector. However, the alt-right absolutely does not offer a viable third way to white conservatives, and it is important for sane members of the American right to point this out. This is true not only for moral reasons (in other words, "racism is bad"), but more importantly because many of the movement's core claims are simply wrong. Speaking as a quantitative scientist, alt-right thinkers regularly make massive empirical mistakes.

They tend to confuse, among other things, (1) cultural variables with genetic ones, (2) "whites" with Caucasians, and (3) racial diversity with ethno-linguistic diversity. The first of these mistakes is the most critical. One of the alt-right's most clearly inaccurate claims also happens to be the movement's defining argument: that massive and almost purely genetic IQ gaps between the races exist.

Dissident right figures such as Jared Taylor make this claim incessantly. In an American Renaissance "classic" article dating back to 1992, Taylor argued, "Study after study has consistently shown that the average Black IQ test score is 15 to 18 points lower than the white average ... the gap starts at about 15 points in childhood and widens to as much as 20 points during adulthood. The gap has remained unchanged for 70 years ... civil rights laws, greater social equality, and affirmative action have not reduced the difference."[11] As a result, Taylor claimed that whites and Blacks have "overlapping intelligence distributions" but only about 15 percent of Blacks have IQs higher than the white average of 99–100. Whites are seven times more likely to test as geniuses or members of the "gifted" population (IQ over 135), while Blacks are about seven times as likely to test as mentally "retarded" (IQ under 70). At the very highest levels of tested IQ, according to Taylor, Blacks can hardly be found at all. Thomas Sowell, no doubt, wept to learn of his nonexistence.

The alt-right claims that crime is also largely genetic, linked to this allegedly almost subhuman Black IQ. In another American Renaissance article titled "Africa in Our Midst," which was discussed briefly some pages back, Taylor explicitly argued that the American Black population represents a dangerous third-world presence inside the U.S.A. Discussing Hurricane Katrina, he claimed that the tragedies accompanying the superstorm were caused not by poor maintenance by New Orleans of its levees and seawalls or by an insufficient federal rescue effort, but rather were due to barbaric behavior resulting from the low genetic capital of the Black population of the city. Taylor's piece is full of histrionic, "Jumanji"-style descriptions of Black behavior during the storm. For example, as rescuers attempted to enter New Orleans, according to

Taylor, "[s]ome Blacks fired on any symbol of authority, blazing away" at the sky in a maddened attempt to shoot down rescue helicopters. He went on to describe rampant robbery, rape, and murder, all carried out by lawless Black men. In contrast, Taylor claimed, fifty thousand equally situated, low-income urban whites would have handled the epic storm splendidly: "They would have established rules, organized supplies, cared for the sick and dying. They would have organized games for children. The papers would be full of stories of selflessness and community spirit."

The problem with this pleasant-sounding stuff, as with "hotep" talk on the Black side, is that there is little or no evidence for any of it. I personally think that a football stadium filled with fifty thousand rednecks and no food during a once-in-a-century tropical storm would have resembled the movie *Gangs of New York* much more than *The Andy Griffith Show*—although the rednecks might at least have decided to just get in their pickup trucks and drive the ten or so miles to higher ground. More seriously, at the macro level, the Black-to-white IQ gap of 15–20 points almost universally cited by the alt-right has not existed for decades. Alt-righters are frequently forced to use dated, unreliable data in an attempt to ignore or deny this fact. The central contention of the alt-right is not true.

As we discussed at length in chapter three, multiple studies—such as the one William Dickens and James Flynn performed in 2006—have shown that the purported IQ gap between blacks and whites has closed significantly just since the seventies. Overall, the *actual* tested IQs for a range of Black populations which were examined in 2002, now almost twenty years ago, ranged from 88.8 to 95.5. The latter figure is 17.5 points higher than the most common Black IQ estimate used by the alt-right. By comparison, the average IQ in the great Celtic nation of Ireland, from whence came many of my white family members, is 92. We African Americans certainly still have some work to do in the classroom, but the American Black IQ has probably not been 78, or 81, or anything similar to that for fifty years.

The racial IQ gap has, if anything, narrowed even further since Dickens and Flynn wrote. Subsequent studies seem to show not only that Blacks have picked up another point or two, but that *multi*racial kids now test identically with whites. In a previously mentioned major 2017 report, the Brookings Institute concluded that "mixed" children and teens now have the same average scores as white kids on tests of science, math, and writing. On tests of reading ability, multiracial students out-perform all other groups, including Asian Americans. Analyst Jonathan Rothwell stated, "These results contradict the controversial hypothesis that between-group differences in IQ result from genetic differences between the races."[12] That one sentence from a serious scholar analyzing foundation-level quantitative data would seem to torpedo the entire alt-right.

It is noteworthy that these impressive recent scholastic perfor-mances by multiracial students do not appear to be due—as some critics have speculated—to the mostly upper-middle-class status of a relatively small cohort of interracial kids. In fact, compared to the parents of "single-race non-Hispanic children," the mothers of multiracial kids are slightly less likely to have a college degree, less likely to be married, and more likely to have been teenagers when they gave birth. The aver-age income for parents of multiracial children was $72,800, as opposed to $118,107 for the parents of white children and $80,700 for all par-ents of single-race children. The success of mixed kids is also not due to the fact that they are genetic outliers—the product of "crosses" between elite Caucasians and high-IQ Asian or West African immi-grants, for example. Most multiracial teens seem to simply be half white and half African American. According to Rothwell, roughly half of multiracial students report having significant Black ancestry, and "white-black combinations are the most frequent interracial origin of multiracial children." The high average performance of individuals who literally embody human genetic mixing seems to hammer another cof-fin nail into the racialist right's arguments.

A final point about the IQ debate: assuming it were true that, with all cultural variables (such as birth weight, father in the home, diet, family size) equalized, the maximal average Black IQ was perhaps 94–95, versus 99 for whites and 101 for Asians, it is not immediately clear why this would matter much at all. As I pointed out in an earlier chapter, the average IQ in Ireland and Greece is 92. That of Turkey is 90, Thailand 91, and the Philippines 86. All of these countries are respected middle-income world powers.

There also seems to be a weak connection, if any at all, between IQ and crime globally. According to widely available World Bank data, many African powers such as Ghana and Egypt, which have average IQs generally in the 80–85 range, average 2–3 murders annually per 100,000 citizens. In contrast, Russia (with a mean IQ of 97) averages at least 10 murders per 100,000 people per year, Lithuania (91) averages 7, and our own United States (98) averages roughly six murders per 100,000 citizens. Even more dramatically, El Salvador, which has roughly the same average tested IQ as low-crime Ghana, posted 70 murders per 100,000 persons in 2011, 41 in 2012, and 40 in 2013. This represented one of the highest overall murder totals in the world. Clearly, the structure of a nation's government, extent of governmental corruption, level of income inequality, level of ethnic tribalism, skill of the political class, and a dozen other things within a nation all predict the level of crime and instability among its populace far better than the average score of the populace on a fallible one-hour test.

Robert Lindsay made essentially this same point in memorable fashion in a piece called "The Skyrocketing Black IQ." Citing the Flynn Effect, which says that rising IQ scores gradually rise over time, he pointed out that the IQ of American Blacks today (say 93) is "equivalent to" or higher than the IQ of white Americans during World War II—which would have been about 86 in today's terms. Simply put, Black IQs in 2019 are not especially low, unless you happen to believe that the legendary white heroes of 1945 were all morons and rubes. The struggles of the Black underclass in the U.S.A. may have many causes, ranging from past racism to incompetent activist-left leadership in many Black-run areas (ding, ding). However, Lindsay noted, "Black average IQ cannot be one of them."[13] He pointed out that the explosion of urban American pathologies such as illegitimacy rather remarkably coincided with an increase of at least 10–11 points in American Black IQ!

In addition to a tendency to confuse genetic and cultural factors and to misunderstand the flexibility of IQ, several other major problems exist with the alt-right's arguments. Most notably and embarrassingly, the leading lights of the movement often appear to confuse racial diversity with ethnic diversity and "whiteness" with membership in the Caucasian genetic group. These may seem like wonky and irrelevant technical points, but they are not. Simply put, *most of the conflicts the alt-right describes as racial are actually between members of the same race.* Alt-righters often describe whites and Middle Eastern Muslims as existentially incompatible populations, but both of these groups are Caucasians in biogenetic terms. For that matter, so are the "light brown men" (Persians, and so forth) and Greeks who were described as implacable enemies by Lothrop Stoddard decades ago.

This is not a minor mistake. Logically speaking, "genetic incompatibility" between different races, who supposedly have vastly different levels of aggressiveness and IQ, simply cannot be the reason for the many conflicts between the groups I have just described. In actual genetic terms, most of America's recent enemies (Afghans, Iranians, and Iraqis) are almost identical to many of her recent immigrants (Italians, "Assyrians," and Greeks).

A brief note on basic racial categories seems merited at this point. Generally speaking, prior to the "social justice" revolution, anthropologists and biologists were in agreement that there are three to four primary genetic human races. The science blog *World Mysteries* lists the three largest groups as Caucasian, Mongolian/Asiatic, and Negroid. All of these groups have recognizable, genetically determined physical characteristics. For example, Caucasians are distinguished by features which include (relatively) light skin, long and narrow noses, "dolicephalic" (longer) skulls, and straight rather than kinky hair.[14]

In contrast, Mongoloid East Asians tend to have wide faces, "slanted" (epicanthically folded) eyes, dark hair, and a few other group-specific traits such as shovel-shaped incisor teeth. Blacks, or Negroids, have dark-to-black-colored skin, flat and broad noses, high foreheads, and generally kinky hair. Others scholars past and present have added a few more races to the Big Three, most commonly granting Amerindians, Malays, and Australian Aborigines an independent genetic status. But the basic idea that a small number of clearly identifiable human reproductive populations exist has remained the same for centuries.

It is worth taking a minute after reading through these descriptions to note that race in some valid sense of the term obviously does exist as a biological reality. Just as with sex and "gender," it has recently become popular to argue that the human races are merely social constructs, not reflective of any objective reality that actually exists outside the human braincase. Qualitative social scientists correctly point out that (1) humans interbreed, and so there are no "pure" races, (2) groups (such as the "non-white" Irish) have previously been misassigned into racial categories, and (3) there exists more variation in traits such as height within racial categories than across them. For example, some whites, such as NBA superstar Kristaps Porzingis, stand more than seven feet tall, while others are dwarfs who fail to reach the four foot one mark. More empirically, some evolutionary biologists point out that there are few or no specific single "genes for race." With the exception of a few regional anomalies like coding for sickle cell anemia, there simply are not biological traits which all Blacks possess and no whites do.

Sure. However, as "race-believing" biologists like Nicholas Wade have pointed out, none of this debunks or even challenges the commonsense claim that there are separate breeding populations of humans from different regions of the world who display different *frequencies* of the genetic sequences that predict skin color, eye shape, hair texture, sprinting speed, and so on. It should not be especially controversial to say that Samoans tend to be physically bigger than Bambuti pygmies, that the two groups look very different, and that there is a genetic explanation for much of this. As Dinesh D'Souza has pointed out, it would not be especially difficult for any intelligent human being to walk into a room containing one hundred Zulu, one hundred Swedes, and one hundred Japanese and sort them all by racial group while making no mistakes at all.

Companies such as 23andMe provide an updated version of that sorting service for the digital era. For less than a hundred dollars, any person can buy an almost infallible DNA test that uses measurable regional variations in human genetics to tell him not only his primary racial/ethnic group, but also his exact historical heritage, broken down in group percentage terms. According to promotional materials and a few low-level conversations with the company, there are "several dozen" common human haplotype populations which compose five or six larger categories centered on regions such as Asia, Europe, Oceania, and North America.

These groups do not perfectly match up with the centuries-old, slightly simplistic racial categories drawn up by the scientists of the past. For example, there exists nearly as much genetic difference between the most dissimilar African populations—for example, West African Bantus and Khoisan "bushmen," who are technically not Negroes—as there is between either one of those populations and a Frenchman. However, this fact in no way means that West African Blacks are not themselves a recognizable population group or that groups that strongly physically resemble one another are not genetically closer than those which do not. In practice, any distinction between the "genetically identifiable and testable regional human groupings" recognized by the DNA services on the one hand, and "races" on the other, seems arbitrary if not nonsensical. Race, like biological sex, is a valid idea based upon an objective, observable reality.

That said—and as previously noted—probably 90 percent of the "racial" conflicts described by alt-righters are actually *ethnic conflicts among tribal groups of the same race.* This does not make such wars among brothers less brutal, but it does mean that atavistic incompatibility between different races logically cannot be the reason for them. To give an example of what I mean here, Jared Taylor and other alt-right writers have referred to Africa's Uganda as both the world's most diverse country and a troubled one riven by tribal conflict. This allegedly indicates that racially integrated societies are less sustainable than racially homogenous ones.

The problem with this argument is obvious after a minute's pause for thought. Uganda is indeed very diverse, containing (among others) the Iteso, Luganda, Luo, Busoga, Konjo, and Sebei ethno-linguistic populations. However, the big problem here for scholars arguing that racial diversity causes conflict is that *all of these groups are Black.* Similarly, the brutal wars in the former Yugoslavia, often cited as an example of the impracticality of multiracial societies, in fact involved Serbs, Croats, Bosnian Muslims, Kosovar Albanians, and so forth. All of these groups are composed entirely of Caucasians genetically indistinguishable from one another.

It may be true, to some extent, that any variety of population diversity can be a cause of conflict in integrated societies. Homogenous Iceland seems a peaceful enough place. However, a quick look through the literature indicates that *racial* diversity has historically been much less of a problem for polyglot societies than diversity of language, tribe, religion, or class. Truly avoiding conflict by avoiding diversity would thus logically require large nations to ban not simply all immigration of individuals who are not part of the current majority race—which the alt-right supports—but essentially all immigration of foreigners whatsoever. This is clearly not a feasible policy for the United States to ever implement. Rather than retreating into utter isolationism, á la 1800s Japan, modern societies need to learn how to manage diversity in order to maximize its advantages and minimize its negatives. The alt-right offers literally no useful guidance on how to do this.

A curious twist to the alt-right's frequent confusion of racial categories and conflicts with ethnic ones is its confusion of the Caucasian race, which clearly does exist, with an invented idea of "whiteness." This matters because Caucasians, when all analyzed together, do not perform dramatically better than East Asians, West Africans, and several other sizable human haplotype groups in terms of IQ or crime rate. The Middle East (Iran, Iraq, Palestine), far Eastern Europe (Moldova, Albania, Bosnia), and even the "Stans" of Western Asia (Afghanistan, Uzbekistan, Kazakhstan) all have almost entirely Caucasian populations. Some of the countries in these regions literally touch the Caucasus Mountains!

However, while I certainly do not believe their citizens to be genetically inferior to anyone else, no one would describe these states as the most peaceful and developed places on earth. Attempts to artificially distinguish the populations of wealthy post-colonial nations in Western Europe from the rest of the globe's genetically similar Caucasians, and then argue specifically for "white" genetic superiority on the basis of the performance of the first of those two groups, is an attempt at logical sleight of hand, and one that fails.

Alt-right thinkers, who obviously tend to disagree, expend a great deal of time and effort defending the boundaries of whiteness and attempting to distinguish "whites" from other Caucasians. Quite a few argue that Caucasians such as Muslims and Jews cannot truly be white, and that conflicts between these groups and "whites" have a genetic or at least atavistic root. For example, in 2016, American Renaissance ran the first of several articles about Muslim "no-go zones" in Europe. Author Edmund Kozak contended that no-go zones, "Muslim neighborhoods ... in which Sharia law is the rule and non-Muslims are attacked on sight," are frequently dismissed by liberals as a conservative bogeyman but are in fact a horrifying reality.

He quoted a Swedish filmmaker who waxed breathless about a fight in the Swedish slum of Husby as saying, "Moments after I stepped into the town, a gang of five clearly Islamic men ... attacked me without provocation. They repeatedly punched, kicked and choked me, as a number of bystanders watched." Husby allegedly does not stand alone. There are neighborhoods like this scattered about Europe, "a devastating testament to the utter devastation wrought on Europe by ... mass Muslim migration." Kozak appears to at least float a genetic explanation for the growth of no-go zones: the almost abnormally "high birthrates" among many Muslim groups. The author and a source, "Hamid," closed by comparing Muslims to deadly diseases: "It's like when you see a cancer cell that is not causing any trouble now, but later on if it is left without intervention it can cause very serious trouble."[15]

Another recent American Renaissance piece is flatly titled "A Muslim Ban Is Logical." In it, author Ilana Mercer argued for the total quarantine of Muslims from the West because of their faith tradition, which "predisposes [them] to violence." She contended that President Trump should expand his proposed travel ban, which was originally designed to bar citizens of six Muslim-majority states that have clashed with the United States from entering the country, in order to exclude essentially all residents of the Islamic world from the U.S.A. She referred to those Americans opposed to this idea as "treasonous."

Once again, deep-seated meta-cultural factors, if not genetic ones, are cited as the justification for Mercer's claims. Islam has yet to undergo a religious reformation, and thus remains a radical and dangerous force, which makes every Muslim into a potential weapon. In what appears to be an entirely genetic sentence, Mercer explicitly says that moderate Muslims should be barred from the United States because they are statistically likely to "sire sons who'll embrace the unreformed Islam." Simply put, Islamic religion is an automatic risk factor that makes Muslim immigrants undesirable: *Their Muslim faith puts Muslims in a security risk group.*[16] None should ever be permitted to permanently enter the U.S.A.

In yet another piece, American Renaissance expresses considerable sympathy for how Russia deals with Muslim immigrants. The *rodina*'s treatment of Islamic sojourners seems to be, by any mainstream normative standard, brutal. Author Yaroslav Lavrentievich Podvolotskiy—wonder where *he's* from—noted that Vladimir Putin banned all foreign immigrants from working as small merchants or from trading in "kiosks and markets," back in 2011. Anyone who broke this law could be summarily deported; 513,000 foreigners have been thrown out of Russia, and another 1.7 million have been banned from entering the country, since 2013. A Russian deportation hearing takes roughly three minutes, with the judge ruling against the defendant nearly every time. Should even this sort of thing not discourage immigration, anti-migrant riots are very common in Russia. In Moscow, after a 2010 fight between groups of Russians and ethnic Chechens, roughly 50,000 Russian citizens took part in bloody anti-Muslim rioting that killed twenty-four people and injured hundreds more.

Once again, American Renaissance presents these clashes as being essentially racial in nature, and sometimes describes them using genetic terms. According to Podvolotskiy, a major source of tension between immigrants and native Russkis is that "ethnic Russians represent only 32 percent of recent immigrants." Another 10–13 percent come from the Ukraine, and the rest hail from former Soviet republics like Uzbekistan, Kyrgyzstan, and Tajikistan. Although the huge majority of these people are genetic Caucasians, Podvolotskiy describes them thusly: "Some of these people look almost white, but they are not Slavs."[17]

He went on to describe much of the former U.S.S.R. as consisting of Central Asian countries hosting a "culturally Asiatic" population. His language calls to mind descriptions of Irishmen and Italians (and Russians!) as "cavemen" and "dirty white people" in the yellow journalist press of the early 1900s, and Podvolotskiy used it utterly non-ironically. White people in the former Warsaw Pact countries, he argued, have a right to protect their "racial … identities," and Americans have something to learn from these unabashed racial nationalists.

Once again, the rebuttal to the argument that Lebanese Muslim immigrants would be eternally unable to assimilate into the U.S.A. or that Chechens or Magyars are so biologically distinct from Russians as to justify their ethnic cleansing is quite simple: all of these people are the same race. In an Al Jazeera piece, Khaled Beydoun pointed out that Arabs are genetically Caucasian, and generally considered white for

Western census purposes. Although Beydoun clearly disagreed with some cultural aspects of this designation, he affirmed, "Since 1944, Arabs have been deemed white by law" in the U.S.A. As the date given indicates, this has been relatively uncontroversial for decades. Beydoun described early Arab immigrants as "pursu[ing] whiteness" and "perform[ing]" it almost perfectly during immigration proceedings. American courts have generally agreed with the immigrants. A 1915 judicial decision ruled (correctly) that Arabs are clearly part of the Caucasian race, and a subsequent 1940s-era case "solidified the legal designation" of Arabs as Caucasian whites.[18]

Most Arabs seem happy enough with whiteness. While a noisy minority are pursuing a "MENA" classification on the census for Middle Easterners and North Africans, a statistical majority of Americans of Arabian descent "embrace and defend" their designation as whites. The almost universal recognition of Middle Easterners as Caucasian provides another hammer blow to the alt-right. If both the most successful societies on Earth (for example, England, Norway), and some of the most troubled and violent (such as Afghanistan, Iraq, Iran) are populated by people who are 90 percent racially identical in genetic terms, race clearly cannot be the reason for the successes of the first set of societies and the struggles of the second set.

So far, this chapter has reviewed a number of major problems with the alt-right as a political movement. Alt-righters are simply wrong in much of what they say about large performance gaps between the races: the IQ of middle-class Blacks in the West is 93 or 95, not 78. They are wrong in what they say about diversity and conflict. *Ethnic* and linguistic diversity, like that found in Uganda or the former Yugoslavia, certainly seems to cause conflict. However, a diversity of largely assimilated genetic racial populations, like that found in New Zealand or Costa Rica, does not. Their railing against Muslims or Middle Easterners in general or Eastern Europeans (usually labeled "central Asians") makes no sense whatsoever; most of these groups are 100 percent Caucasian in genetic terms. However, the most sweeping and effective argument against the dissident right is simpler still: adopting the primary alt-right proposals would destroy the United States.

That is not hyperbole. Probably the most popular political idea on the hard alt-right is that the U.S.A. should be broken up into various racial ethno-states. John Ingram, for example, made this proposal in a widely recirculated article published to American Renaissance. According to him, we need to begin talking about "the specifics of racial separation." In Ingram's opinion, genetic racial differences make any prolonged coexistence between different population groups impossible—out of here with your dreams, Roman Empire!—and only "gradual, mutual, voluntary" total separation can solve this problem.[19]

Ingram is not speaking in vague generalities. Instead, he explains, we Americans need to "get out maps and start marking them up" in order to establish the boundaries of new sub-nations defined by race. Whites might, for example, take over Idaho and the Northern Pacific coast, while Blacks could establish a separate country in the fertile deltas of the South. Remarkably, and rather entertainingly, Ingram invoked the constant racial complaining of Black authors such as Ta-Nehisi Coates to support his ideas: "If [he] says white racism is incurable, this is the solution."

There are books about this idea, including some quite major ones. In a 2013 piece for American Renaissance, F. Roger Devlin reviewed one of them: Arthur Kemp's *Nova Europa: European Survival Strategy in a Darkening World*, an eighty-eight-page plaint from Ostara Publications, which is currently available on Kindle for $5.95. According to Devlin, who philosophizes for a bit before diving into the pages, the traditional racialist strategy of "'awakening' whites and gaining power through democratic electoral means" is currently failing. Not only is the American population shifting demographically, but most whites seem to have little interest in returning to the European-only immigration policies of 1923. As a result, political opportunities for a white nationalist takeover of the government are vanishing and, absent a dictator, "a strategic reorientation is becoming inevitable."[20]

To Devlin, this reorientation should involve a focus on creating autonomous, totally white territories that might eventually become independent nation-states. Like Ingram, Devlin and especially Kemp are dryly technical about how all this should be done. After "mustering the political will," Caucasian would-be colonizers will have to face the task of choosing and taking over specific blocs of territory. There are two approaches, essentially, to how such takeovers might happen. The first is to select small cities or low-population states "within an existing threatened Western state," and somehow "purify" them or keep them all-white.

Should even this fail and Wyoming (or wherever) become more diverse despite the best efforts of racialist settlers, a new America—or France—might perhaps be built in Russia. To Kemp, Eastern Europe seems promising as a destination for future all-white havens. While some former Warsaw Pact states have "substantial gypsy and Turkish populations," which might have to be somehow dealt with, other non-whites comprise no more than 2–3 percent of the region's population. Even better, many East Bloc nations are dubious about Western liberalism and have governments that encourage high white birthrates. *Moldova, Moldova, über alles*!

The enthusiasm on the dissident right for ethno-states such as these stretches, quite literally, into the cartoonish. In a 2018 video called "Wakanda: The Perfect Ethnostate[?]" uploaded to American Renaissance's YouTube channel, Jared Taylor and the American Renaissance crew heap praise on the mythical African nation of Wakanda, the home of King T'Chaka and Prince T'Challa in the movie *Black Panther*. Wakanda, to Taylor, is the "perfect" one-race state: mono-racial by definition, militaristic, nationalistic and proud of it, obsessed with heritage, well-armed, secluded. Alas, of course, the place does not exist.

Proposals like those just outlined may be fun to tweak—one wonders when serious alt-right thinkers will analyze Iron Man's views on late capitalism and the military-industrial complex—but would literally destroy the country if ever adopted, breaking the world's greatest nation into a series of quarreling small states with names like "the Republic of You and Me," and "I'm Not Sure about Me."[21] This, again, is not over-statement. As just discussed, one popular alt-right framework would break the U.S.A. into white, Black, Latino, Asian, and "diverse" Bantu-stans, with Blacks getting Georgia and Alabama and whites the high West. I just quoted you another, which would move most of the country to Russia. Not only would these absolutely zany ideas shatter the territo-rial integrity of the United States, but they would more seriously destroy the large population, financial base, and ethnic and ideological diversity that give us strength.

This is a key point. Large and diverse national populations may indeed experience more internal conflict than tiny, poor, and homoge-nous ones. However, they also operate as engines of change within the countries that contain them, leading to improved artistic and cultural scenes, athletic performance, cuisine, rates of patent and invention, and even human biogenetic potential. An entire empirical paradigm in busi-ness, the managing diversity literature, discusses this phenomenon.

A look at one major street in my hometown, Chicago's Michigan Avenue, illustrates it. A Yelp list of the four- and five-star restaurants to be found within one roughly ten-block area includes Bandera (Southern jazz and blues themed), the Purple Pig (Asian and European pork prepa-rations), The Gage (British gastropub), India House (you guessed it), Quiote (Mexican), Acanto (Southern Italian), Michael Jordan's Steak House (Black-owned and upscale), Grand Lux (Franco-American), and Heritage (a caviar bar focused on Russian and Iranian eggs). Russian Tea Time, the Berghoff (German), Tamarind (contempo-Asian), and Star of Siam can all also be found within about a five-minute walk.

Hard-right conservatives often mock pro-diversity arguments with comments like, "The best thing about multi-culturalism is the food." But food is important! Most people eat three times a day and try to enjoy doing so. The plain fact is that the presence of a dozen or more Zagat-starred restaurants within a city mile is a *good* thing and a major perk of our cosmopolitan society. It is doubtful whether this range can be found even in the global cities located within more monoglot nations, from Oslo to Lagos.

Managed diversity also correlates with improved physical and sporting competition within societies and the performance of those societies on the global athletic stage. According to the athletics website Total Sportek, the United States leads the all-time Olympic medal count by more than 1,000 medals: 2,399 to 1,010. It is no secret that this is due largely to the fantastic diversity of our Olympic teams, which include white swimmers and skiers, Black runners and basketball players, Asian gymnasts and figure skaters, and Hispanic baseball players and cross-country runners.

Second place all-time on the medal count list belongs to the former Soviet Union, which included at its peak not only Russia but also Lithuania, Kazakhstan, the Baltic states, all of Armenia, and so on. Great Britain, now more than 10 percent Black and Asian—and obviously always a conglomerate nation made up of England, Ireland, Scotland, and Wales—brings home third place with a very respectable 780 medals. In contrast, the very bottom of the medal count list is dominated by small, homogenous states such as Bulgaria and South Korea.[22]

Beyond food and ball games, diversity among high-performing citizens also tends to improve the overall artistic and cultural "scene" within their society. While preparing this chapter, I asked my research associate, Jane Lingle, to pick the most exotic form of high art she could think of and see whether it existed at all in the United States. She picked gamelan ensembles, which are Indonesian artistic troupes that put on traditional musical performances involving drums and gongs, "metallophones," and handmade bamboo flutes. As it turns out, there are more than one hundred actively performing gamelan ensembles in the United States, most of them highly reviewed by their local communities. California alone, perhaps unsurprisingly, boasts thirty-four of them. But even such dyed-in-the-wool blue-collar cities as Newark and DeKalb (Illinois) and Lewiston (Maine) boast one apiece, all of which put on "lovely cultural nights" several times a year. At least two thirds of the states in the U.S.A.

have an actively performing gamelan group, and UCLA maintains a series of credited academic courses in the playing of gamelan music. This particular example of the positive benefits of managed diversity was intentionally chosen to be "cute" and whimsical, but—given our nation's remarkable diversity—it is probably no exaggeration to say that many of the best examples of all of the world's great traditional arts can be found here in the U.S.A.

Diversity also affects how Americans and the citizens of other pluralistic societies fall in love and get married, often for the better. Pew Research Center noted that a "record high 12 percent of newlyweds" opted to marry someone of a race different from their own in 2013. This figure specifically does not take into account interethnic marriages such as those between Hispanics and non-Hispanic whites or between Italians and Irishmen, which represent a probable majority of *all* marriages. Even with this caveat, nearly 10 percent of whites, 19 percent of Blacks, 28 percent of Asians, and an astonishing 58 percent of Native American Indians married someone of a race different from their own during Pew's study year.[23] Contrary to the alt-right, these cross-race marriages seem generally to be as happy as any others. They also may have some practical genetic advantages; a major recent study conducted by the University of Edinburgh found that genetic diversity between parents is a key predictor of taller, smarter children.

More seriously—although whether one is able to eat well and marry happily are serious matters—America's status as an anti-racist nation that welcomes selected immigrants from around the world boosts our proficiency in science, technology, and other fields of hard business. In August 2018, the right-leaning *Washington Examiner* noted that an astonishing 37 percent of Silicon Valley employees and executives are foreign-born, with overrepresented groups including Indian, Chinese, and Nigerian immigrants. The overrepresentation of elite immigrants was most notable in the most skilled and demanding jobs. According to the 2016 Silicon Valley Index, roughly 75 percent of "employed computer and mathematical workers ages 25 to 44" were foreign-born.[24]

Legal immigrants—multilingual and sometimes multicolored—also win a staggering percentage of the Nobel Prizes awarded to Americans. Since the year 2000, thirty-three of eighty-five (39 percent) American Nobel Prize winners across mathematics, chemistry, physics, and other honored fields have been foreign immigrants. In 2017, for example, Joachim Frank, an immigrant from Germany, was the sole American winner of the Nobel Prize in Chemistry. His win seems to be more the rule than the exception. Of the most recent twenty-nine American Nobel laureates in chemistry, eighteen have been native-born Americans while eleven came from a much smaller pool of elite foreign immigrants. It should be noted that hauling in these Nobel Prizes is by no means a strictly Western European thing. According to *Forbes*, countries of origin for prizewinners during the past twenty years have included Japan, Israel, Canada, Turkey, Austria, China, and South Africa. An alt-right society would ban probably half of these people from entering America—or at least from coming into the largest "white" fragment left of the old motherland.

Not only would the alt-right's "white homelands" idea dramatically reduce the size and power of our great country, but there are more practical problems with the idea. Perhaps the most basic question that arises is: Who the hell is going to get hundreds of millions of home-owning Americans to leave their properties and travel to wherever "their" new country is supposed to be? As much as Richard Spencer or Vox Day might dislike it, we Americans live amongst one another. A quick look at two typical American cities illustrates this fact. Dallas, as of 2010, was 50.7 percent white, 24.7 percent Black, 2.9 percent Asian, and heavily ethnically Latino. Across the country, Cleveland is (somewhat surprisingly) only 37.3 percent white, 50.3 percent Black, and more than 10 percent Latino. Breaking up the United States into racial Bantustans would require convincing the populations of cities like this to split roughly into thirds and move, with more than 10 percent of citizens leaving their own wives and husbands behind. As an armed interracial

American, I don't plan on moving anywhere, hoss! This idea strikes me as the purest sort of internet masturbatory fantasy: just nonsense.

To some extent, it is not hard to understand the appeal of the dissident right. Many moderate Americans forced to listen to the nonsensical child's prattle of the "social justice" movement—"Illegal immigrants are refugees," "Biological sex is a tricky thing to define," "Islam is feminist!"—certainly may begin to think that swinging hard right is not only tempting but logical. However, there is no succor to be found down that road. The alt-right is wrong about race and performance, wrong about diversity and violence (*ethnic*, not racial, diversity predicts conflict), and absolutely wrong that two-thirds or so of the world's Caucasians are somehow genetically distinct from the "white" race. Its actual solutions to the nation's problems, such as breaking the U.S.A. up into four or five smaller ethno-states, would literally destroy the country. Simply put, successful American resistance to failed foreign ideas such as Communism and post-modernism will not be founded in failed foreign ideas such as fascism. Only by turning back to our own best traditions of non–politically correct scientific inquiry (sometimes tempered by religion or ethics), freedom-loving skepticism of government, and absolute equality for all can we push back the tide of nonsense and taboo.

God bless America.

Acknowledgments

No man is an island, and no book is truly a solo project. For the existence of this one, as with all my past projects and work to come, I owe a debt of gratitude to a good many people.

I'd first like to thank my excellent textual editor (Kathleen Curran) and copy editor (Kathryn Riggs) at Regnery Publishing, who took on the surely not always enviable task of turning my original 220–odd page manuscript for *Taboo* into a finished final book and succeeded admirably! Thanks also to Regnery herself: a solid, right-leaning, nearly century-old publishing house that took a chance on a book which explicitly breaks down all the things one just can't say socially! Most of these topics are not inherently political, but the increasing refusal to discuss them—which I often notice on the other side of the aisle—bodes ill for the republic. Thanks, finally, to Tom Spence, my first point of contact at the publisher, with whom I have easily exchanged fifty emails about my books and writing more broadly. May your tenure as president and publisher be long and fruitful!

The members of the Regnery team do not stand alone. I also owe a considerable debt of gratitude to the writers, journalists, warriors, and social scientists who agreed to read *Taboo* and provide official blurbs for or reviews of the book. The list of them, in alphabetical order, includes Marc Defant (author of *The New Creationists: The Radical Left's War on Science*), Louie B. Free (*BrainFood from the Heartland*), Stephen Knight (*Godless Spellchecker*), Bill Martinez (*Bill Martinez Live*), Andy Ngo (The Post Millennial), John Podhoretz (*Commentary Magazine*), Noah Rothman (author of *Unjust*), Pete Turner (*The Break It Down Show* and *Straight Outta Combat*), Kathleen Wells (the Naked Truth Report), and Toby Young (Quillette). Even closer to home and to my heart, thanks to Jane Lingle, my life partner and—as a way of keeping her hand in while out of the business world—an absolutely invaluable research associate.

Finally, as always, kudos to my beloved mother, Jean Marie Ward, and to East Aurora School District #131, for teaching me how to think—and to the social scientist Thomas Sowell for providing a younger me with a coherent framework within which to do it.

Notes

Introduction

1. It is worth noting that this "unarmed" category would include martial artists, intoxicated individuals who attack armed police with their hands or feet, individuals who attempt to take guns from officers, and so on. Very, very few truly innocent people peacefully making their way to church are shot and killed by police officers.

2. "About Us," Movement for Black Lives, https://policy.m4bl.org/about/.

3. Deroy Murdock, "Black Lives Matter's Numbers Are Bogus," *New York Post*, November 6, 2015, https://nypost.com/2015/11/06/black-lives-matters-numbers-are-bogus/.

4. African Americans are more likely to live in the South, where wages for everyone are lower.

5. "Poll Finds a Majority of White Americans Say Discrimination against Whites Exists in America Today," 2017 Press Release, Harvard T. H. Chan School of Public Health, https://www.hsph.harvard.edu/news/press-releases/poll-white-americans-discrimination/.

Chapter 1
Taboo Obvious Fact #1: The Police Aren't Murdering Black People

1. My previous bestselling book, *Hate Crime Hoax*, can be located and purchased here: https://www.amazon.com/Hate-Crime-Hoax-Lefts-Campaign/dp/1621577783.

2. "About Us," Movement for Black Lives, https://policy.m4bl.org/about/.

3. "Platform," Movement for Black Lives, https://policy.m4bl.org/.

4. "End the War on Black People," Movement for Black Lives, https://policy.m4bl.org/end-war-on-black-people/.

5. "Reparations," Movement for Black Lives, https://policy.m4bl.org/reparations/.

6. "Why Do US Police Keep Killing Unarmed Black Men?" BBC News, May 26, 2015, https://www.bbc.com/news/world-us-canada-32740523.

7. Travis Waldron and Julia Craven, "Here's How Many Black People Have Been Killed by Police Since Colin Kaepernick Began Protesting," HuffPost, September 20, 2016, https://www.huffpost.com/entry/colin-kaepernick-police-killings_n_57e14414e4b04a1497b69ba6.

8. Cody T. Ross, "A Multi-Level Bayesian Analysis of Racial Bias in Police Shootings at the County-Level in the United States, 2011–2014," *PLOS One* 10, no. 11 (November 5, 2015), https://journals.plos.org/plosone/article?id=10.1371/journal.pone.0141854.

9. Interestingly, as we will see when I begin to discuss poor white culture, such cities would hardly be earthly paradises. Rates of suicide, opiate abuse, "perverse" sex crime, and auto wreck would be "through the roof" in an all-white Chicago with income demographics anywhere close to those for the city of today. However, Rubenstein's figures specifically for violent "Index" crime appear accurate.

10. Roland G. Fryer, "An Empirical Analysis of Racial Differences in Police Use of Force," OpenScholar@Harvard, July 2017, https://scholar.harvard.edu/files/fryer/files/empirical_analysis_tables_figures.pdf.

11. Roland G. Fryer, "Reconciling Results on Racial Differences in Police Shootings," *Papers and Proceedings* 2 (May 2018), https://scholar.harvard.edu/files/fryer/files/fryer_police_aer.pdf.

12. If this even needs to be said, Mr. Castile was not in fact the robber.

13. Christine Hauser, "Fresno Police Shooting Video Shows Dylan Noble Ignoring Orders to Stop," *New York Times*, July 14, 2016, https://www.nytimes.com/2016/07/15/us/video-is-released-in-police-shooting-of-dylan-noble-in-fresno.html.

14. Steve Straub, "Unarmed White Man Killed by Black Cop; Here's How the Media Reacted," Federalist Papers, August 21, 2014, https://thefederalistpapers.org/us/unarmed-white-man-killed-by-black-cop-heres-how-the-media-reacted.

15. Danielle DeCourcey, "The Other Group of People Getting Killed by Police That We Can't Ignore," attn.com, July 11, 2016, https://archive.attn.com/stories/9818/media-coverage-of-latinos-and-police-shootings.

16. Kelly Bauer and Mark Konkol, "Chicago Police Stops Down by 90 Percent as Gun Violence Skyrockets," DNAinfo, March 31, 2016, https://www.dnainfo.com/chicago/20160331/bronzeville/chicago-police-stops-down-by-90-percent-as-gun-violence-skyrockets/.

17. We got there: there were 769 murders in Chicago in 2016.

18. Chuck Goudie, Ross Weidner, and Christine Tressel, "Wall-to-Wall: FBI Stats Show All Chicago Crime Up," ABC7 Chicago, January 9, 2017, https://abc7chicago.com/news/wall-to-wall-fbi-stats-show-all-chicago-crime-up-/1694530/.

19. Heather Mac Donald, "All That Kneeling Ignores the Real Cause of Soaring Black Homicides," *New York Post*, September 26, 2017, https://nypost.com/2017/09/26/all-that-kneeling-ignores-the-real-cause-of-soaring-black-homicides/.

Chapter 2
Taboo Obvious Fact #2: There Is No "War on POC"... and BBQ Becky Did Nothing Wrong

1. This, like all hypotheses, is a guess—but an educated one. To test it, simply Google "Trayvon Martin" and then a notable case of Black-on-white violence (Dylan Noble or the Knoxville Horror) and compare the number of returned search results—and, more importantly, the number of CNN, MSNBC, and *New York Times* stories for each of the two cases.

2. Jeandra LeBeauf, "Racist White Man Calls the Cops on Black Woman Using Their Pool at Her Own Complex; Makes Racist Statements & Cops Do Nothing about It (Video)," BSO, July 5, 2018, https://blacksportsonline.com/2018/07/racist-white-man-calls-the-cops-on-black-woman-using-their-pool-at-her-own-complex-makes-racist-statements-cops-do-nothing-about-it-video/.

3. Jessica Campisi, Emily Smith, Eric Levenson, and Kimberly Hutcherson, "After Internet Mockery, 'Permit Patty' Resigns as CEO of Cannabis-Products Company," CNN, June 26, 2018, https://www.cnn.com/2018/06/25/us/permit-patty-san-francisco-trnd/index.html.

4. It is.

5. Gina Martinez, "Woman Dubbed 'Permit Patty' Says She's Gotten Death Threats Over Viral Video of Her Calling Police on 8-Year-Old Girl," *TIME*, June 25, 2018, https://time.com/5320939/permit-patty-alison-ettel-threats/.

6. Whoever's side you take here, didn't any of these people have something better to do?

7. Not crime, heroin, earthquakes, etc.

8. Travis Gettys, "White Woman Calls Police on Black Family during Barbecuing for 'Trespassing,'" Salon, May 12, 2018, https://www.salon.com/2018/05/12/white-woman-calls-cops-on-black-family-for-barbecuing-in-park_partner/.

9. Gianluca Mezzofiore, "A White Woman Called Police on Black People Barbecuing. This Is How the Community Responded," CNN,

May 22, 2018, https://www.cnn.com/2018/05/22/us/white-woman-black-people-oakland-bbq-trnd/index.html.

10. Chris Sommerfeldt, "Trump-Supporting Texas Teen Gets Attacked, Doused in Soda for Wearing 'Make American Great Again' Hat," *Daily News*, July 5, 2018, https://www.nydailynews.com/news/politics/ny-news-trump-texas-soda-hat-burger-20180705-story.html.

11. Kate Taylor, "'We Were Shocked': Texas Cult-Favorite Chain Whataburger Responds after Footage of a Man Taking a Teenager's 'MAGA' Hat and Throwing a Drink in His Face Goes Viral," Business Insider, July 5, 2018, https://www.businessinsider.com/whataburger-responds-video-maga-hat-theft-drink-throwing-2018-7.

12. Lydia O'Neal, "White on Black Crime vs. Black on White Crime: New Statistics Show More Killings Between Races," International Business Times, September 30, 2016, https://www.ibtimes.com/white-black-crime-vs-black-white-crime-new-statistics-show-more-killings-between-2424598. All of these FBI figures are a bit on the low side, as they include only homicides which (1) led to a criminal case and (2) for which the race of the attacker and victim are known. The point, however, remains.

13. Think, for a second, what an odd description this is—based wholly around the idea that most regular white folks are out-of-control bigots. Aren't YOU an "anti-racist," in the sense that you dislike inaccurate genetic stereotypes of people? Me too! When do we get to cash in?

14. Tim Wise, "Race, Crime and Statistical Malpractice: How the Right Manipulates White Fear with Bogus Data," www.timwise.org, August 22, 2013, http://www.timwise.org/2013/08/race-crime-and-statistical-malpractice-how-the-right-manipulates-white-fear-with-bogus-data/.

15. It is worth taking a second here to do some math concerning crime rates. In a U.S.A. with today's population demographics, where all racial groups had similar sociocultural characteristics and no racism existed at all, we would expect the number of Black-on-white crimes and the number of white-on-Black crimes to be nearly identical: (5x [number of white targets] x 1/5x [number of Black attackers]) = (1/5x [number of Black targets] x 5x [number of white attackers]). In fact, the real annual ratio of BoW crimes to WoB crimes is usually in the order of 3–5:1. "Alt-right" scholars often attempt to ridiculously

inflate this ratio figure, by multiplying the original (say) 4:1 metric by five or six, to adjust for the smaller number of Blacks in the country (that is, 4x5.5). After doing this, American Renaissance has argued that the average Black individual is up to twenty-seven times as likely to attack the average white as vice versa. This equation, however, leaves out one critical final step: dividing by 5 or 6, to adjust for the fact that an entirely non-racist mugger or rapist would still be confronted by many more white potential targets than Black ones. It is fair to say that Black-on-white interracial crime is proportionally more common than the reverse, but by a ratio of 300–500 percent rather than 2,700 percent.

16. Jason Lewis, "Black-on-White Crime in America," *Star Tribune*, September 14, 2013, http://www.startribune.com/black-on-white-crime-in-america/223696071/.

17. Jeff Poor, "Coulter Slams Media for Hyping Rare White-on-Black Crime While Ignoring Black-on-White Crime," The Daily Caller, August 25, 2013, https://dailycaller.com/2013/08/25/coulter-slams-media-for-hyping-rare-white-on-black-crime-while-ignoring-black-on-white-crime/.

18. "Brittanee Drexel, Teen Who Vanished in 2009, Was Raped, Shot, Eaten by Alligators, FBI Says," Fox News, August 29, 2016, https://www.foxnews.com/us/brittanee-drexel-teen-who-vanished-in-2009-was-raped-shot-eaten-by-alligators-fbi-says.

19. Veronica Rocha, Joseph Serna, Diana Marcum, and Hailey Branson-Potts, "Hate Crime Is Suspected after a Gunman Kills 3 White in Downtown Fresno," *Los Angeles Times*, April 19, 2017, https://www.latimes.com/local/lanow/la-me-fresno-shooting-20170418-story.html.

20. Reported by at least one source as "God is great!"

21. There isn't much natural snow in Georgia, one of our southernmost states, for my overseas readers.

22. John Dempsey, "Shaun King Fails to Find the Facts Before Sharing Fake Cop Story," *Townhall*, May 25, 2018, https://townhall.com/columnists/johndempsey/2018/05/25/shaun-king-fails-to-find-the-facts-before-sharing-fake-cop-story-n2484362.

23. Shaun King, "When the 'Victim' You Fought for Turns Out to Be the Victimizer: Sherita Dixon-Cole and the Painful Consequences of a False Report of Sexual Assault and Police Misconduct," Medium, May 23, 2018, https://medium.com/@ShaunKing/ when-the-victim-you-fought-for-turns-out-to-be-the-victimizer- sherita-dixon-cole-and-the-painful-cec6ca8f3670.

24. Jason Johnson, "So Trump Is a Traitor. What Difference Does That Make to Black Folks?" The Root, July 17, 2018, https://www.theroot. com/ so-trump-is-a-traitor-what-difference-does-that-make-t-1827654833.

25. Your ideas are insane, Mr. Johnson, but get your hustle on. #BlackActors

26. Logically, in computer keyboard terms, the flip side of the "alt-right" would be the "cntrl-left." This also perfectly describes the endgame goal of most cultural Marxists.

27. Lawrence Ware, "Texas Shouldn't Execute Chris Young for Murder Even Though He Is Guilty of the Crime," *Very Smart Brothas* (blog), July 17, 2018, The Root, https://verysmartbrothas.theroot.com/ texas-shouldnt-execute-chris-young-for-murder-even- thou-1827629372.

28. "Teen" in this case means, as it often does when African American youth or bat-wielding white Occupiers are discussed, "250lb 18-year old man."

29. Greg Howard, "America Is Not for Black People," Deadspin, August 12, 2014, https://theconcourse.deadspin.com/ america-is-not-for-black-people-1620169913.

30. This was a literal example given in the article.

31. Darryl Fears, "Study: Many Blacks Cite AIDS Conspiracy," *Washington Post*, January 5, 2005, http://www.washingtonpost.com/ wp-dyn/articles/A33695-2005Jan24.html.

32. There are more than forty million Black Americans alone, and at least thirty-five million people (including a disproportionate number of Black Americans) have died since the AIDS epidemic began in the late 1980s. In contrast, the famous empirical estimate is that the Holocaust murdered roughly six million Jews.

33. Fears, "Study: Many Blacks Cite AIDS Conspiracy."

34. Simon Wolfe, "Nothing We Do Is Good Enough for Blacks So Stop Trying," *The Iron Legion* (blog), March 20, 2015, http://www.thisblogisdangerous.com/nothing-we-do-is-good-enough-for-blacks-so-stop-trying/.

Chapter 3
Taboo Obvious Fact #3: Different Groups Perform Differently

1. "Race and Crime in the United States," Wikipedia, https://en.wikipedia.org/wiki/Race_and_crime_in_the_United_States.

2. Lauren J. Krivo and Ruth D. Peterson, "The Structural Context of Homicide: Accounting for Racial Differences in Process," *American Sociological Review* 65, no. 4 (August 2000): 547–59.

3. Joseph Williams, "Why Are Blacks Less Suicide Prone Than Whites?" *New York Times*, February 9, 1982, https://www.nytimes.com/1982/02/09/science/why-are-blacks-less-suicide-prone-than.html.

4. Associated Press, "Drug Overdoses Now Kill More Americans Than Guns," CBS News, December 9, 2016, https://www.cbsnews.com/news/drug-overdose-deaths-heroin-opioid-prescription-painkillers-more-than-guns/.

5. Gina Kolata and Sarah Cohen, "Drug Overdoses Propel Rise in Mortality Rates of Young Whites," *New York Times*, January 16, 2016, https://www.nytimes.com/2016/01/17/science/drug-overdoses-propel-rise-in-mortality-rates-of-young-whites.html.

6. Devin Foley, "Chicago: 75% of Murdered Are Black, 71% of Murderers Are Black," Intellectual Takeout, July 27, 2016, https://www.intellectualtakeout.org/blog/chicago-75-murdered-are-black-71-murderers-are-black.

7. Lois Beckett, "Most Victims of US Mass Shootings Are Black, Data Analysis Finds," *Guardian*, May 23, 2016, https://www.theguardian.com/us-news/2016/may/23/mass-shootings-tracker-analysis-us-gun-control-reddit.

8. William T. Dickens and James R. Flynn, "Black Americans Reduce the Racial IQ Gap: Evidence from Standardization Samples," *SAGE Journals* 17, no. 10 (October 1, 2006): 913–20, https://journals.sagepub.com/doi/abs/10.1111/j.1467-9280.2006.01802.x?journalCode=pssa.

9. I love that state, and boy, can they play some football. But honesty compels me to admit that Alabama does not rank near the top of the educational charts for either whites or African Americans. The average white IQ in Alabama seems to be about 95 or 96.

10. Jonathan Rothwell, "Multiracial Adolescents Show No Test Score Gap with Whites," Brookings Institution, July 17, 2017, https://www.brookings.edu/research/multi-racial-adolescents-show-no-test-score-gap-with-whites/.

11. These gaps in income between white and Black families/households are due almost entirely to the much higher percentage of single mothers in the Black community. While some racism certainly still exists, adjusting for the variable of single parenthood almost totally eliminates Black/white family income gaps. As conservative writer Dennis Prager has pointed out, the rate of actual poverty is 7 percent for Black two-parent families and 22 percent for white single-mother households. See Dennis Prager, "The Fallacy of 'White Privilege,'" *National Review*, February 16, 2016, https://www.nationalreview.com/2016/02/white-privilege-myth-reality/.

12. "The Widening Racial Scoring Gap on the SAT College Admissions Test," *Journal of Blacks in Higher Education*, https://www.jbhe.com/features/49_college_admissions-test.html.

13. Admittedly, this figure was for the math portion of the test, analyzed alone. A line or so down, the author notes that 363 Black students posted that score on the verbal exam.

14. David French, "What Ivy League Affirmative Action Really Looks Like—from the Inside," *National Review*, May 18, 2015, https://www.nationalreview.com/2015/05/what-ivy-league-affirmative-action-really-looks-inside-david-french/.

15. "Black Student College Graduation Rates Remain Low, But Modest Progress Begins to Show," *Journal of Blacks in Higher Education,* http://www.jbhe.com/features/50_blackstudent_gradrates.html.

Chapter 4
Taboo Obvious Fact #4: Performance—Not "Prejudice"—Mostly Predicts Success

1. "What Are the Root Causes of the Problems That Black People in America Face Today?" Quora, https://www.quora.com/What-are-the-root-causes-of-the-problems-that-black-people-in-America-face-today#MoreAnswers.

2. Jason Silverstein, "How Racism Is Bad for Our Bodies," *The Atlantic*, March 12, 2013, https://www.theatlantic.com/health/archive/2013/03/how-racism-is-bad-for-our-bodies/273911/.

3. Nick Buffie, "The Problem of Black Unemployment: Racial Inequalities Persist Even amongst the Unemployed," Center for Economic and Policy Research, November 4, 2015, http://cepr.net/blogs/cepr-blog/the-problem-of-black-unemployment-racial-inequalities-persist-even-amongst-the-unemployed.

4. Kim Farbota, "Black Crime Rates: What Happens When Numbers Aren't Neutral," HuffPost, September 2, 2016, https://www.huffpost.com/entry/black-crime-rates-your-st_b_8078586.

5. Jared Taylor, "Africa in Our Midst," American Renaissance, October 2005, https://www.amren.com/archives/back-issues/october-2005/.

6. Thomas Sowell, "Race, Culture, and Equality," Hoover Institution, July 17, 1998, https://www.hoover.org/research/race-culture-and-equality.

7. Thomas Sowell, "Sowell: The Dangers of Isolation," St. Augustine Record, August 1, 2013, https://www.staugustine.com/article/20130801/OPINION/308019975?template=ampart.

8. Dennis Prager, "The Fallacy of 'White Privilege,'" *National Review*, February 16, 2016, https://www.nationalreview.com/2016/02/white-privilege-myth-reality/.

9. June O'Neill, quoted in Dinesh D'Souza, *The End of Racism* (Free Press Paperbacks: New York, 1995), 302.

10. Marianne Bertrand and Sendhil Mullainathan, "Are Emily and Greg More Employable Than Lakisha and Jamal? A Field Experiment on

Labor Market Discrimination," National Bureau of Economic Research, July 2003, https://www.nber.org/papers/w9873.pdf.

11. To be clear, Sander and Taylor focus on academic/educational admissions.

12. "The Consequences of Fatherlessness," National Center for Fathering, http://fathers.com/statistics-and-research/the-consequences-of-fatherlessness/2/.

13. Walter Williams, "The True Black Tragedy," Creators, May 20, 2015, https://www.creators.com/read/walter-williams/05/15/the-true-black-tragedy.

14. Jesse Powell et al., "Births to Unmarried Mothers Exceed 40 Percent; White Fertility Low," Thinking Housewife, April 6, 2010, https://www.thinkinghousewife.com/2010/04/unmarried-births-exceed-40-percent-white-fertility-remains-low/.

15. MTO Staff, "The FBI Just Released the List of the MOST Violent Cities in America . . . and the Most VIOLENT CITY IN AMERICA . . . Is 97% WHITE!! (Don't Let FOX News See This . . . LOL)," MTO News, September 3, 2016, https://mtonews.com/fbi-ust-released-list-violent-cities-amer1ca.

Chapter 5
Taboo Obvious Fact #5: Racism Didn't Cause the New Problems of Today

1. Leanna Garfield, "The 9 Biggest Marches and Protests in American History," Business Insider, January 20, 2017, https://www.businessinsider.com/largest-marches-us-history-2017-1.

2. Wikipedia lists this total as "1," but apparently neglected to add the three deaths from Charlottesville to this total.

3. *Los Angeles Times*, "Bloody Sunday 50th Anniversary: Thousands Crowd Selma Bridge," *Washington Post*, March 8, 2015, https://www.washingtonpost.com/national/thousands-join-second-day-of-selma-remembrances/2015/03/08/60d6784c-c5da-11e4-a199-6cb5e63819d2_story.html.

4. The figure for white children was even lower, stable at 3–4 percent.

5. Rich Lowry, "The Moynihan Report and Ongoing Family Breakdown," *National Review*, May 11, 2010, https://www.nationalreview.com/2010/05/moynihan-report-and-ongoing-family-breakdown-rich-lowry/.

6. The Hispanic decline was probably even steeper than this, since most figures for "Hispanics" as a class separate from Caucasians/whites have been kept only since the early 1970s.

7. Steven Pinker, "Decivilization in the 1960s," *Human Figurations* 2, no. 2 (July 2013), https://quod.lib.umich.edu/h/humfig/11217607.0002.206/—decivilization-in-the-1960s?rgn=main;view=fulltext.

8. Katie McHugh, "Crime Surges as Feds Restrain Police, Relax Sentences, Revive 1970s Just Before 2016 Election," Breitbart, October 6, 2015, https://www.breitbart.com/politics/2015/10/06/crime-surges-feds-restrain-police-relax-sentences-revive-1970s-just-2016-election/.

9. Robert Rector, "How Welfare Undermines Marriage and What to Do about It," Heritage Foundation, November 17, 2014, https://www.heritage.org/welfare/report/how-welfare-undermines-marriage-and-what-do-about-it.

10. Ibid.

11. Eduardo Porter, "The Myth of Welfare's Corrupting Influence on the Poor," *New York Times*, October 20, 2015, https://www.nytimes.com/2015/10/21/business/the-myth-of-welfares-corrupting-influence-on-the-poor.html.

12. The same could be said of mine, to be sure.

13. Leslie Casimir, "Data Show Nigerians the Most Educated in the U.S.," *Houston Chronicle*, January 12, 2018, https://www.chron.com/news/article/Data-show-Nigerians-the-most-educated-in-the-U-S-1600808.php.

14. Amy Chua and Jed Rubenfeld, "What Drives Success?" *New York Times*, January 25, 2014, https://www.nytimes.com/2014/01/26/opinion/sunday/what-drives-success.html.

15. "Appalachian Poverty," Fahe, https://fahe.org/appalachian-poverty/.

16. Dan Nolan and Chris Amico, "How Bad Is the Opioid Epidemic?" *PBS Frontline*, February 23, 2016, https://www.pbs.org/wgbh/frontline/article/how-bad-is-the-opioid-epidemic/.

17. Kevin McKenzie, "Largely White Opioid Epidemic Highlights Black Frustration with Drug War," *Commercial Appeal*, March 26, 2017, https://www.commercialappeal.com/story/money/2017/03/26/white-opioid-epidemic-highlights-black-frustration-drug-war/97694296/.

Chapter 6
Taboo Obvious Fact #6: Anyone Can Be Racist (and "Racist" Has a Real Meaning)

1. Nicki Lisa Cole, "Defining Racism beyond Its Dictionary Meaning," ThoughtCo., July 14, 2019, https://www.thoughtco.com/racism-definition-3026511.

2. Robin L. Hughes, "10 Signs of Institutionalized Racism," Diverse Education, May 29, 2014, https://diverseeducation.com/article/64583/.

3. Thomas Sowell, "Disparate Outcomes Do Not Imply Discrimination," *National Review*, October 5, 2015, https://www.nationalreview.com/2015/10/wage-gap-discrimination-outcomes/.

4. Jasper Hamill, "Search for Truth: Google Promotes Controversial Claim It's NOT Possible for Ethnic Minorities to Be Racist against White People," The Sun, October 3, 2016, https://www.thesun.co.uk/news/1901544/google-promotes-controversial-claim-its-not-possible-for-ethnic-minorities-to-be-racist-against-white-people/.

5. All grammar mistakes taken directly from the original.

6. Ariel Pontes, "Can Minorities Be Racist?" Medium, January 15, 2017, https://medium.com/humanist-voices/can-minorities-be-racist-a9ff8c7bc102.

7. Brian Anderson, "New FBI Stats: Blacks More Likely to Commit Hate Crimes Than Any Other Race," Downtrend, December 11, 2014, http://linkis.com/downtrend.com/71supe/Qj4eW?next=6&page=4.

8. Simon Tomlinson, "Preparing for Race War: The South African White Supremacist Bootcamps Which Are Training Thousands of Youths to Fight Blacks and Create an Apartheid State," *Daily Mail*, April 14, 2015, https://www.dailymail.co.uk/news/article-3038508/Preparing-race-war-South-African-white-supremacist-bootcamps-training-thousands-youths-fight-blacks-create-apartheid-state.html.

9. Both of the previous words/terms should probably be in quotes.

10. That means "one voice crying in the wilderness," YOU UNCULTURED BOOR! #classicalreference

11. Anna Maria Barry-Jester, "Attitudes Toward Racism and Inequality Are Shifting," FiveThirtyEight, June 23, 2015, https://fivethirtyeight.com/features/attitudes-toward-racism-and-inequality-are-shifting/.

12. Kyle Jaeger, "Here's How Big the KKK Really Is Today," attn:, February 29, 2016, https://archive.attn.com/stories/6255/how-big-kkk-is-2016.

13. "Arizona Antifa," Facebook, https://www.facebook.com/arizonaantifa/.

14. Steve Phillips, "What About White Voters?" Center for American Progress, February 5, 2016, https://www.americanprogress.org/issues/race/news/2016/02/05/130647/what-about-white-voters/.

15. The Nation believes, officially, that all people alive on Earth at this time were Negroes. The Egyptians, Ancient Greeks, Sumerians, proto-Celts, and so on—all of whom obviously existed at the time—would no doubt have been surprised to hear this.

16. NOI Research Group, "National Geographic Proves Teaching on Mr. Yakub," Final Call, May 23, 2013, http://www.finalcall.com/artman/publish/Perspectives_1/article_9878.shtml.

17. National Center, "National Council of La Raza," National Center for Public Policy Research, July 11, 2012, https://nationalcenter.org/ncppr/2012/07/11/national-council-of-la-raza/.

18. Peter Hasson, "Black Caucus Members Refuse to Denounce Hate Group Leader Louis Farrakhan," The Daily Caller, February 27, 2018, https://dailycaller.com/2018/02/07/black-caucus-members-refuse-to-denounce-farrakhan/.

Chapter 7
Taboo Obvious Facts #7 and #8: Whiteness Isn't the Only "Privilege"—and "Cultural Appropriation" Is Not Real

1. Peggy McIntosh, "White Privilege: Unpacking the Invisible Knapsack," *Peace and Freedom*, July/August 1989, https://psychology.umbc.edu/files/2016/10/White-Privilege_McIntosh-1989.pdf.

2. Gina Crosley-Corcoran, "Explaining White Privilege to a Broke White Person," HuffPost, May 8, 2014, https://www.huffpost.com/entry/explaining-white-privilege-to-a-broke-white-person_b_5269255.

3. Nadra Kareem Nittle, "A Guide to Understanding and Avoiding Cultural Appropriation," ThoughtCo., July 3, 2019, https://www.thoughtco.com/cultural-appropriation-and-why-iits-wrong-2834561.

4. Maisha Z. Johnson, "What's Wrong with Cultural Appropriation? These 9 Answers Reveal Its Harm," Everyday Feminism, June 14, 2015, https://everydayfeminism.com/2015/06/cultural-appropriation-wrong/.

5. As a note: we have not in fact forgotten.

6. "Is Social Class More Important Than Race Ethnicity in Determining a Family's Characteristics?" debate.org, https://www.debate.org/opinions/is-social-class-more-important-than-race-ethnicity-in-determining-a-familys-characteristics.

7. Sarah Garland, "When Class Became More Important to a Child's Education Than Race," *The Atlantic*, August 28, 2013, https://www.theatlantic.com/national/archive/2013/08/when-class-became-more-important-to-a-childs-education-than-race/279064/.

8. "Affirmative Action," U.S. Department of Labor, https://www.dol.gov/general/topic/hiring/affirmativeact.

9. It is worth noting that attempting to make the elite field of computer software engineering "look like America" is a doomed crusade even by woke leftist standards. According to the data.usa web resource, during 2016, 4,721 bachelors-on-up computer engineering degrees

were awarded to whites, and 1,622 to Asians. The huge majority of these degree recipients—3,626 of the whites and 1,007 of the Asians—were male. In contrast, Blacks of both sexes received a total of 435 computer science degrees, Native Americans received 18 such degrees, and Pacific Islanders received 14 degrees. The total number of Black women receiving specifically a bachelor's degree in computer engineering was 66, and no Native American women received one (one Islander did). Three Black women received a Ph.D. in computer engineering. The fantasy that the nation's elite computer research and design laboratories will soon resemble the nation's general population seems to be exactly that—a fantasy.

10. In an interesting note, while I hardly think of myself as a uniquely elite person, my verbal SAT score was 770 when I took the exam in 1998. It seems this may have been one of the 3–4 highest Black scores in the nation that year. Ah, well: I still never made it downstate as an athlete!

11. William Levinson, "It's Past Time to Acknowledge Black Privilege," American Thinker, April 15, 2015, https://www.americanthinker.com/articles/2015/04/its_past_time_to_acknowledge_black_privilege.html.

12. An unintentional illustration of this point—notice that both Blake and I spell out terms like "honky," but automatically censor the word "nigger" as "the N-word."

13. John Blake, "It's Time to Talk about 'Black Privilege,'" CNN, March 31, 2016, https://www.cnn.com/2016/03/30/us/black-privilege/index.html.

14. I say this sort of thing a lot because it is true.

15. Admin, "Afrikan Student Union at UCLA Releases Demands," Nommo, October 23, 2015, https://nommomagazine.com/?p=2580.

16. "Black Students Demand Segregated Spaces from White Students," Griffin Georgia NAACP, http://naacp-griffinga.org/black-students-demand-segregated-spaces-from-white-students/.

Chapter 8
Taboo Obvious Fact #9: A Sane Immigration Policy Isn't Racist (And We Need One!)

1. History.com editors, "U.S. Immigration Since 1965," history.com, June 7, 2019, https://www.history.com/topics/immigration/ us-immigration-since-1965.

2. Many of the nation's top leaders seem to have had something in common during this period—but I can't quite put my finger on what it was.

3. Altair333, "Tracing Liberal Woes to 1965 Immigration Act (or, How Ted Kennedy Destroyed America," Free Republic, July 4, 2005, http:// www.freerepublic.com/focus/f-news/1436455/posts.

4. History.com editors, "U.S. Immigration Since 1965."

5. Italics mine. Mark Andrew Dwyer, "The Disastrous Effects of the 1965 Immigration and Naturalization Act," Canada Free Press, August 20, 2013, https://canadafreepress.com/article/ the-disastrous-effects-of-the-1965-immigration-and-naturalization-act.

6. It is worth noting that the difficulty level of the SAT has almost certainly been adjusted upward over the past five decades to take into account the "Flynn Effect" phenomenon of slowly rising overall IQ scores. However, the basic idea that an SAT score of 1000 indicates an IQ score of 100–110 (https://www.iqcomparisonsite.com/SATIQ. aspx) and represents high-average intelligence within a generational group remains essentially unchanged.

7. It should be noted that, for whatever reason, SAT scores for all racial and ethnic groups being analyzed here trended a bit lower during the three years under review than was the case during other representative years discussed elsewhere in the book. However, the gaps between racial groups remain almost identical in size and should be fully comparable.

8. One wonders what their position on the agency might be.

9. Sean McElwee, "It's Time to Abolish Ice," The Nation, March 9, 2018, https://www.thenation.com/article/its-time-to-abolish-ice/.

10. Quick note: not to be mean, but ICE is literally by definition not terrorizing legal "American communities."

11. Amy Gottlieb, "It Is Time to Abolish ICE. It Cannot Be Reformed," *Guardian*, June 23, 2018, https://www.theguardian.com/commentisfree/2018/jun/23/it-is-time-to-abolish-ice-it-cannot-be-reformed.

12. Roque Planas, "16 Reason Why Opening Our Borders Makes More Sense Than Militarizing Them," HuffPost, September 2, 2014, https://www.huffpost.com/entry/open-borders_n_5737722.

13. Tim Cavanaugh, "Open the Borders," *Reason*, April 16, 2006, https://reason.com/2006/04/16/open-the-borders-2/.

14. Rutger Bregman, "The Surprisingly Compelling Argument for Open Borders," *Fortune*, April 17, 2016, https://fortune.com/2016/04/17/immigration-open-borders/. It must be noted that those numbers represent a truly remarkable rate of immigration—essentially all of it apparently illegal. If we accept Bregman's data, at least 7 million persons crossed the U.S.–Mexico border every year during the decade of the 1970s, and fully 10.5 million of them remained in the United States. In contrast, Border Patrol data for the "busy" year of 2018 reveal "only" 396,579 apprehensions at the border: https://www.cbp.gov/newsroom/stats/sw-border-migration/fy-2018. Even if that latter figure represents only 30–40 percent of all illegal border-crossers who entered the U.S.A. during 2018, illegal immigration seems down to roughly one-seventh of earlier high-water marks. Without meaning to, Bregman may in fact be making the steel-man case for walls.

15. Andrew Lam, "Is America Still a Nation of Immigrants?" HuffPost, February 8, 2017, https://www.huffpost.com/entry/is-america-still-a-nation_b_14643610.

16. Randi Weingarten and Maria Teresa Kumar, "America Is a Country of Immigrants," *The Hill*, February 28, 2017, https://thehill.com/blogs/pundits-blog/immigration/321602-america-is-still-a-country-of-immigrants.

17. D'Vera Cohn, "How U.S. Immigration Laws and Rules Have Changed through History," Pew Research Center, September 30, 2015, https://www.pewresearch.org/fact-tank/2015/09/30/how-u-s-immigration-laws-and-rules-have-changed-through-history/.

18. Andrew R. Arthur, "Two Reasons to Amend the Public Charge Ground of Inadmissibility," Center for Immigration Studies, May 7, 2018, https://cis.org/Arthur/Two-Reasons-Amend-Public-Charge-Ground-Inadmissibility.

19. African Americans, Appalachian whites, and so forth are all obviously included within the "native welfare users" figure.

20. Jason Richwine, "The Cost of Welfare Use by Immigrant and Native Households," Center for Immigration Studies, May 9, 2016, https://cis.org/Report/Cost-Welfare-Use-Immigrant-and-Native-Households.

21. Alan Gomez, "Report: More Than Half of Immigrants on Welfare," *USA Today*, September 2, 2015, https://www.usatoday.com/story/news/nation/2015/09/01/immigrant-welfare-use-report/71517072/.

22. "Examples of Racial Microaggressions," University of Minnesota, https://sph.umn.edu/site/docs/hewg/microaggressions.pdf.

23. Mark Friedman, "The End of the Melting Pot," Fiscal Policy Studies Institute, April 5, 2006, https://resultsaccountability.com/the-end-of-the-melting-pot/.

24. Maisha Z. Johnson, "4 Lies You've Fallen for If You Think the US Is a 'Melting Pot,'" Everyday Feminism, August 29, 2016, https://everydayfeminism.com/2016/08/melting-pot-lies/.

25. Ann Coulter, "Coulter: Democrats' War on America Turns 50," *Clarion Ledger*, September 30, 2015, https://www.clarionledger.com/story/opinion/columnists/2015/09/30/coulter-democrats-war-america-turns-50/73122980/.

26. If this figure seems low, recall that young people of all races tend to lean further left than their elders. Young people are also more likely to have no strong political opinions and simply not vote.

27. These last two provisions might in practice operate together so that outside of certain situations of contagious disease, an immigrant who is not "able-bodied" could be admitted upon absolutely demonstrating employability in a white-collar field, such as computer science. Obviously, the goal of this policy is reducing the size of the welfare rolls, rather than gratuitous cruelty to those with workplace or battlefield injuries. In essence, I favor expanding the scope of the public charge rule so that it requires immigrants to positively demonstrate employability before being admitted into the United

States, rather than only barring the small number of immigrants who are provably unable to work from admission into the United States.

28. Charlotte England, "Sweden Sees Record Numbers of Asylum Seekers Withdraw Applications and Leave," *Independent*, August 25, 2016, https://www.independent.co.uk/news/world/europe/refugee-crisis-asylum-seekers-sweden-applications-withdrawn-record-numbers-a7209231.html.

Chapter 9
Taboo Obvious Fact #10: The "Alt-Right" Has Nothing to Offer

1. This point is frankly less "taboo" than the others laid out so far, but the reasons underlying it are almost never explained in an intellectual and rational fashion. There are many arguments against ethno-nationalism besides waving one's arms and screaming, "You are a Nazi! Orange Man BAD!!!" This chapter aims to provide them.

2. *Discrimination in America: Final Summary*, NPR/Robert Wood Johnson Foundation/Harvard T.H. Chan School of Public Health, January 2018, https://cdn1.sph.harvard.edu/wp-content/uploads/sites/94/2018/01/NPR-RWJF-HSPH-Discrimination-Final-Summary.pdf.

3. Given the affirmative action statistics discussed earlier in the book, this latter figure probably represents a substantial underestimate, perhaps due to colleges and universities almost universally misrepresenting the "sausage-making" realities of academic admissions.

4. Dan Gonyea, "Majority of White Americans Say They Believe Whites Face Discrimination," NPR, October 24, 2017, https://www.npr.org/2017/10/24/559604836/majority-of-white-americans-think-theyre-discriminated-against.

5. Ariel Edwards-Levy, "Nearly Half of Trump Voters Think Whites Face a Lot of Discrimination," HuffPost, November 21, 2016, https://www.huffpost.com/entry/discrimination-race-religion_n_5833761ee4b099512f845bba.

6. Robert Kraychik, "Moore: Whites Afraid 'to Be the Minority in This Country,'" Daily Wire, November 13, 2016, https://www.dailywire.com/news/moore-whites-afraid-be-minority-country-robert-kraychik.

7. Tom Jacobs, "Fear of Coming Minority Status Drives White Opposition to Welfare," *Pacific Standard*, June 4, 2018, https://psmag.com/social-justice/fear-of-coming-minority-status-drives-white-opposition-to-welfare.

8. Two notable findings of this experiment seem to reach beyond "racial resentment." First, almost all whites want to cut the welfare budget by tens of millions of dollars. Second, most citizens have no idea how large the government is, and radically underestimate the size of the cuts that would be needed in order to significantly affect the welfare budget. Fifty-one million dollars is a lot of money, but, according to www.usgovernmentspending.com, the annual non-Medicaid welfare budget is $482 *billion*.

9. "Hate Hoax Map," American Renaissance, https://www.amren.com/archives/reports/hate-crime-hoax-map/.

10. "Map of Trayvon Martin Revenge Attacks," https://www.google.com/maps/d/viewer?mid=1n7SWoBIZ6lKHbp8UF19IO9JG9Dw&ll=34.91746683786479%2C-97.91015600000003&z=4.

11. Jared Taylor, "Race and Intelligence: The Evidence," American Renaissance, November 1992, https://www.amren.com/news/2017/07/race-and-differences-in-intelligence-evidence/.

12. Jonathan Rothwell, "Multiracial Adolescents Show No Test Score Gap with Whites," Brookings Institution, July 17, 2017, https://www.brookings.edu/research/multi-racial-adolescents-show-no-test-score-gap-with-whites/.

13. Robert Lindsay, "The Skyrocketing Black IQ," American Renaissance, October 12, 2007, https://www.amren.com/news/2007/10/the_skyrocketin/.

14. "How Many Major Races Are There in the World?" *World Mysteries* (blog), February 18, 2011, https://blog.world-mysteries.com/science/how-many-major-races-are-there-in-the-world/.

15. Edmund Kozak, "Hundreds of Muslim 'No-Go' Zones Take Root in Europe," American Renaissance, December 13, 2016, https://www.amren.com/news/2016/12/hundreds-muslim-no-go-zones-take-root-europe/.

16. Italics Mercer's. Ilana Mercer, "A Muslim Ban Is Logical," American Renaissance, November 4, 2017, https://www.amren.com/news/2017/11/muslim-ban-logical/.

17. Yaroslav Lavrentievich Podvolotskiy, "How Russia Deals with Immigrants," American Renaissance, January 27, 2017, https://www.amren.com/features/2017/01/russia-deals-immigrants/.

18. Khaled Beydoun, "Are Arabs White?" Al Jazeera, July 16, 2015, https://www.aljazeera.com/indepth/opinion/2015/07/arabs-white-150716110921150.html.

19. John Ingram, "Why We Push for an Ethnostate," American Renaissance, November 17, 2017, https://www.amren.com/commentary/2017/11/why-we-push-for-an-ethnostate-racial-separation/.

20. F. Roger Devlin, "A Home of Our Own," American Renaissance, June 21, 2013, https://www.amren.com/features/2013/06/a-home-of-our-own/.

21. A tip of the hat to P. J. O'Rourke for this joke.

22. To be fair, Total Sportek's list focuses on the top twenty overall performers at the games. But the same point is true writ large: France, Brazil, and South Africa far outperform (say) Sudan, Moldova, and Paraguay.

23. Wendy Wang, "Interracial Marriage: Who Is 'Marrying Out'?" Pew Research Center, June 12, 2015, https://www.pewresearch.org/fact-tank/2015/06/12/interracial-marriage-who-is-marrying-out/.

24. Anna Giaritelli, "37 Percent of Silicon Valley Foreign-Born," *Washington Examiner*, February 12, 2016, https://www.washingtonexaminer.com/37-percent-of-silicon-valley-foreign-born.

Index

The Black-White Test Score Gap,
    69
toxic masculinity, 90
Trump, Donald, 26, 37, 48, 94,
    151, 167, 177–79, 190

U
U.S. immigration policy, 56, 149–50,
    153–54, 161, 168, 172–73
University of California, Los Ange-
    les (UCLA), 74, 147, 197
USA Today, 163

V
Vanity Fair, xv, 4
Ventura, Melissa, 26
Villanueva, Pedro, 26

W
Wall Street Journal, 28
Washington Examiner, 197
Washington Post, xiv–xv, 25, 51,
    95
Washington Redskins, 136
Waters, Maxine, 129
Weingarten, Randi, 159
West, Kanye, 81
Western civilization, 81
Western Europe, 101, 189
Whataburger, 37
Wheatley, Zora, 82
white privilege, xiv, xviii–xix, xxii,
    73, 77, 84, 126, 133–37, 139,
    141, 144, 147–48
White, Alicia, 17
Williams, Joseph, 60
Williams, Walter, 90, 96
Wilson, Darren, 49
Wise, Tim, 8, 38–39
Wolfe, Alan, 141
World War II, 40, 98, 184

Y
Yakub, 126–28, 130
Yanez, Jeronimo, 19–20
Yiannopolous, Milo, 179

Z
Zimmerman, George, 18, 53, 180